Brains,

Living The Autism Life

by

Alicia Hart

Cover Art: Ewan Nees and Tera Swango

Editor: Brianne Bolin

Published by Alicia Hart

Copyright 2011 by Alicia Hart

For my son, Ewan, and my father, Terrill.

Table of Contents

Prologue 5

Chapter One 7

   A Strange New World

Chapter Two 18

   The Infant Insomniac

Chapter Three 38

   The New Normal

Chapter Four 50

   Out of Wedlock and Into the Trenches

Chapter Five 63

   Express Train to Rehab

Chapter Six 75

   A Word, an Identity

Chapter Seven 88

   I Want a Name

Chapter Eight 97

   You Can Always Go Home

Chapter Nine 129

   Sweet Home Illinois

Chapter Ten 140

   A World of Possibility

Chapter Eleven 158

   Building Bridges

Chapter Twelve 165

   The Creole Incident

Chapter Thirteen 179

The Education of Ewan

Chapter Fourteen 186

This

Chapter Fifteen 200

A Recipe for Success

Chapter Sixteen 211

A Quilt of Connections

Chapter Seventeen 225

The Invisible Wall

Acknowledgements 231

Definitions... 236

Resources.. 239

About The Author.. 241

Sneak Peak... 242

Prologue

I am normally a very private person. Not many people know everything there is to know about me. With the exception of my husband, most people, even my own family, get the abbreviated version of my life. Most people know of my devotion to pajama pants. Some people know of my addiction to chocolate snack cakes and coffee. Few people know the legend of my husband and I. Fewer still know the tale behind the tale of both our weddings. There is a greater story to be told, yet most friends and family only get a chapter here and there. Most get the CliffsNotes version. It is not secrecy I seek, though. It is a retreat behind a protective veil of laughter and superficiality, isolating the troubles of the past from catching up to the daydreams of the present. It is what keeps me sane. There are some things I cannot constantly relive over and over again. So the façade has been built as a shadow falls over the past. The past has been put away, relegated to a dusty box in the corner of the attic. In opening the box, in retelling the story, there is more than memory. There is pain, there is sorrow, there is life and there is death. All the things I'd rather not face. But I cannot always run and hide from the history of this life.

When I started this book, the overall plan focused more on educating parents and others about topics all across the autism life. The story I started with was personal but not too personal, it was inviting but not too intrusive. It was funny and lighthearted. It was self-help laced with sarcasm and jokes about my obsessive need for pajama pants, snack cakes, coffee and various other caffeinated beverages. It opened only a sliver of that dusty box. Yet my editor, my guide and my guru, Brianne Bolin, directed me away from the self-help guide toward the greater narrative that lay buried beneath the laughter and the jokes. Image by image and word by word, she helped draw out something greater than all the how-to thoughts and concoctions. Her mantra repeated over and over again: 'Slow the story down.' I would have preferred to rush through the personal in order to give the advice. Yet the frantic pace did not do the story justice. That dusty, old box had to see the light of day. Before you read the how-to's, you must first hear something much more private and intimate. Before we walk together through the autism life, you must first see the beginning of a journey that began nine years ago.

This is the story of that journey.

Chapter One

A Strange, New World

On the morning of September 11, 2001, I woke to my phone ringing. I had spent the previous few days out of town visiting my ex-husband. We were in the process of reconciling, and I had been traveling back and forth between my new home in Indianapolis and his home back in Illinois. It was the beginning of fall, and that bone dry harvest air was playing havoc with my sinuses. The throbbing pain between my eyes had taken its toll on my beauty sleep. I thought an extra forty winks that Tuesday morning seemed like a good idea. Thinking that it probably wasn't important, I let the phone ring. And ring. And ring. But when I realized that whoever was calling wasn't going to stop anytime soon, I picked up the phone and croaked out a groggy "Hello?"

My sister's panicked voice burst out of the receiver and flew straight to my spinal cord, "Turn on the TV *now*. I don't know what's going on in New York, but this is freaky." My sister, Heather, has this knack for giving me information in a way that sends an electric shock through my heart faster than a double shot of DayQuil and espresso. Falling out of bed with a lead balloon for a head, I sleepily tripped my way to the living room. I clumsily searched through every couch cushion 'til I found the remote lodged between 50 cents and a hairbrush and turned on the TV. Squinting through swollen slits I normally call my eyeballs, I watched the first tower burning as smoke drifted across the New York skyline. A national disaster was unfolding before my eyes, and I hadn't even had a cup of coffee yet.

Heather and I were discussing whether or not this was just a plane crash when the second plane flew straight into the building. At that moment, we knew this was indeed a terrorist attack. The world stopped spinning in that single moment of searing heat and smoke. In my young life I'd rarely witnessed such violence. Even watching bombs over Baghdad through an eerie night vision lens did not compare to the scene unfolding on CNN that morning. I stood frozen in terror as I watched the footage repeat itself. Watching the towers burn was an otherworldly experience. I was a voyeur into the death of hundreds of people, a private grief made public for all to see. It was easier to assume all that fell from the buildings were merely debris rather than bodies. Panic rose in my chest as I watched thousands of New Yorkers, blackened by smoke and ash, run away from the terrible scenes of violence. Hysteria spread like an infectious agent as airports across the country shut down and the skies emptied into a mournful silence. My own unease grew ever greater as my mother, my daughter, and I lived just a handful of miles from the Indianapolis International Airport. In all the months we had lived there, the skies had never been silent. The roar of an engine was always humming in the background like a thousand bees. But now, the sky was still as if even the birds knew the world had suddenly stopped. The silence between my sister and I was broken as the call waiting erupted into an endless stream of clicks. My mother urged me to hit the grocery store and stock up on non-perishable items, and my ex-husband fervently wished my mom's house was further away from the airport.

    I spent the next few hours vacillating between phone calls to my loved ones, pulling my then six year old daughter to my side, and watching every second of news coverage. Two burning towers scorched into my memory. Of course, the attack did not end in New York, and as the coverage came in from the Pentagon crash and the field in Pennsylvania, the collective anxiety of all Americans reached its peak. I couldn't sleep. I couldn't watch anything else but the continuous loop of falling buildings. I could barely leave the house for work and shopping. With more rice and beans than a small country, we waited for the next explosion and attack. War was inevitable. For the time being though, war had come to my doorstep, not to some distant, foreign shore. I would wake in the middle of a sound sleep just to turn on the news and see if the world had erupted in a tower of flames. The sound of breaking news was constantly screaming from the television. I was an edgy, jumpy mess. There was not a movie or book that could distract me from the news coverage. After a few weeks, the subsequent theories and threats left their toll on my psyche. Exhausted and discombobulated, I began to wonder if some sort of Post Traumatic Stress Disorder had settled in.

    At the time, I was working as a phlebotomist as an effort to get some hands-on experience before applying to medical school. Blood and guts don't bother me much, so I knew something was amuck the day a seven foot tall Viking offspring and I turned mutually green in the middle of a blood draw. As we raced to the solo bathroom stall in that tiny little laboratory, an epiphany penetrated my seasick brain. I was not suffering from Munchausen by Proxy for my Viking comrade, nor was I suffering from some sort of collective American PTSD. I was pregnant.

This baby, coming amidst a strange, new world of chaos and terrorism, had put everything into perspective. My husband, Anthony, and I had been divorced nine months when we realized that it had been a mistake to give up so quickly on our marriage. Anthony and I were the classic on-again, off-again Ross and Rachel couple, but this baby brought my husband and I back together again in a way no amount of couple's counseling ever could. Fighting over Chinese food, patio furniture, and a host of other things suddenly no longer seemed important.

My mother, who had been perfectly happy to see those divorce papers signed, was now confused and exasperated to find out Anthony and I were not only reconciling, but also in the market for a baby on board bumper sticker. My father had died just a few years earlier, and my mother was not ready for what she considered another loss. My daughter Skye and I had been living with my mother since the divorce, and to be honest, my mother couldn't have been happier with that situation. Our presence filled the void left from my father's passing, and any change in the status quo was met with fear and anger. She was not ready to let go of a normal she had so recently found.

My daughter Skye, although happy to see mom and dad together again, radiated four feet two inches of pure jealousy at the thought of having to concede the six year run of her 'only child' title to an unknown usurper. Her new role as big sister left her insecure and skeptical. Friends and family were exasperated and surprised to hear that we were giving it yet another go. But for whatever reason, life made sense to Anthony and I as Providence brought us back together. Timing is everything, and this child's life sparked the possibility of a new life for us all.

That November, amid the turkey and stuffing preparations, the date of my 'would be' second wedding anniversary approached. Under gray skies and with little fanfare, Anthony and I found ourselves in front of a judge pledging our lives to one another yet again. The judge seemed to have gotten a kick out of our story and added a little extra here and there about promising to cherish one another despite errant Chinese dishes and lavish patio furniture purchases. It was as different from our first wedding as night to day. The first time there was a flurry of plaid, bagpipers and family. The second time, we said our vows in front of only a judge and our daughter, promising to love and honor each other for as long as both shall live. Rather than celebrating the night together, I had to drive back to Indy while he stayed behind in Illinois. Our second wedding night was spent apart. Anthony was forced to stay behind until he could find a job in Indy.

      We decided that marrying on our original wedding date would save us from mixing up or forgetting any important milestones with the excuse, "Oh I thought you meant the *other* anniversary." Our anniversary is close to Thanksgiving, and every year we remain thankful to still be together. Needless to say, we never forget our wedding anniversary—what we *do* forget is how many years we've been married. Should we count from the first or second anniversary, or should we just be thankful we're still married at all? Usually we just end up teasing each other about being stupid enough to marry each other twice, and I always add, "You know you could end up divorced twice too, Bucko."

      By January, Anthony found work at a restaurant on the south side of Indianapolis and moved in with my mother, Skye, and I until we could find our own place. Since the divorce, I had taken all the furniture and household goods, which meant Anthony had about two suitcases to his name. In the middle of a snowstorm, I met him in Terre Haute and threw his meager belongings in the frozen trunk. The glacial winds and the hazardous drive on ice-covered roads were nothing compared to the frosty reception we were about to receive from my mother. With the new family dynamic, we were experiencing growing pains of more than just an exponentially expanding stomach. The air between us was practically toxic. My mother would tersely stare off at the TV, creating a chill in the air colder than any Canadian high pressure system. She could be happy when Anthony was out working, but the minute he stepped back over the threshold, her whole face and body language changed to a neon unwelcome sign. She may have loved Skye and I, but there was no room in her heart for Anthony. The 2500 square feet of her house offered no relief from her anger, and I have rarely felt more trapped than in those days. The rage and frustration rolling off of my mother left me burned, scarred and exhausted. It was hard to breathe in that house then. The air was so polluted with pain that my lungs seemed on the verge of collapse. The entire house was holding its breath not wanting to bear witness to the internal despair building inside us. While I could forgive Anthony, she could not, and I was left in the middle between a man I loved and a mother who hated everything to do with him. She has never quite forgiven me for choosing him, choosing to be with him, and choosing a life I could truly call my own.

After months of tiptoeing around a myriad of explosive situations, Anthony and I moved out into an apartment of our own, determined to make it work. It was spring, and the Midwestern weather had turned stormy and turbulent. Every other afternoon we found ourselves crouched under the table as tornado sirens wailed in the background. In the months before the baby came, we faced a barrage of floods, winds, and hail the size of golf balls. While the weather raged on in a tempestuous mix of seasonal rotation and rain, inside our new home peace reigned eternal. Anthony worked long hours in a restaurant as Skye and I prepared a baby's room. I went from a house of anger to a quiet house of solitude. Skye was in kindergarten at the time, and I spent most days alone in the house. It was easy to breathe again. Away from the slow burn of my mother's hostility, I could simply be a pregnant wife and not a single thing else. I could enjoy the thought of motherhood again and touch my pregnant skin with a trembling anticipation. Anthony and Skye may have been gone all day, but I was never truly alone. The child inside created a rhythm all its own, a soothing lullaby to ease the pain of the previous few months. My father dead and buried, my mother lost in her melancholic sorrow, I had to step away from the family I grew up with and toward a family of my making.

In due course, we found out I was giving birth to a son, and we decorated the room in shades of brown and Noah's Ark, a fitting tribute to what we had weathered both literally and figuratively. Like Noah, we had survived the initial deluge that threatened our happiness and marriage. Our forty days and forty nights lingered much longer, yet we always emerged into the bright sun of serenity. Two by two, a daughter and now a son, our equation had balanced itself quite nicely. The only missing variable was a name, and this boy had to have *a name*, not just any name, a name to match the incomparable beauty of his sister's. We couldn't raise a Skye and a Bob. We had to have a Skye and a Phillipe or some such novel moniker. Noah would have been a fitting name for this child, yet in my heart I knew that wasn't the one. I deliberated over Skye for weeks and months. I have to say the name and yell it out over and over to see if it flows off the tongue when screaming, "Skye, what on earth are you doing? Get back in this house!" We are the same way with pet names. Much deliberation has gone into the names Moses, Wilbur, Simon, Boris, Grace,

Sophie, Iggy, Oscar, Norman, and Frank—all former dog and cat names in our household and all with significant meaning for pet and owner. The same amount of care and argument went into our second child's name. I would say, "How about Gavin?" and my husband would reply, "No, I went to school with a Gavin, and he looked at me funny during math class," or some such nonsense. So back and forth it went between old classmates and neighbors, until we settled on Ewan. Some of you might argue that this name is a rather peculiar choice for two Midwesterners, but for my husband and I, it was perfect. Ewan was just the right blend of uniqueness and Scottishness we had been looking for (oh yes, we claim a fair amount of Scottish ancestry, and I have a picture of a Scotsman over my mantle to prove it). I someday hope to be like Stuart and May Mackenzie from *So I Married an Axe Murderer* and have my own Scottish Wall of Fame. Quotes like "Heed Move" and "Let's Get Pissed" are regularly uttered in our household (in fact that last one was uttered at my wedding, also). If you have no idea what I'm talking about here, I command you to rent that movie, pronto.

We were stuck on a middle name, though—it was between Terrill, my dad's name, or Anthony, after my husband, so we made a bet. If this little boy was born with black hair, he would be named after his Grandpa Terrill, and if he was born with blonde hair, he would be named after his daddy. Now to be fair, I think I got the short end of this deal since I was advocating for Terrill. My hair has its blonde moments, and my husband is decidedly towheaded, so the likelihood of this munchkin's hair being black was zero to nil. And so we waited and waited for our son to grace us with his presence as bets flew back and forth regarding color prediction like it was a Clairol convention.

~

It was June, and not only was I at the awkward and uncomfortable last leg of pregnancy, I was miserably hot. The air was so thick with moisture that a simple trip to the store left me drained and sopping wet. The restlessness of impending motherhood settled on my shoulders like a heavy cloak of irritability. My skin and my patience were stretched to the limits. After many false alarms and backaches the size of Rhode Island, this week-overdue woman finally reached her breaking point and gave the doc a green light for labor induction. We packed our bags and parked ourselves at the hospital, ready for the rollercoaster to begin. As we checked in to the hospital and settled into our room, a nurse came in with some initial paperwork. While I changed into a hospital gown, she threw a series of questions at me with a slightly suspicious look on her face. When she asked me if I had any other children, I answered, "Yes. My husband and I have a seven year old at home waiting to meet her brother." Her eyebrows shot straight up into her hair line, and she bit her lip as she walked back out to get some supplies. Rolling my eyes at Anthony, I jumped in the bed and waited for her to come back with the IV.

The nurse returned with several compatriots, all laughing and smiling, and when I asked what the joke was, she replied, "When you walked in here we thought you had to be the youngest mother we'd seen all year. You've got your hair up in pig tails, and you and your husband look about as old as couple of junior high kids. When you said you had a seven year old, I had to run back out and check your chart to see how old you were. We had a bet at the nurses' station, and we were shocked to see you were 27, not 14!"

Soon my smile matched her own. It wouldn't be the first or last time someone would mistake me for a much younger, naïve girl. I simply replied, "Well, this *much older* lady has suffered through 41 weeks of pregnancy, and I'm ready to get the show on the road. Let's move on to betting how long it takes 'til this baby is born. Last time it was a mere three and a half hours." Seeing her dinner break evaporate before her eyes, she reluctantly started the IV and kick started the labor process. Within minutes, the oxytocin was running through my veins, accelerating and amplifying the childbirth process. As the nurses hooked me to multiple wires, electrodes and machines, the miracle of birth evolved into researching a laboring mother's tolerance for irritation. Since my delivery with Skye, the world of obstetrics had changed into a quantitative analysis of the endless data strips printed from each machine. Hooked to an IV along with internal and external monitoring systems, I was not free to move an inch. Induced labor was turning out to be a complete 180 degree different experience from my first delivery. In the beginning I bravely said, "Oh, no drugs for me, thanks; I've done this before without drugs, and I intend to do it again." In hindsight, let me just say there are two phrases that should never be uttered together: labor induction and natural childbirth. Natural childbirth is an amazing and beautiful thing, unless you are giving birth to a small walrus. This *au naturel* philosophy lasted long enough for me to realize this birth was quite a bit different from the last time. The pain of induced labor came at a pace my body was not prepared for. Caught by surprise attack, my internal coping mechanisms were completely overwhelmed and rendered totally useless. The wired chains held me in a prison of immobility that no amount of breathing exercises could break through. Amidst a relentless procession of beeps and alarms, I could not find the peace to let nature take over. I could not find the focus to work in sync with my body as I walked out of step through one of nature's greatest acts. In a haze of pain greater than I had ever experienced, I wisely remembered a friend saying, "You know they don't hand out badges for women who do natural childbirth—TAKE THE DRUGS." So I caved, demanded an epidural and smiled with glee when the anesthesiologist walked in the room. Peace finally came to me in the form of 12 inch syringe.

It was a good thing I did take the drugs, because the small walrus I was about to give birth to got stuck. Apparently this little guy wasn't so little, and my doctor debated the pros and cons of an unplanned cesarean. His mammoth size might have been because I gained like 60 pounds to my normally thin frame and ate like Armageddon was going to happen at any given moment. There was a time toward the end of my pregnancy where the whole family got together for a buffet of ribs. It was a rare moment of kinship and laughter during my pregnancy, free from the strain we all so often felt. As I devoured my plate, everyone was staring at me as if I might turn cannibal at any moment and eat *them* when my brother-in-law said, "Umm, you've got barbecue sauce on your nose, cheeks, and forehead." My rather voracious appetite made for a bouncing baby boy that turned out to be a whopping 9 pounds, 4.5 ounces. All I can say is that the epidural saves lives, people. As my labor progressed, my husband, sister, and I all hung out laughing and watching TV thanks to the miracle of regional anesthesia. My mother was even able to come and set aside her animosity for a few short hours. But when she thought you weren't looking, it was still easy to catch a glimpse of both sadness and resentment that always seemed to hover near the surface. Even now, when I look at the photographs from that day, one can see an odd mixture of joy and sadness frozen across her face. For my husband and I though, there was only joy. Our fondest memory of Ewan's birth was of my husband eating Funyuns and drinking Vanilla Coke while the Ob-Gyn played video games. After plenty of laughing and pushing and whopping amounts of halitosis, Ewan came into the world replete with a head full of black hair.

Ewan Terrill it was.

This wet, slippery mass of goo was unceremoniously flopped upon my chest. It was so hard to hold on to him and keep him from falling. I sometimes still feel that way about Ewan, and he's nine. The epidural was a good one because I couldn't move my legs to save my life, and holding on to this slippery little sucker was a superhuman feat. The nurses saved me the embarrassment of dropping my second born in that initial moment of motherhood and cleaned him up. It was within these first few moments that we knew this child was like no other. As the nurse scrubbed and rubbed all the goo away, my brand new baby boy reached up and started grabbing her stethoscope and her nametag. My sister, who is an occupational therapist, watched this in awe. She said, "Whoa. Look at him, *look* at him grab that. I have *never* seen a newborn do that."

The nurse replied, "I've certainly never seen a two minute old newborn do that." For an exhausted and starving mommy, who endured labor watching her husband happily munch Funyuns and Vanilla Coke, it wasn't all that interesting. But when they handed him over to me, the awe shifted from the audience to me. I have never, in all my life, seen a newborn that was so intense. It was if this child was trying to take the whole world in all at once for fear of being put back in that warm, dark bathtub he'd been in for nine months.

Ewan stared up at me with wide dark eyes. It wasn't as if he were trying to focus or see, it was as if he *could* see me just as clearly as I could see him. He nursed immediately with absolutely no hesitation. He nursed as intently as he looked around. His dark eyes stared up at me as if to say, "Ok, what else you got?" Everyone took turns marveling at his intense stares, even my mother. I wondered if this boy could heal what had been broken between us. I wondered if Ewan could replace but an ounce of her grief with love. For Anthony, this was a unique moment of fatherhood as he had not been there to see Skye born. This time, he had borne witness to both the pain and joy of birth. My sister had delivered both of her children by cesarean, and I think the entire experience was good for her. She was flushed with the excitement of the delivery as we took the first pictures of her and Ewan. I was exhausted and drained, despite the epidural, and lapsed into a short but deep slumber. It was the last moment of peaceful sleep I'd have for several weeks to come.

Later that night and into the wee hours of the morning, Ewan continued to be awake and needing *more*, although I wasn't quite sure what. Problem was, no one else seemed to know what it was he wanted either. He cried so often and in such a high pitch that my 'mommy hormones' went on overdrive, and I demanded to keep him in my room. I also had a sneaking suspicion that the night nurse, who I had renamed Nurse Ratched, was bound and determined to give my son a bottle. Now, I'm not some kind of *Blue Lagoon* breastfeeding purist here, but I wasn't about to let all the sore nipples be in vain—this baby was nursing, not bottle-feeding. The nurse reluctantly brought him in with me to stay, although she couldn't resist a parting shot, "That boy is crying because he is hungry. Just a little formula will settle him right down."

I smiled sweetly back and said, "Thanks, but we'll be just fine together," all the while flipping her the bird in my mind.

That night and throughout the quiet hours of the morning, Ewan and I got to know each other, exploring fingers and toes, legs, tummy, ears, eyes and lips; his skin both soft and wrinkly, his raven hair so fine and smooth. It was just the two of us as everyone else had gone home to sleep. The first moment without monitors or onlookers, I could finally welcome my son to the world in peace. His fingers gripped tightly around my own, and the warmth of our bodies rolled back and forth like the tide. I changed his diaper just for the sake of seeing him not so tightly wrapped and covered up. His limbs were so long and full that he dwarfed my memories of what a newborn should look like. His eyes held the wisdom and mystery of a thousand different lives. His thick dark hair, a gift from the one life I had so cruelly lost. I ran my fingers through the black curls, astonished at my good fortune. I didn't want Ewan to be my father, he was his own person to grow and become who he chose to be, but to see some part of my father in him gave me such comfort. For a brief moment, everything felt connected and part of some grander design. In that second, I could see that I had been given back a piece of my heart. Unaware of his place in the wider universe, Ewan simply continued to gaze at the world with the fervor of a Nobel laureate in physics just as he continued to nurse with the rapacious appetite of a starved post-hibernation bear.

That very night I started to notice how sensitive Ewan was to sound and movement. As he slept in the bassinet to next to me, he would violently startle awake every time I would flip over to my side. He would also startle at the distant noises coming in from down the hall as nurses and patients moved throughout the hospital. He would literally do the textbook version of the Moro reflex while lying in the bed or in my arms: arms and legs tightly curled then quickly spread out, and then back again.

This boy would have me jumping through hoops in the next few weeks trying to be as quiet as possible and to move as little as possible in his presence. If I picked him up and he fell asleep in my arms, I had to move as little as possible in order to keep the startling from waking him. My new mantra became 'Still as a statue, silent as a snowflake.' As I held him to my chest, it almost seemed as if breathing too deeply might startle him awake. I was holding my breath on the edge of some unknown precipice, waiting to see what would happen next.

The next day, the pediatrician came in to check on Ewan and did all the routine tests. She, too, noticed the startling but just chalked it up to being a bit jittery and maybe hungry. They may have checked his blood sugar, but apparently all was within normal limits since she said as my milk came in more, he would most likely settle down and become accustomed to the environment. We got to stay in the hospital another night, thanks to a rather large episiotomy and a mommy hobbling around as if she were 105. The next night was much of the same, startles to noises and high pitch cries that shattered the silence. He was the edgy, jumpy mess I was just nine months earlier. Born into a strange new world of terrorism and war, he was cloaked in the apprehensive mantle that we all now shouldered. It was if he had taken in all our fears and forebodings and made them his own. Ewan was born the original worrier. The next morning, my husband and I took our little worrier home to begin one of the longest journeys of our life.

Chapter Two

The Infant Insomniac

    Anthony and I brought Ewan home on a Saturday afternoon, and by Monday morning I was on the phone with the pediatrician's office. Now, I was not a brand new mother, so I knew what newborns did and did not do. I'm here to tell you this was no ordinary newborn. This little boy would stare up at me with those wide, dark eyes for hours on end. He would stare at the ceiling fan, the blinds, the shadows on the wall, anything but the backs of his eyelids. When I called the doctor, the receptionist, who happened to be my mother's neighbor, said, "Well, you must have eaten a lot of fish when you were pregnant with that little one." My sleep deprived brain did not comprehend what on earth this woman was rambling on about. I failed to see how eating fish had anything to do with a baby that did not sleep. Literally.

    My reply was, "Huh? Fish? What do you mean?"

    "Oh, I just meant he must be one smart cookie. You know what they say about moms who eat a lot of fish!" Obviously, I was not aware of this ever so popular theory on fish consumption, brain capacity and lack of sleep, so I asked for a little explanation.

    "You think the reason why he's not sleeping is because he's smart? What does that have to do with it? I just want a *little* bit of sleep. I'm not asking for a weekend at the spa here, just a chance at a glimpse of sleep!" Obviously, my snarky attitude was enough to get us in, and besides, Ewan needed a newborn check, so off we went into the stifling summer heat.

    Sometimes, I think office staff and physicians don't understand exactly what patients and caregivers are trying to explain. To be fair, sometimes parents are living on no sleep and are exceedingly unrealistic about what a stethoscope and a reflex hammer can do for their child and situation. Certainly this would describe the amount of hope and faith that went in to my son's first check up and discussion with his doctor. This pediatrician was new to us, and we had no relationship with her, let alone trust. But she was an M.D., and at the time, I believed those two little letters conferred an almost mystical power to the person wearing the white coat. Sitting in the waiting room with a romanticized belief of medicine, I believed she could soothe my worried son into a peaceful consciousness. It wasn't as if I expected medication or surgery or some revolutionary new product on the market. Rather, it was about the wisdom and experience that surrounds the idea of the white coat. In my own naïve manner, I thought surely she had seen something like this before and that surely there was a simple explanation with a simple solution—as if the answer had been before me all along and I was simply too tired to see it. Staring at Ewan, I tried to see it, whatever *it* was, but the answers were just out of reach.

When they called us back, they put us in one of those cutesy pediatrician-type rooms. You know the kind, very colorful walls with a nice little alphabet border in primary colors traversing the room. Posters and little dangly toys were plastered everywhere. Ewan was in stimulation heaven. At only a little under a week old, Ewan sat on the examination table twisting and turning, desperately trying to move in all directions trying to see it all and take it all in. When the nurse and doctor came in to examine him, they both were stunned, "Wow, he is *so awake* and he *really is* looking at these things. This is really unusual." No shit, Sherlock. Apparently, my happy go lucky epidural from the week before had finally worn off as I failed to see how they did not grasp the fact that I explained all of this *before* we came. Yet as they checked his vitals and all the other things that might stand out as being wrong, they fell back on their 'smarter than the average baby' and my overconsumption of seafood products explanations. With a pat on the back, they ushered me and my unease out the door with a very bright and very awake new son. This simple solution just didn't make sense though, and my faith in this new doctor went down a notch.

The next few weeks were a bit of a blur, as it is for all new mothers and fathers. My husband was not in a position to take a few weeks off, so he was back at work already, and this mother was stuck at home with a sleepless wonder. My only comfort was a thick pediatrician's guide to raising infants and toddlers. Poring over the chapters again and again, there was nothing that came even remotely close to explaining or describing my son. So I bought a second, even bigger, book of babies. Nothing in there either. This boy defied modern child development standards and theory. The answers wouldn't come from a book; I was truly on my own with this child. Ewan and I spent the next few weeks searching for a routine simply through trial and error.

The days passed by like a breeze in summer. The humidity seeped into our apartment despite the overworked air conditioner. For all the moisture soaking the indoor air, I was constantly thirsty. There wasn't enough water in the world to quench my thirst. I chugged milk by the gallon. I was breastfeeding, and the sheer work of feeding this child was exhausting me. He nursed and nursed and nursed, and, oh yeah, nursed. His appetite was insatiable. While I may have been thirsty, he approached life like a shipwrecked sailor desperate for any drop of moisture to quench his desiccated mouth. My friend came to visit with her six month old daughter one day for a few hours. She too, was not a new mother, and noticed how awake and how hungry he seemed to be. Ewan continued to nurse every 45 minutes, and she mentioned how odd it was that he would need to nurse that much. We discussed the principles of breastfeeding like we were solving peace in the Middle East, looking for anything that might call a stalemate to this voracious cycle. Maybe he wasn't nursing completely on one side, or maybe he was not getting that rich hindmilk. Maybe the letdown was too fast, too great for him. Maybe he needed it warmer in the house, or maybe he was too hot. We thought about it all, and yet nothing seemed to change either his startled, jittery personality or his near starvation-like cravings. Finally, when my sister came by, she noticed he calmed down when swaddled very, very tightly. He needed to be wrapped up like a little human enchilada. So I would practice over and over getting that burrito blanket as tight as I could while managing to still allow for blood flow and breathing. Pacifiers were of no use; this boy was an instinctive thumb sucker. Wrapping him up and letting his thumb take over helped create a better sleep schedule. We got into a routine, and at around a month old, he did start sleeping. In fact, he went the other way. He slept all night. As a new mother, I thought to myself, "I don't care why, I'll take what I can get!" and slept blissfully through the night.

Of course, you knew that paradise wouldn't last long. It never does. A couple of weeks later, we were back to a schedule only 20 year old frat boys can handle. And I was neither a 20 year old, nor a frat boy. The two of us would often escape into the early morning coolness of the dawn. He and I drove through quiet streets looking for sleep where we could find it. At the end of our daybreak journeys, we usually found ourselves at Wal-Mart shopping through deserted aisles searching for some miraculous sleep aid around every corner. I bought fans, humidifiers, noise machines, ambient sound CDs—you name it, I tried it. I pored over every sentence in that big book of babies, yet nothing in it could bring sleep any closer. Infant massage, scented blankets and pillows, scented lotions and soaps, warm baths replete with candles and potpourri. Nothing. The infant insomniac continued to haunt the midnight hours.

My brain and my body were pushed into survival mode, and I was left to the mercy of my autonomic system. Breathing and blinking were all that I could effectively accomplish at times. Days turned into weeks and weeks turned into months. Time passed by, and my life dissolved into a hundred million seconds of confusion. A nauseating fatigue washed over me, and I was powerless to stop any of it. Family and friends tried to help, but it was of little use. So much of what is used for typical babies had no effect whatsoever on Ewan's system. A lot of the time, typical remedies only seemed to make things worse. Someone bought a really nice swing for Ewan, but he couldn't stand it because the movement was too much. He wanted to be held but would change his mind almost as soon as you would pick him up. He liked being left to his own devices, finding solace in the isolation of his crib watching the mobile and tuning into the details on the crib and blankets.

When Ewan was about two and a half months old, my mom and I took a trip down to Nashville for a day of shopping. We walked in and out of climactic zones as we went from shop to shop. Switching from blistering cold blasts to sweltering waves of heat made it difficult to keep Ewan comfortable. Within a short time, Ewan was an irritable and uneasy mess. We called it a day and retreated to the steady comfort of an air conditioned car. While we cooled down, I looked over at Ewan. He smiled real big, and I will swear until my dying day that he said, "Hi!"

My eyes about popped out of my head, and I said, "Mom! Did you hear that? He just said hi!"

Of course, my mom, being realistic, said, "Oh honey, it just sounded like that, he's only making noise." There were other times where it sounded like he was saying or repeating honest to goodness real words. But then at around three to three and a half months, Ewan and Skye both suffered from a series of ear infections and colds. It was then that he went fairly silent, and for many months I would only hear grunting, screeching, and weird noises, nothing that sounded like the English language anymore at all.

As the world of consonants and vowels crept toward the shadows, I noticed that Ewan preferred the simple solitude of his crib rather than my embrace. I, being the intense mother that I am, wanted nothing more than to simply hold him, shove my way into his world and become something of significance. Yet he did much better and was much happier when left alone. All that made for one very frustrated mother. The whole experience of motherhood felt skewed this time around. Now I thirsted for more than just water. I yearned for a child who needed me for something other than just nutrition, a task I could barely keep up with. The more I pulled him to me, the harder he pushed away. The ceiling fan held his attention more than I ever could. There was nothing in that big book of babies to help me connect with him, and I continued to flounder in my trial and error parenting experiment. All my instincts were wrong this time around. What worked with my daughter, seven years before, wasn't working now. I was lost in a sea of parenting advice, tips, and tricks that served no purpose with this child. He was simply different.

    Nursing him was an arduous process for us both, and it was only through an iron will that we persevered. Our problems weren't anything that any breastfeeding manual or website could help with. This wasn't in my big book of babies either. In my desperation, I ended up at a WIC office. They were kind enough to try and help, but again, this child defied every possible rule of childhood. Even their professional big book of babies could not set us straight. We ended up back at the doctor's office, hoping to find that simple solution yet again. Like the last time, though, there were no answers and there were no tricks of the trade. This time around, the doctor hinted at the need for more invasive testing, like a scope of his esophagus and stomach. The very idea of such a procedure on our baby terrified us, and we refused to take such drastic measures. I was still looking for that simple solution, and surgery wasn't simple enough for me.

    It was a vicious cycle of need and refusal. I would nurse him and he would latch on just fine, dive right in and take a few big gulps only to push and turn away. He would arch his back and turn his head from me but then take a big breath to dive right back in. He would do this for every single nursing session, and it was becoming increasingly more difficult to hold him. I was never one of those blasé moms with a baby deftly wrapped in a sling shopping for butter while unknowingly nursing the invisible infant. I could barely walk through the house with him without setting up a safety zone of pillows and blankets because he would so forcefully throw himself backwards that I was afraid I'd be the proverbial mother to drop him right on his head. Needless to say, I developed some really kick ass forearms and learned to keep an emergency inflatable exit at my feet in case he pushed too hard away from me.

Late that fall, the nursing demands and sleep deprivation began to take their toll on my psyche. My frustration was so profound that it spread like a living organism throughout the house. Every night I stared at that big book of babies, willing it to explain my son and unlock the secrets. Every night, that big book of infants and toddlers lay silent as my son grew more mysterious by the day. By this point I looked a little like an extra from *Night of the Living Dead*, and I told the pediatrician to do something *or else*. I didn't care if the answer was simple or complicated or anything in between. I needed help. I left it up to her what a sleep and caffeine deprived woman who barely had time to shower might do if she ignored me. So, the pediatrician ordered an overnight sleep study at a hospital where my son would be hooked up to more wires than the Matrix in order to see exactly what his brainwaves were like. My sister drove Ewan and I to the hospital that evening. For the entire 45 minute drive, Ewan screamed like the devil himself was chasing us through the wet November night. Drops of rain glistened on the window, reflecting every light that flashed past us, creating a whirling distorted feeling. I tried to block out the screams and focus on the watery splashes of light, but my ears were close to bursting from the sound. This was becoming a new problem. Going anywhere in the car was sheer torture for Ewan and anyone else within a five mile radius. Movement like that was not soothing for him. Now, my daughter and I can fall asleep in the first 10 minutes of the car ride. Not so with this little one. The screaming reverberated off the doors and windows until we pulled into the brightly lit parking lot and stopped the car. As my sister waved goodbye, she joked, "Well, let's see what kind of super brainwaves they find on Mr. Ewan— they'll probably resemble the brainwaves of a 40 year old physics professor." Since I was a graduate of the history department, I did not find this statement comforting in the least. I did not have the brainwaves of a 40 year physics professor, and I certainly wouldn't understand a six month old who did.

The sleep study was an interesting way to spend six hours, note the sarcasm in this statement. First, they put my fully awake son in a crib that looked like a jail for criminal babies and then tried to attach hundreds of wires and electrodes to him. Because he had pretty good aim, grasp, and hand control, keeping those electrodes and wires where they should be was an exercise in futility. After wrestling him to the ground with moves that would impress Rowdy Roddy Piper, Ewan was able to sleep enough for them to gather some data, but nothing came back to explain why my son was so alert and awake. They didn't find any secret 40 year old physics code in there, either.

Because my sister is an occupational therapist, I called and harassed her over every little thing. Why won't he do this? Why does he do that? Shouldn't he be doing this? Shouldn't this be something he does much, much later? She earned her degree in those months and years that would follow. When the sleep study came back normal, she suggested that maybe early intervention should come out and do an evaluation on Ewan to see if they could help. They were able to come out at seven months, and the only things we could comment on being wrong were things early intervention really didn't cover. He didn't sleep, and they had no answers. He didn't eat much, and they had no answers. He couldn't stand to be in a moving vehicle, and they had no answers. He threw himself backward every time he was held, and they had no answers. In some ways he was very odd, and in other ways he seemed 'advanced,' something early intervention definitely didn't cover. All in all, he was not delayed enough in any area to get any services at the time. At only seven months, assessing language delay was difficult, and he was on target—if not ahead of schedule—for everything movement-related. At the time, self-regulation was not a category that early intervention could or would do anything about, and yet again, we were left to our own devices waiting to understand our son.

While Ewan excelled at movement, it was a difficult issue for him. When we forced it upon him, it was a nightmare he suffered through. When it was something he initiated, it was so much more than just a joyful discovery. Ewan wanted and needed to move, but only on his terms. If only I had known then, what I know now. The entirety of our lives would be on his terms, when he was ready. While I waited with bated breath for each and every milestone, Ewan moved through life without even the slightest thought to the child development chart hung on his pediatrician's wall. His need for independence was obvious even then. He has always walked to the beat of a different drum, even in infancy. In the beginning, we waited for that first milestone of turning over. I wanted something tangible that I could check off from that big book of babies list of skills. I wanted something, anything, to be in that damn book. Because of a cranium reminiscent of the "Heed move" scene in *So I Married an Axe Murderer*, we wondered if he would ever make the turn. Finally, the day came at four and half months when the momentum pushed him from front to back. Yet in those early days, Ewan hated to lie on his stomach, and he would just keep on rolling to reach the safety of his back. He quickly went from turning to sitting up, and shortly thereafter, he was sitting tall all on his own. But it wasn't enough. He wanted more than just a better view, he wanted to move. It didn't take long for Ewan to figure out the motions from sitting to crawling, even if it was an odd way to crawl. In the beginning, he did a Navy Seal-like combat crawl. Then, he skipped to a funky bear crawl with his arms and his legs stuck straight out. Big sister, the OT, said this was just a way for him to get as much input to his joints as he could. She told me to try it and see how different it felt from regular crawling. Yeah, I thought, you go first.

  From rolling and crawling, Ewan sought out the next step on the horizon. He wanted to stand, and by five months he was using the furniture to do so. *Harry Potter* had just come out, and mom, Skye, and I had gone to the movies while Anthony stayed home to watch Ewan. When our trip to the land of myth and magic was over and we walked in the door, Anthony excitedly said, "Hey, look what Ewan can do." I'll be honest, I was a bit worried about what daddy and son had been experimenting with in my absence, but I was more surprised to see Ewan holding on to the furniture standing up all by himself. There were those strong little legs working hard to do what his brain so badly wanted to do. My own son seemed as mythical and magical as the movie I'd just seen. Defying expectations, living outside the big book, he was more legend than fact. All along I'd been looking for answers in the reference section when it was clear I should've been reading fiction.

  Ignoring every norm and standard, the drum roll began, and Ewan started walking to the sound of his own bewitching beat at only seven months of age. No longer imprisoned by his own body, his soul was free to travel the earth. Ewan had finally deciphered the mobility code, and for once in his young life, his body could keep pace with the terminal velocity of his mind. By Jove, I think it was the best thing that could have happened to the kid. Long before Ewan actually started walking, he had been practicing. When he was only three months old, we would hold him semi-upright, and he would tense his little legs as if he were truly trying to stand. My sister said something about hypertonia and excessively tense muscles, but he was able to control it and relax, so it never seemed too much of an issue—just interesting. He had been ready to go and explore from day one, and now his body had caught up with his mind. It took a lot of pressure off of my husband and me because we were, quite frankly, running out of toys to occupy his mind. We would have to go to second hand baby stores and buy new toys every couple of days. As soon as he would figure out a toy, he was completely bored and uninterested in it. If the mystery was solved, he saw no reason to continue playing with it. I will forever be grateful to that store for letting us bring toy after toy back and exchange for something else, something novel. Now the simple act of movement could occupy his thoughts. If Ewan marched to the beat of a different tune, then surely his tempo was a sporadic drum roll. He went well past crawling and standing and went straight to running. We've been struggling to keep up with him ever since.

    I was wrestling so many different monsters then. Sleep was elusive, yet Ewan was stuck in overdrive. His path through life was vastly divergent from my own and from what I knew about infants. Just when I thought I understood him, life would change drastically. Things would come in big spurts, take huge steps backwards, or not happen at all. Ewan has always had that rather baffling asymmetrical and asynchronous development. His enigmatic brain defied every parenting book on the market. On one hand, we were happy to see Ewan occupy his mind with movement, and on the other hand, it was exhausting to keep up with the inhuman pace he set. I hoped the movement would wear him out, yet it was like fuel to the flame as his energy levels reached the speed of a particle accelerator. My body couldn't handle the strain and the lack of sleep began to affect my grip on reality. At some point a human being cracks under the strain of insomnia, and I was cracking at every seam. I remember an anatomy professor once describing the brain and how it functions while we are awake. He described the actions of the brain as one big hug between all the systems, and at some point when the brain and body cannot take anymore, everyone stops hugging and the lights go out. I was at that point. My brain was no longer hugging anyone and sleep was going to come whether I willed it to or not. When a parent is this ultra-stressed and exhausted, rational thinking is well beyond grasp. I couldn't think, I couldn't function, and I couldn't think beyond 'breathe in and out.' Every minute I stood in the twilight of sleep, yet Ewan would wake and keep me from the arms of Morpheus. Tears came easy, and my whole body was a clenched fist of frustration. I don't know how my husband or my children made it through all this without being scarred for life.

One day I stood on the edge of a nameless void of stress, and the next day I plunged head first into the Stygian darkness. I absolutely lost it. It felt like I was headed straight for the middle of madness. My feet couldn't take me far enough away and I ended up driving down a country road to nowhere. I didn't care where I went as long as I was moving and putting some space between me and that house. I wondered what would happen if I just kept driving. This child was the sphinx, and I wondered why God had given him to me and not a mother with more patience and a case of insomnia to match his. After a few miles and an earful of AC/DC, I knew the answer even if I didn't fully understand it. I believe God puts us where He wants us, and He puts us where we may have the greatest impact on another human being. It was during the chorus of "Highway to Hell" that the epiphany hit. This wasn't about me. It was about a boy who saw more than I did, who understood life in a way I did not. It was about Ewan. God gave me this child for a reason, even if I couldn't fully understand the rationale behind it. In the middle of a dirt road, I turned around and headed home. This was *my* son, and I was just going to have to suck it up and figure him out. I had to make myself see what I was missing and remember that "This too shall pass." By the grace of God and Angus Young, my car found its way back to the driveway. Anthony approached me like I was a rabid wolverine, but I grabbed his hand and headed inside. For whatever reason, the path before us was the one we were meant to be on, and in 20 years I knew I would look back and see the plan laid out in all its glorious complexity and understand how simple it all is. Someday I would decode the inner workings of his mysterious brain and I would know why God gave *me* this child.

Making that decision to see the bigger picture, I resolved to find a way to keep Ewan and I both happy, so we moved everything around and gave him the space he needed and his own room (even though we didn't really have the square footage to pull this off well). This way, he could be up all night and not totally affect me, and I could turn from side to side in bed without affecting him. I still had to get up and nurse him, but the time was getting a little longer in between sessions. He was still not sleeping for long stretches at a time, yet in the quiet of my own room, every now and then Morpheus would patiently lead me to the land of dreams.

While I may have had the god of dreams in my life, I really needed Asclepius. Skye and Ewan continued to battle cold after cold that winter, and a visit from the god of healing and medicine would have been helpful. No amount of hygiene or warmth could keep the insidious germs at bay. We all had the sniffles, but Ewan and Skye just couldn't shake the illness off. They were both on a series of antibiotics and pain relievers, but no amount of acetaminophen could ease the discomfort in Ewan's ears. He would bang his head and slide his ear across the floor screaming in pain. In his discomfort, he turned to nursing. At around eight months he was still nursing about every two to two and a half hours and kept the same schedule as a newborn. Nursing was an equalizer for him. He didn't nurse solely for the purpose of nutrition. This boy was born large and stayed on that trajectory until he turned out to look like Paul Bunyan's genetic offspring. Nursing for Ewan fulfilled many needs: nutrition, hunger, sensory, comfort, and more. He would nurse and rest for about 15 minutes and then seem completely refreshed and ready to go, ready for something. It wasn't as if he was crying all night. From across the hall I could hear him coo and screech in an effort to entertain himself. Throughout the night he vacillated between under and overstimulated, seeking a balance between body and mind.

As the year progressed, March brought with it a sliver of warmth for the spring thaw. Ewan continued to suffer a series of ear infections, and both he and his sister battled a consistent wave of illness. The pediatrician rolled up her sleeves and tried to hold back the tide, yet no amount of antibiotic could keep up with the stream of ailments. When the doctor had no answers, the burden lay at my feet. When medicine offered no panacea, comfort was found in the healing power of a mother's compassion and love. Ewan's rampant ear infections and Skye's ongoing immune issues kept us on our toes and kept Tylenol's profit statements in the black. With round the clock medical care, I felt like the reincarnation of Florence Nightingale. Through the midnight hours, my weary soul tended to the ills and pains of two equally tired children. It didn't matter that I was sick, too, for Florence Nightingale cannot afford to take breaks. I was at the front line and the rear, digging trenches and evading gunfire, holding the enemy at bay with no reserves in sight. In the darkest of nights, I was the lady with the lamp called to care for every cough, to heal every ache, and to nurse every fever. For the woman who had wanted to be a doctor, I was now the nurse straining to hear the patient down the hall.

It took multiple antibiotics and two shots of Rocephin before we threw in the towel with Ewan's pediatrician. That spring marked the end of our time with that pediatrician as we decided to find someone else we could connect with. Skye shed weight as if it were tears. Both children ended up at a friendly ENT office where we scheduled a set of Eustachian tubes for Ewan and a series of tests for Skye. The internal hostilities between Skye's white blood cells and some foreign entity had reached a stalemate. After throwing thirty different antibiotics at her, she was subjected to a series of tests and procedures while Ewan and I navigated a series of waiting rooms and diagnostic clinics. A CT scan gave us an inside view of the destruction with ground zero being her sinuses. Two surgeries were scheduled back to back: one for Ewan's tubes and one for Skye's sinuses. Not only was I drafted into Ewan's insomniac army, I was now a battlefield medic running here and there between the two children dispensing acetaminophen and love.

While the Eustachian surgery itself is nothing more than a 15 minute fix, the before and after were a big ordeal. Keeping Ewan calm enough to get the medication in and dealing with the after-effects of the anesthesia was extremely difficult. He woke up rather combative and surprisingly strong for a nine month old, and we were quickly ushered out of the recovery area and into our car. The tubes were a blessing, though, because soon after Ewan began sleeping. It wasn't perfect, but I no longer felt the press of insomnia upon my mind. Yet as one part of life evened out, another careened out of control. As Ewan began to sleep, Skye's health continued to decline. While the sinus surgery corrected a lot of the damage, they also discovered polyps reminiscent of cystic fibrosis. Our new pediatrician was kindly but not the brightest bulb in the bunch. Recognizing his limitations, he deferred to Skye's ENT, who suggested a simple sweat test. As we struggled to maintain a sense of normalcy with Ewan, we held on by our fingernails as Skye was tested for the deadly disease through a procedure that collected and analyzed the sweat from her skin. When the first batch of sweat testing was read as borderline, Skye was sent to the local children's hospital for an appointment with an expert immunologist. After many more tests, antibiotics and IVs, we managed to flush out a negative result for cystic fibrosis and come back with the diagnosis of an overworked and overtaxed immune system. With a great deal of patience and an immune team on call, Skye slowly clawed her way out of the gaping hollow of illness.

~

With the approach of summer came the whisper of a hope for normalcy. We found ourselves healthy and antibiotic free. Everyone was finding a rhythm to life that had been missing over the past year. The medical appointments slowly tapered off, and we found ourselves at home rather than in a clinic. We were able to simply live without stress for a short time. Ewan was still moving a million miles an hour, but the stress of understanding him lessened for a time. We accepted that Ewan was Ewan and learned to ride the waves of his asynchronous life. As I thought about how this boy approached life, it became clear that the stars were never fully in alignment for him. He still marched to the beat and tune of his own drum, and we could not force him to hear anything else other than the atonal tune he started to hum. Every day Ewan conducted a calming effect of movement and vibration. Every single day he composed a symphony of serenity through instruments only he could play and only he could hear.

It was a trade off. When one system righted itself, the next one seemed off kilter and worked twice as hard to catch up from the lack of attention. It almost seemed as if his brain was taxed by a multi-system disruption and could only attend to one aspect at a time. We simply held on to what was in front of us and surfed each wave of development and delay without really seeing the bigger tidal wave around us. Our new normal was everyone else's Mr. Toad's Wild Ride.

The storms of spring were over, and we emerged from the trenches battle weary and ready for a truce. I was shell shocked from the constant strain and stress detached from my normal self. The hypervigilance of the combat medic evaporated, leaving a temporary numbness in its place. As the explosion of warmth and life surrounded us, the sickness and insomnia of the past year crept to the shadowy spaces in between. With the sun came hope and the summer wind breathed new life into my pores. The siege had ended and I was ready for the next phase of life. It was June again, and somehow we had managed to make it through the first year of Ewan's life. When I think back at that first year, it's clear we were all in survival mode. For twelve months, I had lived in a constant state of fight or flight, pushing myself onward and forward through it all. We had been thrown in the deep end of the ocean and had been treading water the whole time just trying not to drown. We kept our head above water though, and managed to swim to shore. It was probably the hardest thing I've ever done. Harder than what was to come, even if I didn't know it at the time.

For Ewan's first birthday we decided to have a Thomas the Train birthday party. It was one toy that he continued to gravitate toward when we would visit the local book store. My husband and I both thought that it would be a good toy to encourage play and other skills, and it was the classic boy toy. So for his first birthday, all the grandparents and family members chipped in to get Ewan the whole Thomas the Train table and train set. That day, we set the table up in the living room for the party and let the fun begin. Only Ewan completely ignored all the people in the room and focused on the trains and not anyone or anything else. The train had eclipsed the house and left all of us in darkness. This eclipse in our life would last not just an hour or a day, but years, and we had no idea what we had just set in motion with those innocent little trains. Ewan was walking around and around the table pushing trains to and fro, completely mesmerized but not seeing the bigger picture, not noticing the balloons, the presents, or the cake.

My sister said then, "You know, I'm worried about his eye contact. He's not really looking at us or you for that matter, and you're his mother."

I defended my son's so-called lack of eye contact by saying, "Look there, he *is* looking at me. Didn't you just see him look at me?" I could tell by my sister's lack of enthusiasm over the half a millisecond glance my way that she did not believe he really was *looking* at me.

She then said, "Call his name, see if he'll really look at you." I did call out. Over and over. Ewan never turned towards my voice. He was lost in the magic of the trains. It was then my sister mentioned that Ewan reminded her of children she worked with, children with autism and Asperger's Syndrome. A moment frozen in time, she was the first of many to tell me my son had autism. Neither shocked nor angry, I merely stared at my young son wondering if anything could ever define him. Marching to the beat of his own drum, his short life had been miles apart from normal. The trajectory of his life followed no known chart or curve. He walked his own path. While I stared at Ewan, Anthony stared at me. Willing me to look at him, my eyes found his as my husband shot me a warning glance from across the room. He didn't want to hear or believe that anything was wrong. Any mention to Anthony of Ewan's eccentricities led to a clenched jaw and a stubborn refusal to talk about any of it.

In the dark, though, we whispered the things we couldn't say in the light of day. Later that night, in the solitude and privacy of our bedroom he finally broke the silence, "My son does not have ASS burger's or anything else. He's fine." The late nights and persistent nagging thoughts of the previous year had worn his patience thin. With a deep sigh he said, "Why can't you just let him be? Why does everyone have to try and diagnose every little thing? We've spent the past year in doctor's offices and poring through books and what has it done? Nothing, it hasn't done a damn thing. Let it alone. He's fine, Skye's fine, we are ALL fine."

I whispered, "Don't you see it, Anthony? He's different. There's something about him and it may not be autism and it may not be anything, but he *is* different. I can *feel* it Anthony."

With a huff he replied, "So what, you think you can fix him? He doesn't need to be fixed because there is nothing *wrong* with him."

"It doesn't have to mean that there is anything wrong with him, but if we want to help him, we need to understand him. In order to understand him, we need answers and I can tell you the answers sure as Hell aren't in any book. Trust me, I've looked. For the past year, I've pored through every book I own looking for something to help us and there's no words of wisdom to be found."

"My cousins have autism, Lisha, and I just don't see it. Leave it be. For God's sake, just leave it be." He turned to his side then and refused to say another word.

I really had no knowledge of autism and had never even heard of Asperger's syndrome. I didn't know if there really *was* a word or a book that could ever explain Ewan. But long after Anthony went to sleep, my mind was racing with what my sister had said. Given that Anthony's two cousins had autism or autistic-like disorders (one has Fragile X), I would have thought he might have reacted with a little less anger and surprise. Yet, to accept that something, *anything*, might be wrong with your child is a tough pill to swallow for any parent. Moreso for fathers than anyone else, I think.

Anthony was steadfast in his belief that Ewan was fine while I mulled the word *autism* over and over. Long after Anthony had fallen asleep, I stared into the night looking for answers. I knew so little about autism that I couldn't blithely dismiss it the way Anthony had. This word stood before me in the dark, a monolithic and mysterious force. It was the first time anyone had ever said the word to me and I wondered if it would be the last. In three syllables, autism had suddenly forced its way into my reverie and worry. Before sleep pulled me under, I thought of all the reasons Ewan might be autistic and all the things I told myself autism could never explain about him.

Over the next few days and weeks, I looked at Ewan and thought about what my sister had said. I could see what she was trying to show me and tell me about Ewan, but I didn't know what *to* do. I had already called early intervention once and they had not been much help. They came, they saw, they said, "We'll call you back later," and in the meantime, I was left treading water in the deep end of the ocean without a life raft. It seemed like I was stuck between indecision and action with no discernible plan at all. I didn't know what to do or how to do it, and I didn't even know where to start. Our new pediatrician sat on the sidelines sticking with Ewan's first doctor's 'smarter than the average baby' assessment, leaving me to figure things out by myself. These were the loneliest times of my life with Ewan. No one there to guide us, no one there to show us the way—we were lost and alone in a sea of confusion, waiting for the Coast Guard to find us on the radar.

~

After weeks of soul searching and staring at Ewan's every move, life continued to move on around us. The next month, Anthony and I found ourselves alone for a night out in Chicago for a wedding. We hadn't been alone since before Ewan was born, and it was exhilarating to spend just a few hours *sans* children. We took off from Indy around 11 a.m. on a Friday morning to make it in time for a rush hour 4 p.m. ceremony. Our grand adventure turned out to be a series of traffic nightmares. First was the unexpected, one lane, crawling traffic on I-65. After 25 miles, the traffic cleared, and we breathed a sigh of relief, hoping we'd still make it on time to the wedding. Then came I-80 and Gary, Indiana. In all my life, I hope to never drive on I-80 on a Friday afternoon ever again. Traffic didn't just slow down, traffic came to an absolute standstill. Tumbleweeds blew past us as we realized the interstate system had just transformed into a desert of idling vehicles. Here we were at 3 p.m. after five hours of driving, most of which was non-stop, because of the earlier traffic snafu. It didn't help that just an hour before we'd gone through a Wendy's drive-up and I ordered the largest Diet Coke the restaurant offered. We were stuck in eighteen lanes of gridlock, and I had to pee like you wouldn't believe. There was no exiting this logjam to look for a rest area or gas station. We couldn't even move five inches, let alone across five lanes, to find an exit. There was no way but forward, and forward was moving at a snail's pace. While Anthony eyed the suspiciously low gas gauge, my brain was focused on the alarm bells blaring from my urinary tract. I shifted in my seat. I bit my fingers. I did everything I could think of to ignore the screaming in my bursting bladder. When I started to sweat, my husband pointed out the fact that the oversized Wendy's cup was now empty. I stared at the cup and then looked back at him. He raised his eyebrows at me and cocked his head at the cup again and said, "When you gotta go, you gotta go."

I about cried as I replied, "You think I'm going to pee in that cup?!"

Anthony said in his practical and impatient way, "My Lord woman, you have to pee, there's a cup, now do it!"

For another 25 minutes I held out, thinking this God awful bumper to bumper traffic was going to suddenly break wide open. When my eyes began to water, I knew it was either pee in my pants or pee in that cup, so I chose to save the upholstery and jumped in the backseat. My husband delicately looked the other way and didn't start laughing 'til I had crawled back into the front again and didn't stop laughing until we pulled in an hour late for the wedding.

We missed the wedding and ended up getting to the reception just in time. Originally, we had planned to drive back home that same night, but there wasn't enough money in all the world to get me back in a car so soon, so we ended up grabbing a hotel room for the night. Intermittently throughout the night, Anthony would burst out laughing, and my face would turn bright red until I, too, giggled like a school girl. It was nice to laugh just for the sake of laughing. A year's worth of stress and worry was wearing off with each passing minute of laughter and festivity. It was a wedding, and we were miles and hours away from the mountain of responsibility that had piled up over the past few months.

Uninhibited by the lack of children and overwhelmed from a year of insomnia and sickness, Anthony and I found ourselves swept up in a wave of spontaneity. Catching his glance across the room, I knew where we were headed. In a crowd of people, I wanted nothing more than to be alone with him. We found ourselves drifting away from the party to find comfort in the quiet of our room, entwined in a tangle of limbs and sheets. We existed in those hours simply for the pleasure of each other's company. Breathing a sigh of relief from months of stress, in one long and languorous night Anthony brought me back to sanity. Little did we know, the next time we'd find ourselves alone in the quiet of a hotel room would be five long years later.

    Returned and rejuvenated from our night away, smiles came easier, laughter lasted a little longer, and we found ourselves hopeful that maybe the worst was behind us somewhere on I-80 near Gary, Indiana. For a time, I tried to ignore the obvious and kept quiet and hopeful when Ewan ignored me. Ewan was still eccentric and obsessed, and while Anthony hoped it was just a phase he would outgrow, the unease grew in my heart. I think Anthony hoped to one day wake up and find the passion for locomotives pushed aside and replaced with a passion for real live people. I simply prayed that somehow it would all work out. Skye was growing up too, and while she was now healthier, she struggled with returning to school and the rigors of second grade. She had missed so much school during her first grade year that she was behind and confused much of the time. As Ewan retreated to the comfort of his trains, Anthony and I sat down each evening for homework duty with one frustrated little girl. My husband had found work outside of a restaurant for the first time in his life, and because he was working more regular hours, he was able to participate in the rituals and routine of home life. Although he commuted a long way every morning and afternoon, he seemed to be happy with his new job. On a hot August night, Anthony said out of nowhere, "Why don't we go out to eat tonight? I know this great Japanese restaurant over by where I work. You'll love it." My husband's work was about 45 minutes away, and this meant we had to endure 45 minutes of pure terror emanating from the back seat. If one thing had not changed, it was Ewan's fear of a moving vehicle. But my husband and I are willing to endure quite a lot for good food, so we innocently set out on what we thought was a simple night on the town. We packed up Skye and Ewan and headed to an experience on the NE side of Indy that would change our lives for years to come. Who would've thought that an innocent Japanese restaurant would be the pivotal moment of realization for our family?

    We opened the door to that restaurant and walked into a potpourri of sound and smell. The kitchen was open to the rest of the restaurant, and you could see the rapid actions of seven chefs at once. In a flurry of movement and noise, dishes of various aromas flew out of the kitchen and onto the table. Chefs enthusiastically shouted out orders and playfully chopped and minced a thousand ingredients at once. Every so often, a bell would randomly toll, and the chefs would break out into a raucous chorus of giggles. It was a wholly interactive environment, and I briefly wondered how Ewan would do with this mayhem. We nestled Ewan into a high chair at the end of the table and waited to see what would happen. Would he think it was funny, or would he want to run from the building? When we first sat down, he seemed okay, so we breathed a sigh of relief and ordered a round of Teriyaki chicken and Asian seafood. Ewan was sitting so that he could see the outside, the rest of the people, and the flurry of activity in the kitchen. The view might have been entertaining for the typical toddler, but for a child with such a sensitive system it was way, way too much. Right about then a couple came and sat down behind us and attempted to engage Ewan by smiling and waving at him. Any other child might have been entertained by two elderly individuals being incredibly silly in order to gain favor with a toddler. Ewan was not like other children, though; he was literally trembling from head to toe in a state of near shock. Anthony nervously asked, "What's wrong with him? Is he hurt or something?"

I replied, "I don't know but he looks like he's going to be sick." I picked him up and ran off to the bathroom, worried he was going to vomit all over some unsuspecting diner. He was still trembling, and in the quiet of the stall began crying hysterically. Nothing I did could bring him out of this state. He refused to nurse, which was a sign that the world had turned upside down. I knew we had no other option but to leave. I went back to the table with an obviously unhinged baby and told Anthony to box up my food as Ewan and I headed over to the sanctuary of a neighboring bookstore. I had hoped to find the one thing that might put the proverbial train back on track: a Thomas train table set. Yet the hysteria continued to hold Ewan in its grip no matter how many times I shoved Percy and James under his nose. In the end, we fled that bookstore as well, seeking the security of home to put things right again. Anthony and Skye came out of the restaurant with a pile of Styrofoam containers, our fun evening cut short by some invisible force. Just when I thought I understood this child, something completely illogical would push me back into confusion. Home was 45 minutes away, though, and the car was the last place Ewan wanted and needed to be after such an experience. I tried to nurse him in the backseat, but he wanted nothing to do with me and continued to scream bloody murder all the way back.

In desperation, I said, "Dear God, I wish early intervention would just call back. I can't seem to do anything right with him. Look at him Anthony, what kind of mother has a child that screams like this? What are we doing wrong here? I swear I'm going to call them and beg them to help us, I don't care what their tests say."

My husband took a deep breath, looked at me sheepishly and said, "Well, they actually called yesterday to check on us but I told them my son was fine and he didn't need any more evaluations."

I stared back at him with a mixture of fury and awe as I pointed to the nuclear bomb in the back seat, "Does it *look* like he's fine, Anthony? *Does it*? Does it look like *I'm* fine? We're not okay here, do you not see that we need help?"

The next morning I was on the phone setting up an appointment for early intervention to come, and at the same time, I gave my husband strict instructions to never answer the telephone again without my permission.

Chapter Three

The New Normal

December 2, 2010

Early intervention is a program that is near and dear to my heart. Early intervention is a program that saved my sanity, forever changed the developmental trajectory of Ewan's life, and ultimately gave me the tools I needed to help him live a life of possibility and hope. Early intervention is a program that is often under-utilized, under-funded and completely misunderstood by those in our neighborhoods, communities, and legislatures.

Right now, many state programs are facing a critical mass. Right now, our program to help those at risk is at risk itself of dissolving in front of our eyes. And if we fail to act now, millions of children face an unknown future where possibility and hope cease to exist.

I remember the day early intervention came into my home and into my heart. First came the service coordinator, then came the therapists, and progress followed them both—progress in my understanding of the true nature of my son's needs and progress in my son's abilities to walk, talk, understand, and learn. All the coordinators and therapists knew what we needed before we knew ourselves. They not only worked with my son, but they gave me the tools I needed to succeed as this child's mother.

Our special needs children don't come with a manual, and often mothers, fathers, and caregivers find themselves lost and confused in a sea of terminology and tears. Early intervention is a life-line for those of us raising a special needs child. And without it, many families will drown in the waters of depression and overwhelming emotion.

Every single day I look at the young man my son has become, and I thank a higher power for the gift of early intervention. Every success he has now started when he was in early intervention. Every inch of progress began when he was but 14 months of age, and the lasting effects of every minute of therapy will be felt throughout his lifetime. And I know when he graduates from college some day that I will think of how early intervention was there to shape his life. I will remember the day the service coordinator walked through my door and brought hope into my life. I will remember the day all our lives changed in an instant, and I will fight to keep early intervention alive for all the families that come after me.

In states across the country, early intervention services are being cut back and altered drastically in an effort to keep these programs afloat. Misunderstood and under-funded, these programs are losing quality therapists by the truckload. Therapists who have spent their professional careers advocating for our most precious children. Therapists who are even now sacrificing so much just to show up at the homes of those they serve. Therapists who work without pay in some situations. I ask that you join me in this fight to save early intervention across the country by advocating for early intervention on a state and federal level. I ask that you stand up for these children and families when no one else will.

In the next few months and years, early intervention across this country will face lean times and those who will be most affected will be the children early intervention is supposed to serve and protect. These children will grow up without the benefit of early intervention, will start school with more drastic delays, and may not reach their highest potential into adulthood because the lack of early intervention will fail them and their families. If there is but one program I had to choose that would make a difference in the life of a child, I would choose early intervention every single time. Today, right at this very moment, you have the opportunity to truly make a difference in the life of a child. Make early intervention a priority in your community and in your state. Call, write, and advocate for a program that changes a life every single day and provides a moment of possibility and hope for families across this country. Choose possibility. Choose hope. Choose it today, tomorrow, and next year. Support early intervention now.

Once early intervention was able to get past the gatekeeper, otherwise known as my husband, we moved through the paces pretty quickly. We were crossing into a new frontier by opening the door to these strangers. In a week, there was an evaluation team in my home settling into the living room couch with clipboards and ink pens ready. After a quick hello and how are you, they proceeded to ask me every conceivable question about Ewan's life and, really, about all of our family. I was thankful that someone, anyone, seemed interested in helping us, but I was still confused about where these questions might lead us. Early intervention hadn't done much the first time around. I knew someone came to your home, and I knew someone worked to help your child meet certain goals, but what I didn't expect was the overwhelming presence of several 'someones' in my life. It felt odd to have strangers come into our home and ask such personal questions. They wanted to know about me and about Anthony. They asked about every facet of life from our income to what diapers we used. Questions flooded our living room as if I were on trial. When did Ewan do this? How do you react when he does that? What do you want Ewan to do? And of course, I felt like every little thing I did as a mother was under the microscope. Set in a petri dish in the middle of a room, every action and reaction was judged by a team of strangers.

Deep down, I wondered if the problem was me. On every level you want conflicting information from these people. On one hand, you want them to validate your feelings that you are not crazy and you are not a bad parent. I tortured myself over action and reaction and presided as judge and jury over my own conscience. How could I be a good parent to one child, and flounder with the other? On the other hand, you want them to say that everything really is fine or that we can fix this very quickly. I wanted a simple solution and a magic wand to fly me back to normal. I knew my sister had thrown around the words 'autism' and 'Asperger's,' and I knew my husband's family had two children with autism, but what I didn't understand was the depth of the issue. I thought after a few short weeks, this intrusion would fade from my life, leaving a well-adjusted toddler in its wake. When Ewan started speech therapy, I thought to myself, "Well this is just playing, it should be easy to fix this," and I didn't fully understand the work that lay hidden underneath all the play. I didn't understand how the therapist was getting Ewan to participate or interact and when he ignored such interactions what it really meant. In my own head, I hoped this was a simple fix—talk to him, play with him more, interact with him more, and voila, problem solved. I didn't understand how pervasive the issue really was. I couldn't see the layers of circumstance that kept him from connecting to a wider world of humanity. I was blind to the layers of scaffolding it would take to build the bridge from his world to ours. It is only now, after all these years, that I truly understand why the term pervasive is used with autism spectrum disorders.

Given our Japanese restaurant fiasco, our first concerns came from the prison we all felt trapped in. There was no blithely leaving the house.

Driving in the car still reduced every occupant to tears. Ewan out of fear, the rest of us out of frustration. Our other major source of worry was Ewan's lack of language. Speech is the quintessential parental concern. This child could have all sorts of problems with walking, playing, eating, seeing, and just about any other issue, but a parent's number one issue will always be speech. We all want the same thing—we just want to hear our child speak. The most important sound in the universe is the dulcet tones of this child's voice. While my husband took a wait and see approach, believing that the words would just magically begin to flow one morning, I remained doubtful. In my head, it was a runaway snowball and if we didn't slow it down now, we'd soon be buried in an avalanche of delay. Without speech, how could we connect with him at all? If we didn't even know what he wanted to eat, how would we ever really know his greatest thoughts and desires? It was no surprise to the professionals in my living room that we yearned to hear Ewan's voice, and that we would prefer to hear it outside the confines of our home.

As the evaluation team settled in for hours of assessment, it became obvious that Ewan would not engage them in any way. He couldn't communicate with them, and they couldn't break through his barriers. Without a way to connect, Ewan remained light years away. Lacking the sounds to signal home, he remained a distant planet rotating around the quiet edge of space. For the most part, he ignored everyone and much of those first reports relied on my answers to questions about what he couldn't do and what we wanted to see as parents, rather than Ewan demonstrating what he could and could not do. Anthony and I wanted Ewan to become more comfortable around people so that we could leave the house, but also so that therapy might actually have some meaning for him. It was pointless if he could not or would not engage with others, including his own family. When people tried to force themselves into his personal space, his usual response was a retreat to the periphery, often the safety of his room. Even now, his room is his sanctuary when the world demands too much from him. Many times, the autistic child is thought of as 'the easy child' because he is happiest when left to his own devices. This was Ewan. He did not need to be entertained, he did not need constant attention or to be the center of the universe. Ewan was quite happy to be Pluto, floating at the edge of the cosmos. Yet I wanted Ewan to be closer to the action, I wanted him to revolve around our family a little closer than just the edge and I wasn't willing to settle for anything less than Mars.

The evaluation team asked us how much had changed since the last time they graced our doorstep. They wanted to know where he had been, where he was now and what we had gone through to get there. They watched me uselessly attempt to feed Ewan lunch. They watched him struggle to finger feed himself a few drops of cereal. At the time, he could pick up some things, but a fork and spoon were far out in left field. He mostly relied on me to feed him food from a short list of room temperature items. While we had moved past the boot camp breastfeeding of his first year, Ewan still struggled with every aspect of food and eating. It just wasn't instinctual for him to reach out for food. It was a struggle to get him to eat anything with any sort of regularity. At a little over a year old, he still mouthed everything that wasn't food, yet anything edible was thrown across the room in disgust. He simply had no interest in the world of food.

Ewan had started sleeping better, and the zombie days of his infancy were now just a faded nightmare. His new sleeping habit consisted of waking intermittently to play alone in the crib all through the night. In the privacy of his own room, he giggled his way through the night entertained by everything but Anthony and I. Naps were more about privacy than they were sleep. Rather than spending each afternoon zonked out, he simply enjoyed the time alone. I learned to give him the space he needed and simply let him be. Unlike other toddlers his age, sleep was limited to just a few short hours each day. Ewan was energized by solitude, not the proverbial forty winks. He simply didn't seem to need as much sleep as everyone else.

We watched therapist after therapist try to engage Ewan in play, yet he continued to play with toys 'his way,' and he liked to play alone. Even the family dog could not entice him into play. Ewan had no interest in such things; in fact, he was downright terrified of the unpredictable habits of such an overly friendly species. While he preferred to play alone, when he needed something he would suddenly remember my existence. In that moment he would reach out, grab my hand and drag me to whatever 'it' was. I was a tool, not a playmate or a mother. And when separated from his lifeline, he would experience a terrifyingly intense separation anxiety. We were chained to each other, in a wordless dance of unspoken needs. As the questions flew back and forth from therapist to therapist to me, Ewan ignored us all. He would flit about on his tiptoes around the edges of our circle of conversation in constant movement, creating his own circles as he spun around and around in an orbit of his own.

He rarely held still in those days. Even changing his diaper was a struggle as it took all my arms and legs to pin him down in a prison of stillness. He had been in constant movement since seven months of age. It was if he were a wind-up toy; every morning he hit the ground running. Movement was limited to the kind he created, though; strollers, cars, wagons, and any other assisted movement were thoroughly rejected. Car trips, no matter how long or short, continued to evoke screams of bloody murder. If he couldn't control it, he wanted no part of it. It wasn't as if he were hyper, though; it was if he couldn't help himself. He was a juggernaut of perpetual motion. Ewan had started bouncing in place then like our very own jack-in-the-box. He would even sit on the couch upside down or try to stand on his head. We all tilted our own heads in wonder as Ewan tried over and over to look at the world from an upside down view. If he wasn't spinning his world into order, he was inverting our reality into another equilibrium.

Ewan continued to move to his own beat and would not be deterred by changes to what he perceived as 'the plan.' Any attempt to shape his activities or to guide him toward something more structured was met with an excessive, trembling fury and frustration, that when provoked, often took hours to soothe. We were prisoners of routine and inmates of our own home, as he never left the house willingly. It was only through repetition that Ewan could find comfort. He needed the same blanket, the same cup, the same video, and the same foods day after day after day. Our life was a constant moment of *déjà vu*.

I struggled to find an anchor in those moments, but nothing about our life was normal. Despite his persistent need for consistency, Ewan was the most inconsistent element of all. Throughout Ewan's infancy and toddlerhood, he would often forget how to do something. We would teach him some skill, or he would discover something out for himself only to find his memory had failed him just a few days or weeks later. Just when we thought we were climbing the path of development, we found ourselves back at square one. This happened most often with language and motor skills. One day he would say a word just fine, and the next it was gone, lost in a jumbled mass of gibberish. One week he could drink from a straw, and the next he was completely lost as the liquid spilled forth from his lips. It was a frustrating process for us, as conquered lands became foreign time and time again.

That day I watched as therapist after therapist placed toys in front of him only to be ignored or tossed aside. He didn't approach toys as if they were fun and had no idea how to play. In the beginning, if he figured a toy out, he immediately stopped playing with it. For him, the novel and the unique were the only things to keep his interest. He didn't really *play* with toys, but rather, he *solved* them. His approach to the toy aisle was less about imagination and interaction and more about some invisible mathematical equation in the parts and pieces. He didn't know how to play, and I didn't know how to teach him.

The ink pens continued to scribble across paper after paper as the therapists on the couch noted every aspect of our existence. The scribbling grew more intense as the questions continued, sounding like static from the radio. With each stroke of the pen, I could see our troubles grow into a billowy mass of clouds blocking my view of the future. The silence lingered as they continued to write down everything he did and did not do. My pulse quickened and my stomach churned as I waited for just a word of comfort. But they had none to give. A veil had been drawn over our future, and these strangers couldn't see through it anymore than I. The day ended as these strangers packed up their clipboards and ink pens and slowly trudged out the door. Apologetic glances shot my way as they left me in a vacuum of confusion.

~

In just a few days, a new team of strangers returned to deliver the news I already knew. This time they had found Ewan delayed in several areas, and my 'dream' of this all being in my head ended abruptly. Our clear skies had just been eclipsed by an atmospheric anomaly no one could see through. While there was no name for the why of Ewan's delays, the percentiles were too great to ignore. Chart after chart was shoved in front of me, translating Ewan's life into a series of diagrams. In one moment, a whole new world entered my life, a world of therapy, doctor visits, medications, evaluations, IFSP (individualized family service plan) meetings, six month reviews, therapeutic toys, support groups, and the world of 'special needs.'

Being the parent of a child with special needs requires a crash course in a multitude of disciplines. Like a medical resident, special parents live, eat, and breathe every single body system. We know more about human anatomy than Henry Gray. Like a post-doctoral student, we get excited every time Steven Pinker comes out with a new book. Before long, our libraries overflow with reference texts, as the fiction section grows ever smaller. There is an alien feeling a parent experiences in raising a special needs child. While typical parents are cavorting between t-ball games and taekwondo, we are commuting between waiting rooms and specialty clinics. Our typical friends cannot truly grasp the polarity of our lives. No matter what the special need is, there are experiences that only a few can truly comprehend and sympathize with. Only a few have walked a mile in those same shoes. Only a parent who has held their child's hand while vomiting up chemo meds can understand that heart wrenching pain. Only a parent who has had to insert an NG tube into their child's nose can understand that fear and guilt. Only a parent who has watched their child stand alone in a crowd of children can understand that sorrow. The special needs world is an alien world. It's a world walled by hospitals drenched in disinfectant, the smell burning through your nose and lungs. It is a world where therapists walk in and out of your house like family. It is a life where doctors know more about you and your child than a grandparent does. It is an existence where every nurse calls you by your first name because they've talked you through emergency after emergency. It is a life where the receptionist, who refuses everyone else, manages to slip you in between patients because they've seen you so many times.

  Our lives are transparent to the world. We don't even blink twice when someone asks for IRS papers, pay stubs, doctor notes, and medical test results. Our lives are open books to every professional that crosses our path. Privacy no longer has the same meaning. It is a humbling and, at times, belittling experience. We find ourselves in line for services we never thought we'd have to use in order to survive. We can rattle off our child's medical history faster and better than the child's own doctor can. We don't pause for a second thought at vomit, diarrhea, special formulas, wheelchairs, crutches, tubes, monitors, communication devices, sign language, picture books, or anything else. Soon the alien world becomes your own, though, and you learn to navigate through the darkest waters and the most difficult seas. You become a voyager discovering new lands and conquering them in the name of your child and family. You have crossed over to a new frontier.

I knew my life was different. I didn't sleep. I nursed and tried to feed Ewan constantly as a baby. I pushed play and toys every chance I had. I felt like we were constantly trying to 'teach' him about life and being a child. I felt like a parent on speed—parenting combat style. It seemed that the moments to just 'be' with my family were less and less. I was always 'doing.' I was an action verb. I was always thinking of the next thing, and what had to be done to get there. One day, while flipping through a catalog, I came across a sign that said, "Be Still and Know That I Am," and I remember thinking how hard this was for me to achieve. Sitting still in my head meant there was something I wasn't doing that I could be doing, and guilt would drive me from my complacency. Looking back, I can see where my approach was much more like a sprint; I was constantly racing to get to the end, but in reality, this was a marathon, and I didn't realize that there was no end.

~

It was September before therapy actually started. The dry, dusty air of harvest time had returned. We were done with evaluations and the endless procession of questions, and, like the farmers around the Indiana countryside, it was time to get to work. We eased into this new normal with therapy just a few times a week. Starting early intervention seemed like a life-line for me even if I thought of it more as a quick fix than I did a complete overhaul of how I understood my son. I wanted functional goals—I wanted to leave my house when I felt like it, and I wanted to know what my son was thinking, what he felt, and what he needed. It sounds simple, and to be honest, it was and still is very simple for us, as we want Ewan to be as functional as possible. What looked like a quick fix, though, quickly spiraled out of control into a complex web of deficit and delay and therapy reports. My quick fix was evaporating before my eyes as the days became months and the months became years with therapists coming and going like a revolving door of rehabilitation. What we didn't know in those early days was just how many more goals and outcomes there would be in this child's life before he could go forth and speak. What we couldn't see were the miles of objectives and benchmarks ahead of us. And what started out as two simple goals multiplied into an intricate labyrinth of cascading developmental stages and abilities.

Our new normal came upon us like a whirlwind, and before long there was a constant stream of therapists in our home. Speech therapists, occupational therapists, or developmental therapists, every part of the rehabilitation alphabet made their way to my living room. There were times that I thought therapy was silly and didn't fully get what the therapists were trying to do. There were times that I didn't get along with the therapists because our personalities didn't 'jive,' and we switched providers often trying to find the right fit. In the beginning, because I didn't fully understand the depth of the problem, we would cancel or miss therapy. Those who know me now may never believe that, but it's true. It wasn't until Ewan's first speech therapist made a list of goals that went along the lines of getting Ewan to say a two word utterance and follow a two step direction that I understood the depth of the problem. We were sitting in the middle of a ball pit, surrounded by every color in the rainbow, when she handed me a list of her clinical goals. Scanning the list, I asked very naively, "Oh, how long do you think this will take, a month, maybe two?"

I will always remember her face when she slowly turned to look at me, her eyes full of apology, when she quietly said, "This may take years, Alicia, these kinds of goals are going to be very difficult for him." Her face and expression have been burned into my mind. I couldn't stand to look at her or her list another second. Turning to the side, I closed my eyes and remembered Skye at this same age. I thought of a time when I didn't have to worry about therapy, a time when words and thoughts easily flowed from my daughter's lips. It was another life then, another child. Opening my eyes, I saw the son before me now, and it was only then that I realized how much work there really was to be done and how far we had to go.

His first speech therapist began by teaching him sign language. I didn't quite understand how he was going to go from signs to speech, but I sat by quietly watching her hands as she taught us both signs for 'more,' 'milk,' 'dog,' 'eat,' 'bubble,' 'open,' and 'please.' She explained that sign language was merely a stepping stone to something greater and would help reduce his frustration until language came easily. As his signs increased, so too did his vocalizations, but these were still very inconsistent and easily lost one week to the next. At that point, language was neither consistent nor clear, but the sign language became a dependable force in our lives. Out of the chaos of loss, sign became our lighthouse in the harbor, guiding us home. Once we saw the value of these silent conversations, we thirsted for more and more signs. We grasped at the one thing that had attracted his linguistical curiosity. His first speech therapist was just the right mix of youth and knowledge. Her frank assessment of the long road ahead of us, combined with a perky determinedness to get us there, made me see the sheer possibility of what early intervention could actually do for this child and our family.

The rest of the eccentricities took much longer to affect through therapy. Overall, Ewan was a happy child if left to his own devices and the safety of his routine and home. Once removed from these things, though, the meltdowns continued. His 'plan' remained the theme of our life and generally consisted of moving his trains back and forth over and over again in some pattern that made sense only to him. He learned to tolerate and then enjoy most of the therapists in his life, though. There were some he did not connect with, and they soon faded from his life. There were a few I did not connect with, and often those too would fade from our lives. He made the most progress with those that made an impact on both his life and mine. Because while therapy may have had an enormous influence on the outcome of his life, it was only for 60 minutes here and there. Real progress had to come from all the hours in between therapists, and all the times spent with me working through our goals day after day. Whether I wanted it or not, I had officially been moved from civilian to private in Ewan's Therapeutic Army. Over the years, I have gone from a lowly private to a Five Star General, but the person leading this army is, and always has been, Ewan.

As I began to understand the whole picture of what was before us, I also began to hope for the possibility of a larger world outside the four walls of house and home. I couldn't see the future, but with our first steps of progress, I realized therapy could have an effect on his life. Targeting goal after goal, I began to dream again. I could see my son at school, like everyone else. I saw my son playing sports with all the other boys. I saw my son at the prom with his girlfriend. I started to believe that we could graduate from this therapy life and move on to something else. I began to grasp the long road ahead of us, yet I wasn't afraid; I knew I wasn't alone anymore. I now had direct access to some of the best minds in the special needs community, who were coming straight to *my* door. In those next few months and years, I questioned everything, as I wanted more than just a generic answer. I wanted to understand everything I could about this new world of therapy and ability. If Ewan needed a guide through this life, then dammit, I was going to be the best possible guide this life had to offer him.

I came to this understanding far sooner than my husband, because while there was much work to be done, much therapy to attend to and practice, many appointments to go to, many signs to learn, all on top of everyday life, I shouldered much of that responsibility. Not to say that my husband did nothing, that is not at all what I am implying. He was at work, and since I was a stay at home mom, he and I had come to an agreement on the responsibilities. But his world was not always my world. While he sweated it out at work both figuratively and literally, I immersed myself in all things Ewan-related. I read child development books and books on language development, found videos and toys that Ewan could connect to, and drilled the therapists about what to do, when to do it, and how to do it. I lived, ate, and breathed this nameless 'special need.' The boundaries between myself and my son became very blurry. It was hard to figure out who I was anymore. I wasn't the woman I had started out as. Ewan changed me, his world changed me. Sometimes for the worse, but more often for the better. I shudder to think of where our family would be without his larger than life personality. Ewan has pushed Anthony and I to live more fully, to appreciate more about life and differences, and to redefine what normal really means. Normal is a subjective term to us now, and your normal is not always going to be our normal.

Chapter Four

Out of Wedlock and Into the Trenches

My husband and I have weathered storm after storm since our first, *and then second*, marriage. In the beginning, before Ewan came into our life we were often selfish and self-indulgent, wrapped up in the importance of all the trivial sides to life. Superficial and shallow, we rarely thought of a life beyond the immediate here and now. We were stuck fighting over Chinese food and patio furniture. I fell in love with a man with many vices, yet for all that we've been through, I wouldn't change a thing. We have grown so much over the years, it's hard to imagine what our life would be like or who we would be had life been different. My husband and I are very different people, and we are the proverbial 'opposites attract' cliché. Despite the rough waters, we continue to emerge from the tempests like the sailor from the sea.

We are an odd couple made even stranger by the circumstances in our life. Anthony and I probably couldn't be more opposite. Where I am quiet, he is the life of the party. At times, I am at the vanguard, driven to change mindsets and attitudes, while he is content to simply follow along the trail. While I have no problem demanding the CEO's home phone number, he is passively content with the answers and solutions given him, even when in disagreement. In other situations, the positions are reversed and he leads me out of the safety of my routines. Where I am ambitious, he is content with the simpler side of life. He lives by the rules of 'buy the cheapest one,' and 'if it's not broke then don't fix it.' If it weren't for my love of all things technological, we would still be using a VCR and cassette player (both of which have been relegated to his garage-based man cave). Once I sent him out for extra chairs to fix a holiday seating problem, and he came home with four cheap, red plastic lawn chairs that I swear were payback for what we refer to as the Patio Furniture Incident.

The Patio Furniture Incident started out seemingly innocent enough, but as my husband often reminds me, he wouldn't have lost his temper had he bought the cheap patio furniture he wanted, i.e. the kind you don't have to put together. We had been together for quite some time, but had only been married a short while. We had our first home together, and I wanted it to be as perfect as it could get. And, I wanted patio furniture. My husband is quite utilitarian. Patio furniture is for fancy people. He prefers the plastic and metal, old school, 1970s style folding chairs. Anything more is simply frivolous. Yet I was dead set on a patio set that had a nice rectangle table, six chairs complete with matching cushions, a porch swing, and the now infamous hose reel. Let me first explain that most of these items came in a box, unassembled. My husband, my love, my wonderful other half, is not mechanically inclined in any way. Hanging a picture is a strain on his handyman capabilities. While I have spent hours on getting Christmas tree lights to twinkle properly, he has absolutely no patience or tolerance for putting things together. It is well-known among his friends and family that when I purchase something, it either better come pre-assembled, or they know we'll need their help on a Saturday afternoon to put it together. Luckily, Anthony had an entire crew to help him with the swing and the patio furniture. His friends all congregated to our backyard to sort through the cardboard boxes and directions, lest they lose their friend to a freak aneurysm from part C of section II of the instruction manual. After they assembled a variety of swings and chairs together, Anthony promised to handle that little hose reel all on his own. Actually, I believe his comment was, "Come on guys, it's a hose reel! How bad can it be?" Smirking at each other, his friends filed out to await the near nuclear screams that this innocent little hose reel would incite.

 Seeing his friends depart *sans* complete hose reel, I cautiously said, "Um, honey, if you want to get dinner, I can always get the hose reel."

 Scowling to his toes at my unmanly suggestion, he replied, "For God's sake, woman, it's a hose reel! I'm not a complete idiot." Realizing I wasn't getting anywhere with his machismo attitude, I stood back and admired the fireworks display that was about to begin. Amazingly, the Krakatoan eruption didn't occur 'til almost the very end of the project. The last piece, that one that would allow the hose to easily wind and unwind, just wouldn't go in. For 45 minutes, my husband wrangled that hose every which way but the right way, and in an explosion of four letter words ended up launching the entire hose and reel clear across our own yard and into the neighbors.' The primal scream originating from the backyard was my clue that the volcano I had married just erupted. Unfortunately, when Anthony gets mad, I get mad. And when I get mad, he gets even madder, and that hose reel just sent us both over the edge. In all my outdoor adventures, I'll never be able to own another one again.

While we both have colossal temper tantrums, most people consider me bookish and prickly, whereas he is jovial yet uncultured. Anthony hates to read while I could happily read a book every day of my life. I wake up early, he sleeps in. I pee in the toilet, and well, Anthony thinks it's amusing to be more creative. I remember one beautiful summer Midwestern day, my sister came over early to get me for a long day of shopping. As we walked out my front door, we stood under the awning while I locked the door up. Suddenly, we heard the distinct sound of water hitting the roof above us and trickling down onto the concrete. Confused about the sudden change of weather, I looked out at the sky and saw not a single cloud. Heather looked at me and said, "I didn't think it was supposed to rain today?"

Just as my sister was about to walk out from under the awning, it dawned on me where the sudden shower had originated from, "No! Don't walk out there! It's not raining, Heather! That's my idiot husband peeing out the upstairs window." Cupping my hands I yelled up to the window, "You idiot! Walk down the stairs and use the bathroom! You almost peed on me and my sister!" Looking at my sister, I simply shrugged my shoulders and sighed, "It's Anthony. The man is a moron."

This man may irritate the living crap out of me on any given day, and yet I find myself hopelessly infatuated with his devil-may-care attitude. He is immature and impulsive and regularly described as my fourth child, yet he is the love of my life. Anthony is the source of laughter and frivolity most usually through his Ronnie Dio impersonations. This is the man who sings '80s metal ballads with gusto and glee in the shower, in the living room, and in the front yard, oblivious to the stares from our neighbors. This is also the man who, in his late night solitary boredom, fell into an infomercial sinkhole. One night, while I was tossing and turning in the bedroom, he gleefully ordered a month's supply of oral cleaning products. Only there was some type of confusion, and he ended up ordering a year's supply all at once. When I got the phone call from our bank explaining that a rather large withdrawal had gone through and we were now hopelessly $600 in the hole for all the other bills I had paid, I knew exactly where to look. Anthony. With detective skills usually only found within the ranks of Homeland Security, I managed to ferret out a confession from my husband about the late night impulse purchase. Calling the company for a refund was about as productive as watching paint dry. Thanks to the internet, I then tracked down the CEO's home phone number. That's what you get for volunteering at the annual golf club fundraiser, I guess. In one call, I had a fervent apology for the mistake, and I even got my 600 bucks back. Anthony now manages to get by with the cheapest dental floss money can buy. My husband is a rare man. Fancy cars and six figure salaries do not impress him. But oral cleaning products at 1:00 a.m., on a Friday night? Well now, that's a different story.

Yes, my husband is quite the character. This is the man who goes out for pizza and comes back with a White Lion cassette. He is also the same man who ran out to get some milk and came back with over thirty VHS tapes he had found at a garage sale for eight bucks, and that was just last week. He provides the comic spontaneity, and I provide the cautious and wary approach to his hair-brained ideas. We are two very different personalities that often balance each other out. Without me, Anthony is reckless and off course, given in to his ADHD side and addictive personality. The root of our problems lie not with the mundane, but with something much more pervasive. For years he has struggled with his addictive personality, including everything from food to beer to drugs. He has struggled to put himself and his family before the addictions, but it has not been easy for him. Where he tends toward excess, I am more restrained and force him to think about the bigger picture. While Anthony walked away from that lifestyle years ago, it is hard for him not to replace one thing with another. For the guy with ADHD, the life of instant gratification is a difficult thing to give up. With a family now, our life is much slower and more restrained than it was in our youth. We may be as opposite as night and day but together, there is a certain symmetry to our life. Separate, we are an absolute mess. Despite our vast differences and despite our rocky start, we manage to find harmony through love and laughter.

His jokes are juvenile, and almost every story in his arsenal revolves around something bowel-related. Anthony's favorite story to tell revolves around a popular American dinner item, meatloaf. Anthony and I had only been dating for a few months when one of those pivotal relationship moments occurred, one we refer to as The Meatloaf Incident. We were students at Southern Illinois University and had been home for a short weekend visiting family and friends. Before we left to go back to Carbondale, Anthony and I stopped at his grandma's house to say a quick hello. Thinking Anthony was too thin, she fussed over him until he ate a plate of meatloaf. It says a lot about this man that he willingly ate meatloaf for his grandma. He hates meatloaf. But he quickly ate it, kissed his grandma goodbye, and off we went for the three hour interstate drive back. Anthony had his own dorm room but usually stayed with me as I had no roommate and he hated his. In a full size futon, he kissed me goodnight and turned off the light around 11 p.m. that night.

Sometime around three in the morning, Anthony noticed his stomach grumbling in a rather unhealthy fashion. Thinking it was just a case of ill-timed gas, he thought a quiet bit of flatulence might diffuse the situation. Unfortunately, what he thought would be a silent squeak turned out to be an episode of violent, explosive diarrhea. I continued to blissfully sleep through this explosion while Anthony, in his total and complete embarrassment, planned a way to fix the situation without waking me up. Sitting in his own filth for a good minute, he debated whether or not he should just run out the door and wondered if I might not notice that my bed was covered in shit when I woke up. Realizing that unless he could adjust the time space continuum in the next 30 seconds and rethink that bit of gas, he was going to have to wake me up and explain that he had just crapped in my bed. I felt a reticent tap on my shoulder as Anthony quietly whispered, "Um, Alicia? Um, I think I'm sick."

I groggily rubbed my eyes and tried to see him through the dark while I croaked out, "What's wrong?" Silence ensued. "Anthony? Are you ok?"

Finally, he just blurted out, "Yeah, Lish, um, I just shit in the bed."

Whether it was because I was still half-asleep or because this kind of thing just doesn't bother me, I sympathetically said, "Oh, it's ok. Here, get up and get down to the showers at the end of the floor, and I'll clean this up." While I grabbed sheets and blankets, Anthony hobbled to the door as I threw him some Kleenexes for clean up duty.

Embarrassed and humiliated, he thought to himself, "This chick is going to kick my ass out and lock the door behind her." With a pink towel quickly wrapped around his waist, Anthony tip-toed down to the girls shower on my floor and took the quickest shower in history, hoping he wouldn't have to cross campus in that same small towel in the off chance I locked him out. As he turned off the hot water, he thought to himself, "My God, I think I love this woman." Running back to the room, he found the door still unlocked as I had cleaned up the room and the bed. For the next three days, he suffered the humiliating effects of food poisoning while I took care of it all, nursing him back to health. And when Anthony tells this story, he ends it with, "And that's how I knew this woman was my future wife." To this day, my husband refuses to eat meatloaf, and I know better than to serve it lest I wake up to such interesting sights again.

We both have had our issues with food over the years. He refuses to eat meatloaf, and I refuse to eat certain kinds of Chinese food. Without Anthony, I am stuck in my own head and reluctant to try even the newest restaurant out. When I'd like to just stay home, he lures me out with talk of the world's best hamburger and fries. Many of our marital fights have been about food, though, and the night of the Chinese Food Incident sparked a decade-long argument over what type of Chinese food is appropriate to order one's wife. The Chinese Food Incident went as follows and started with my husband saying to me, "I am not cooking tonight. Let's just order Chinese food."

Me in my starved state said, "Sure, Chinese sounds great. You order, you know what I like." Now, my husband emphatically points out that I left the ordering up to him as I never specifically stated exactly what I wanted him to order. I counter such arguments by saying, "Why on earth wouldn't you order something you *know* I will eat and order one of my regular favorite foods?" As it happened, though, my husband ordered something that I did *not* normally eat. Upon opening the little white box, my face fell, and in my starved state I yelled, "Ugh. What the Hell is that? I don't eat anything with white sauce! When's the last time you've seen me eat something like this?" In my brusque and openly hostile tone, I ended up hurting Anthony's feelings as he really didn't know that I thought chicken with snow peas was as equally disgusting to me as meatloaf is to him. Frustrated with something he thought he had done right, he ended up storming out of the house and called his best friend. In the middle of the back yard, he broke down, thinking Chinese food was going to end our marriage. We were struggling at the time with a host of problems including an overwhelming addiction to pot (a story for another chapter). While the divorce was about more than chicken with snow peas, the Chinese Food Incident marked the beginning of the end of our marriage. Anthony didn't think he could live with me anymore, and I was so frustrated with him that when he tried to leave that night, I ended up throwing the car keys out into the dark. He left to hang out with his friends, people he understood because I sure as Hell wasn't one of them.

Between the patio furniture, Chinese food, and heavy pot use, my lawyer cited 'irreconcilable differences' while a judge approved the divorce.

After the Chinese Food Incident, Anthony ended up living with a group of Lamda Chi Alphas from the local university. The ironic part to this was that Anthony was neither a college student nor a Lamda Chi Alpha. He was a divorced and carefree 26 year old, and these guys pretty much let him live in the basement. In the divorce, I took damn near everything. I walked away with the beds, the furniture, the kitchen ware, and the shampoo. He walked away with his wedding ring, his favorite Lollapalooza t-shirt, and all his underwear. As soon as he signed the divorce papers he went straight to a local t-shirt shop. There, he had the first page of the divorce packet heat transferred onto a plain white t-shirt. He wore it out to every bar in town before the ink was dry on the divorce decree and proceeded to get drunk. Just about every person who read his shirt bought him a free drink that night and every other night he wore it out. He took his wedding ring and put it on his right hand, relieved to be away from the hostility of our marriage, but refusing to give it up completely. For months, he wore his wedding ring on the right hand until late one alcohol soaked frat night, he sat on his back porch in the pitch black staring at that ring. Looking at that ring, he thought of one of the happiest days of his life, yet sitting on the steps of a remodeled frat house, he wondered where tomorrow would take him. Searching the Celtic knot design for answers, he waited for some kind of understanding about the future of his life. Depressed and discouraged, his carefree life not quite as carefree as he thought, Anthony took off his ring and flung it out into the night. Thinking our marriage had been lost forever, he was finally ready to move on. Ironically enough, one single week later, we started talking again and were on the road towards reconciling and our second wedding. While we searched for that wedding ring, we never found it. His first ring, a hand-made band from the Shetland Islands, was gone, and we ended up at a discount store one afternoon to purchase a simple band of gold. This ring has never left his finger.

The couple that no one believed would make it past year one *or year two*, has made it through 10 *or 11* years of marriage, depending on how you count. Our marriage and our life have revolved around our children, all of our children. We are homebodies, often preferring the comfort and familiarity of hearth and home to that of anything else. We have often forsaken the route taken by others to live a simpler life devoted to family. We have struggled through finances, doctor appointments, and a host of little, and not so little, issues. And while Ewan's needs have swirled and twisted around every aspect of our life, they have never threatened to overcome or separate us. It is all those things before Ewan was even born that sometimes haunt our lives. In Anthony's youth, he did what he wanted when he wanted, and the arrival of Skye just wasn't enough to pry him away from that lifestyle. It wasn't until the middle of a terrorist event when I told him we were expecting our second child that his life took a decidedly different turn.

And, after 10 *or 11* years of marriage, we are still *in love*. The passion of our youth refocused towards something greater. This complete opposite and I have rarely spent more than just a handful of nights away from each other after our remarriage. One particular weekend stands out in my memory. That weekend, Anthony had to go back to our hometown for a funeral while Skye, Ewan, and I stayed behind in Indiana. Despite the situation, I think he was relieved to have a break from the demands of parenthood, hoping to find a glimpse of the life he had before Ewan was born. Looking to catch up with old friends, he packed an overnight bag and headed out for a few nights without diapers, wet wipes, or worries. His first day back he spent the whole day golfing with one of his closest buddies, and with these guys, golf is never just about golf. Golf is about how many drinks one can have and still hit the ball straight. After a long day of bad golf, beer, and a million laughs, he ended up staying with some old roommates. Walking into that converted fraternity house filled with college guys living the single life, Anthony realized his life was infinitely different than theirs. That dark living room, mildewed from the beverages spilled at countless parties was nowhere near as welcoming as our living room filled with toys and blankets and all the comforts of home. In one moment, he realized how much he liked being a husband and father. For once, he wasn't fighting the roles he'd been offered. Looking around the room, he saw the boy he once was, and a longing for home completely rushed over him. Whether it was from too many drinks or too much sun, he ended up calling me on the phone that night, "Lisha?"

"Anthony?" I answered, "You sound terrible, what's wrong? Are you ok?"

Sniffing back tears, his voice broke, "I'm fine, really I am. I just want to come home." Sounding desperate, he continued, "I know you just dropped me off this morning, but my God I just want to be home with you and the kids. I can't stay here all weekend, I just can't. Please, Lisha, just come get me."

Wondering what had caused such a dramatic change in my husband's mood, I asked, "Anthony, what happened?"

"It's stupid, really, I just want to be home with you. My place isn't here hanging out with twenty year olds, it's at home with you. Please, just come get me."

"Ok, ok, but it's kind of late and by the time I get over to Illinois and we get back, it will be the middle of the night. Can you wait 'til morning or do you want me to leave now?"

More sniffling and a long pause, "It'll be fine, get me in the morning. I just want to be home." When he hung up, I thought about what a change the past year and a half had been for my husband. The man who fought the mantle of adulthood every step of the way had finally embraced it. The next morning I picked up an exhausted and embarrassed husband in Terre Haute. With a hug and a kiss for each of us, he sighed and said, "I'm just glad to be going home with my family. The days of my single life are far behind me." Later that night, in the quiet of our bedroom he whispered, "I don't know what I'd do without you. You have saved my life and have given me two beautiful children. I cannot tell you how grateful I am for that. I finally see what we have been missing all these years."

Before Ewan was born, it was hard for us to get our lives and priorities straight. Our free and easy good-natured daughter rarely challenged us as parents. As an infant, toddler, and preschooler Skye was along for the ride, willing to go where we led her. Ewan, of course, challenged us every minute of his early life. He pushed us to think about the bigger picture, one that didn't revolve around the two of us and our eccentricities. During Ewan's first year, we struggled to just keep it together long enough to remember our first names. We lived like refugees in a war torn country then, simply squeezing our eyes shut against the bombardment. We were inundated on every front and pushed to the very edge of our coping skills. We were tired, we were confused, and we were clueless about where our life was headed. Anthony was in denial for a long time about the true nature of Ewan's development, and all I really wanted was a normal life. Yet just when normal seemed within reach, another pitfall would open up under our feet. While we were on autopilot, our finances crumbled, and it would have been easy to just give up on the whole enchilada. Be that as it may, we had tried to live apart in the past and continue to find ourselves drawn back to each other time and time again.

While there may have been little time for romance, intimacy was limited to bits of time stolen from sleep in the midnight hour or the early morning hours of the dawn. These stolen moments kept our hearts and minds going when everything else was falling apart. I gave him what I could, when I could, because no matter how busy and distracted I was or am, he will always have my heart. After 10 *or 11 years*, our passion for each other has not lessened. If there is one thing I crave every day of my life, besides a Diet Coke, it is his touch. It simply takes one lingering look or one brush of his fingertips and all I want or need is a few minutes alone with him. With one glance, he knows he is and always will be wanted. His silent reply sends a siren song through my veins. I cannot help myself but to move to his side and seek out his touch. In one moment, the cares of the day and the stress of the world melt away. The world could burn around us, and it is nothing compared to the fire I will carry for all eternity. In those moments, everything is right. There are no problems, there is no fear. There is nothing but joy. I need him in every possible way even if I become distracted by every facet of our out of control life. For I am still *in love* with my husband.

Love is what held us together during those early years of Ewan's life. Well, love and maturity. Had Ewan been our first child, I'm not so sure we would have ever made it through. For all that we had been through as a couple before Ewan, it was nothing compared to what we would see post-Ewan. I may not have been the best wife nor he the best husband back when Ewan was an infant. We got by with what we had, even if it was just four walls and each other. Surely if we can get through all that, we can get through just about anything. I know, without a doubt, I could have been a better wife to him then, but I was too busy being a mother. The moments for just us were limited to those hours between midnight and dawn. With two sick children and then therapy at my door, I was too busy with doctors and therapists to always be there for him from sun up to sun down. He was working erratic hours and was in and out of the house as often as the therapists. We usually caught each other coming or going.

At the end of the day, I was so exhausted from being pulled in a thousand different directions, I likely wasn't the best conversationalist in the world. Without a doubt, I tended to unburden myself completely upon my husband the second he walked in the house. I saved up *all* the language I didn't get to use during the day for the second Anthony's toe crossed the threshold of our doorway. I would tell him about therapy, what Ewan was doing, what he was supposed to be doing that he wasn't, and what Skye had done in Kindergarten all before that second foot crossed the doorstep.

There was a rare moment when Anthony and I were watching TV one late night after the children had long gone to bed. After a parade of children's shows, it was refreshing to watch something without animation or costumed teenagers dancing about like a bad Broadway musical. We happen to come across a Chris Rock comedy show on cable. He was talking about men and women and how when men walk in the door, women immediately start in about what happened, what needs to happen, yack, yack, yack. We were laughing so hard as he said, "He got to do something to prepare him for all the talking he gonna hear when he get home. Ladies, it ain't that you talk too much. You just talk too much as soon as we get in the f*@ing door. …Soon as you take one step in, 'You're not going to believe this!' Let me get my other f*@ing foot in the door! Let me get something to eat! Let me get something to drink!" Anthony and I just looked at each other and burst out laughing. This was our life. We didn't have cell phones, and I couldn't always call him at work. The minute the garage door opened, I pounced on his ear with a verbal barrage of therapy notes and motherly musings. While I threw every minute of the day at him, he merely put his feet up and sighed.

Because Anthony and I had such a hard time in the beginning of our relationship, I think people wondered if we really would make it this second time around. Most especially because of all the stress that we were under. We had two children, one of whom required a lot of work, and someone had to be there for therapy, so that meant only one income at the time. My husband didn't have his Bachelor's degree then, but I had done graduate work in history. Theoretically, I could have made more money than him, but I was the one that excelled at the whole therapy and child rearing part, so I stayed home. He worked at jobs he hated, went to interviews he would never have gone to, and worked next to people he couldn't stand all to bring home a paycheck. I don't regret any of the choices we made about who did what; they were equally difficult.

We had to move back in with my mother at times because finances were so tight. The situation was difficult for everyone involved. My mother was one of the people who didn't really believe that my marriage was going to survive round two. She continued to harbor that ship of resentment toward Anthony, and trying to live together under one roof was draining. Yet despite her anger toward Anthony and the direction my life had taken, she was always willing to help us. And in those early days when life was so disordered, we needed help from any direction it came from. We had to rely on her many times to get by, and I can never thank her enough for her generosity even with the hostility and lack of faith about my marriage. If you can imagine the well-meaning advice one gets from parents about raising children, you can imagine that advice multiplied by a thousand when you live under a spurned grandmother's roof. Surprisingly, though, it was my mother who happened to be at the intake evaluation for early intervention when the service coordinator asked about Ewan's temperament. I couldn't quite explain him very well when my mother piped up, "The thing about Ewan is that no matter what he does, he does it with an extreme intensity. If there is one word that sums up Ewan, it is 'intense.'" For all the ups and downs we had at my mother's house and for all the distance she tried to put between us, she was, at times, able to put a finger on the situation better than Anthony and I could.

Ewan was, and is, a wonderful child despite all his intensity and needs, but he was a very different baby and toddler. Anthony and I didn't always get what we needed as parents. My husband and I were so enamored with the idea of having Ewan that I think we felt a little cheated out of a baby that didn't like to be held often, that did better on his own than with us, and that seemed so into his trains rather than people. He would look so intently at the faces on his Thomas trains, and I wished for the same kind of scrutiny from him. He was close enough to touch yet still so far away.

Seeing my friend's daughter didn't help either. When we would visit, it was easy to compare her to Ewan since they were close in age. She hardly ever let her mother out of her sight, loved to be held, would stare at me down to the depths of my soul, and was saying word after word and even beginning to say phrases. It was difficult to be around them. Her daughter, so tuned into the rhythm and patterns to family life, was drastically different from Ewan. Where Ewan revolved around the trains, she clung to her parents, seeking out their comfort and their arms. Rather than folding himself into my embrace, Ewan ran to the safety of his trains. My friend, who was always kind, would say, "She's a girl and has two older siblings, of course she is going to say more and do more at her age than Ewan. Boys are just different." I wanted and needed more, though, and I remember talking to my husband when Ewan was a little over a year about my need for another baby. At first, he was more than a little shocked to hear this from the woman who spent the better part of a year unshowered and stressed. He was also worried about money since we were certainly not rolling in cash. He knew how hard Ewan's first year had been and thought I was insane for wanting to jump back in it so soon. I think he was also worried that our next baby's first year would be equally difficult.

   I cannot explain the lure of this next baby, but I needed it like the air I breathed. I was lost in the trance of maternity and was sure of what I wanted. He had just finished a program to be a real estate appraiser, and the economy looked like it might prove to be as good a time as any. I remember being in this café where Ewan and I had met Anthony for lunch one day. We were sitting in the booth and Ewan was moving all around the place doing everything but eating. As I wrestled Ewan into a sitting position only to see him pop right back up again, Anthony giggled at my frazzled determination. He stared down at Ewan and a wide smile spread across his face. He then confessed that he, too, wanted another baby. When we thought about all the 'what ifs,' we simply thought to ourselves, "So what!" We believed (and still do) that if the new baby ended up like his brother we'd be more prepared, and if the baby wasn't, then he'd be a built-in playmate for his or her brother. We both decided to just let nature take its course and what would happen would happen.

Chapter Five

Express Train to Rehab

November came, and as Anthony and I celebrated another anniversary, we were surprised to find that nature was in a hurry. Our mutual gift to each other was a baby. We would be welcoming a new child come July. Staying with my mother, we briefly thought of combining our two families under one roof. My mother was lonely from my father's passing, and Anthony and I were trying to get back on our economic feet. Yet as we prepared for Christmas and decorated my mother's cabin with lights and tinsel, we realized our different personalities would never fit under one roof, despite the financial benefit. In some ways, it was the simple things: she likes doing her dishes before bed, we like doing them in the morning. And in other ways, it was the complicated past standing before us all, preventing life from moving forward. While she made an effort to fold our families together, she held on to those remaining strands of resentment towards Anthony, making a unified home impossible.

Because she couldn't move forward from the past, staying in my mother's house was often awkward and strained. Inside the four walls, we tiptoed through a disquieted setting. Outside those four walls lay a serene and harmonious landscape. She lived in a cabin deep in the woods that during the summer was surrounded by a dense thicket of greenery. In the autumn, the woods slowly shifted into shades of mahogany and caramel. When the sun strikes the trees, the whole forest looks ablaze in an all-consuming fire of color. In winter, the leaves abandon their post, leaving the skeletal branches to brave the snow and wind, while ice holds every inch of nature in its brittle grasp. It was easy to fall in love with the landscape, yet we were merely tenants in someone else's home. It was not our home and comfort, true comfort, was hard to come by. That Christmas, as the indoors held an edgy silence, the wintry outdoors soon became my sanctuary. The woods surrounding the house insulated us all from the chaos of the world. When the storms raged, the wind was but a whisper among the leaves and trees as the roots seemed to grow down to the very center of the earth. Yet the time had come for our family tree to branch away from the roots my mother had set down.

This baby forced us to push away from her home and helped us strike out on our own, whether it worked or not. The moment had come for Anthony and I to steer our own course, for better or worse. It was the last time we would find room and board under her roof as we swore to make it on our own from then on. We were not ungrateful for everything she had done, but rather, we were not willing to settle for anything less than our own destiny. We needed the freedom to make our own choices, both good and bad. For far too long, I had relied on being able to go back home when life threw too much at us. From then on, Anthony and I were on our own. We refused to look back.

As we thought about the new direction of our life, we looked for a suitable place for us all. My sister just so happened to be moving but hadn't sold her first house yet. Her idea was to rent her first house to us, and maybe we would be able to buy it someday down the road. Hoping for some space, we packed up and moved away from the thickets of the woods. We traded the forest for the quiet stillness of the Indiana countryside. Leaving the comfort of the woods for the open cornfields, it was both a geographic and philosophic move. It was time to build our own life with our own home and our own traditions free from the judgments of the past. It was time to start anew.

There was a storm brewing the day we moved, and our first frigid night at the new house was spent unpacking and preparing for snow and ice. From that point on, Anthony and I were determined to keep our lives much more private than we ever had before. In the past I had shared too much of my private life with both my mother and my sister, and it was time to keep the marital issues between husband and wife rather than the whole lot of us. That time in our lives marked a distinct shift in the way Anthony and I approached life as we clung to each other and no one else. All of a sudden, we were thirty miles and a field of freedom away from everything and everyone. For the first time in a long while, it was just us.

Living in the boonies may have fostered a sense of self-determination, but it was not always easy. It was more than a bit of a drive across snow packed country roads for just a gallon of milk. It took forever for my husband to get to work, for me take Skye and Ewan to the doctor, or to see my mom and sister. But we had plenty of space for us all and then some. Ewan had his own room and even had his own 'Thomas the Train' room with all his trains and tracks. Even the unborn baby had a room of his or her own. The problem with this new house was never size.

The problem was becoming the increasing expenses and dwindling income.

We had very little money, and my husband's career as a real estate appraiser had fallen through. What had looked like a good economy in reality was a black hole of expenses. He was working as a server at a busy Indy restaurant and was bringing in some money, but it was very sporadic. There were times he would come home with a roll of bills, and there were times he'd walk in the door with just a few bucks. Those nights with only five dollars and some change in his pocket were the hardest of all. The price of freedom and independence was proving to be more than we could bear. Bills were piling up, and the baby was coming in just a few months. Anthony was still looking for a job as an appraiser, hoping to pass the state test, but it hadn't happened yet. My belly was getting bigger by the minute, and our bank account was getting smaller by the second. Our plan to start over fell apart in front of us. We were beginning to reach the pinnacle of stress and pain for our family, only we couldn't see a way out. It felt like no matter what we did, we always chose wrong. There were times I questioned whether or not we were meant to be together at all, and there were times that I felt just as trapped with Anthony as I did with my mother. Stuck between nothing and less than nothing, I couldn't seem to make things work out to our advantage. I looked out at the sea of houses and families around me, wondering what we were doing wrong that they had all seemed to figure out. We didn't want much, we just wanted our bills paid and bellies full. With no answers in sight, we put one foot in front of the other and kept going, day after day.

All the while, therapists still made their way to our doorstep, and every day presented a new challenge and goal for Ewan. That unnamed presence in Ewan's life still held us in its grip despite the hours and hours of therapy. Therapy is hard enough, but therapy without a reason is even moreso. It's one thing to dedicate yourself to a mission, to an idea, to a belief, but we were dedicating our entire lives to the unknown. We were left without a reason, and it often left us floundering and grasping for stability. I needed to know where life was going to take us, and I needed to see through the billowy mass of clouds that had blown in with early intervention. I needed to see a future, no matter how difficult it would be to envision. With no name for the therapy and no goals in our life other than survive, it seemed we were racing towards some unforeseen collision.

Between the bills, the pregnancy, therapy and everything else, our house of cards barely held it together.

In the meantime, we struggled to transition from one early intervention team to another and settle into a routine at the new house with new therapists, a new service coordinator, and a new pediatrician. We were also struggling to keep Skye afloat as she seemed more behind than ever. She had missed so much in first grade because of illness that we wondered if maybe she should have been held back. Since we had moved, she had switched schools, and it only pushed her further into confusion. Finally, after seeing that she didn't qualify for serious help and that no one seemed to have extra time to help her at school, Anthony and I made the decision to homeschool her. We hoped it would only be 'til the end of the school year, and she could rejoin her class come August. Every day, I woke up facing hours of therapy and hours of home education. While Skye practiced multiplication drills, Ewan and I practiced our signs in front of a string of therapists. If we couldn't be financial moguls, well then, we'd just have to settle for being really good parents. I may not drive a Beemer, and I may not live in a suburbian mansion, but my children and my husband will always be my priority. We pushed through what we could and tried to ignore the rest as we faced a series of new visits and therapists and math equations.

After settling in to a new routine, I looked to find a new pediatrician closer to our new home. That February, we went to see the new pediatrician for the first time. I bundled Ewan up in layers of thick, winter clothes and took off for a drive through the country. This combination of heavy clothes and a vehicular jaunt to a new place completely threw him off. Ewan didn't like surprises or new places, and this doctor's office was certainly new and surprising. After walking in to a cramped office with the heat stuck on inferno, I knew we were in trouble. We found ourselves stuck in that waiting room Hell where many special needs parents find themselves for more hours then we really care to count. But that day if felt like we had been waiting for what seemed an exceptionally long time, even for Doctor Land, where minutes are counted as hours and a day can miraculously disappear in between over-bookings and pharmacy sales reps. Many families had been called back, and every time the nurse would come out, she'd call anybody's name but ours. I was starting to get a panicked feeling that someone had forgotten to put our name down in the big book—I looked at that receptionist and her appointment book like she was St. Peter holding the keys to the Kingdom and wondered if this really was my own special form of purgatory. Ewan was unraveling before my eyes with all the people coming and going, and he was getting more irritable by the second—my ticking time bomb was about to go Hiroshima on this office. But the icing on the cake was when a little boy, a few months younger, came over and innocently tried to play with Ewan. You would have thought this little boy had been holding a poisonous South American snake or something the way Ewan reacted. He screamed at the top of his lungs and tried to escape this younger nuisance. Despite my son's serious overreaction, this brave little boy tried again and again to engage Ewan to absolutely no avail. Ewan wanted no part of this interloper's fantasy of joint attention and parallel play—he wanted to be left alone to line his blocks up along the wall.

Finally, in the midst of this ear piercing scream, the nurse called Ewan's name. Actually, she called Evan's name, and this would be the first of many nurses and receptionists thinking the chart had a misprint dyslexically replacing the W with a V. Since this was a new office, they, of course, had a different routine. Normally, Ewan was allowed to keep his clothes on to be weighed, and, depending on his mood, the nurse might just guesstimate his height and weight. But here, the staff was very strict, and we had to pry Ewan out of the numerous layers of winter clothes just to get his weight. Now for Ewan, getting clothes on and off had become a challenge of epic proportions. He was awkward and didn't always 'help out' like another child his age might. He didn't push his arms through the sleeve or step into pants. It was a lot like dressing a scarecrow made of heavy putty. So getting him undressed, getting him to sit still on the scale, and then getting him dressed again was almost more than either of us could bear. With an hysterical Ewan, we were ushered back into an examination room as the nurse frantically tried to get some vitals on him. We tried distracting, redirecting, bribery, you name it, but nothing could get him to stop and relax. There was this little fishing toy in the corner of the room behind me, and Ewan gravitated toward the safety and shelter of the corner and the colorful plastic fishes. While I stared out the window at the falling snow, the pediatrician came in and looked at the picture before her: a child engrossed in the mechanics of plastic fish heads and a mother staring out in an unknown future. She knew before she even sat down how this visit would unfold. Completely different from our last pediatrician, she was younger, more energetic, and she tuned in immediately. Time seemed to slow down in her presence, and the rush so often felt in a clinical office disappeared. She was simply interested in finding out more. As if we had placed a puzzle before her, she sought to find the answers we so obviously needed. As she shook my hand she asked, "So why the big tears, Mr. Ewan? Don't you like my office?"

Ewan thoroughly ignored her as he focused on the plastic fish heads, so I answered, "I think it was the little boy in the waiting room that set him off. Well, that and the whole getting undressed thing."

Tapping her chin in thought, she methodically began to pick out details of our life to see the bigger picture before her. As she combed through a giant stack of paperwork from his therapists, she asked me where I felt Ewan was developmentally and all the things that had or had not happened in his development. I confessed, "We started early intervention last September, and to be honest, I thought we'd be moving on by this summer. But I get the feeling his therapists see something I don't. I get the feeling there's more to the story here." With a slight frown on her face she glanced from Ewan to his therapy notes and back again, seeing all that I could not.

She noted his need to be as far away from her as possible and his refusal to acknowledge her existence and asked, "Is Ewan always like this with people, or is it just because I'm a stranger?"

I replied, "He is generally aloof and off to the side of the action, even in our living room, but we manage to get his attention in therapy and throughout the day."

Watching Ewan out of the corner of her eyes she asked, "How do you do that? What is he so focused on at home?"

"He is obsessed with trains. It's been like this for about a year. He literally lives, eats, and breathes trains. If we want his attention, we generally have to pick up a train and jump into the action."

"And he's ok with that?" she asked.

Smiling, I said, "Oh no, not always. Ewan generally has what we refer to as *a plan*, and sometimes his plan and our plan are at opposite ends of the rainbow."

Still tapping her finger on her chin, she said more thoughtfully than I thought possible, "Hmmm." As she continued to watch, Ewan grew uneasy with the scrutiny and grabbed my hand to place it on the doorknob. Her eyes narrowed when she asked, "Is that how he gets what he wants? By using your hand? Does he ever say what he wants?"

Blocking Ewan from making an early exit, I said, "Most of the time, yeah, this is what he does. It seems like the easiest way to get what he wants, I guess."

"Easy, yes, but it's not what we want for him. We're going to have to push him down the more difficult path. You've got to make him wait and see if we can push him towards language in his frustration."

Snorting, "I'm sorry, did you just say you want me to irritate him? On purpose? When Ewan gets mad, I mean, this doesn't just last for a minute or two here. You're asking me to give up half a day over a glass of milk."

Patting my hand, she said, "I know what I'm asking you, but trust me, the pay off will be huge. We need him to connect with language, with his actions, and the actions of others. We need him to see that he is separate from you." Then she turned her attention back to Ewan and his 'play' with the fishing game as he hit the same fish over and over and over again. Pointing to the plastic fish head, she said, "Look, do you see the way he is playing right now?" Seeing me nod, she continued, "It's not really play, not the way that we generally think of play. It's what we call perseveration. It's more of a repetitive action that he finds calming rather than any kind of true play. I'd bet that the play you are seeing with trains at home is also what we would call perseveration."

Frowning, I replied, "But he makes such elaborate track designs, and even though I can't understand it, I think he's talking in his own way as he plays."

"Ahhh, but is he playing or is he re-enacting? Does he also watch Thomas videos?" Seeing me nod yes again, she said, "Next time, sit down and watch the videos with him. I bet you a hundred dollars, he's merely re-enacting what he sees in the video, including the dialogue. If his language were better, you'd hear it. Probably word for word. It's what is called echolalia, and it's something we see with children who have autism. I'll be honest, he's got a lot of big red flags waving in the wind right now. If we ignore them, these big red flags are going to turn into bonfires. We've got to do more than what we are doing now or risk letting this turn into an inferno."

I interrupted her, "More? More? You want us to do more? I mean, we already have therapists in and out all day long. What more can we do?"

"Well first, we need to confirm these suspicions because without a diagnosis we're going to be left spinning our wheels. We'll miss the bigger picture as we put out fire after fire. We need a plan, we need to think about the future. I'm a pediatrician, not a specialist. We need someone who can confidently tell us the rest of this story, as you say. Early intervention will end and soon he'll be in school, and trust me, that's when it gets really hard." In one moment, that billowy mass of clouds lifted and a future emerged, even if it wasn't the one I had originally planned for. I didn't know what tomorrow or the next day would bring, but she was the first person to give us an action plan beyond day to day therapy. She was the first person to ask me to think about the next phase of life.

While I stared back out the window at the snow swirling in the air, I watched one large snowflake lazily hover in the air. In a gust of wind, it blew out into the gray sky and into the unknown. Ewan was that snowflake and I was the wind. It was time to push us all into a future we had been too busy and too worried to see. The doctor then handed me two scripts for visits to a pediatric neurologist and medical geneticist and put her hand on my shoulder, "We'll get through this. He's my patient now, and I'll do as much as I can to help him and you." Patting my stomach, she said, "I see I'll have another patient soon." She started out the door and turned to say, "Take care of *all* my patients," and pointing to me she added, "even this one."

She was the first medical professional in a line of diplomas to apply the A word to Ewan. And she was the first white coat to realize we needed more help than what we had been getting. She saw the future through a clouded veil and wanted more for Ewan, for me, and for our family. With a stack of referral papers, she sent us out the door and into the Express Train to Rehab.

This new pediatrician pushed for some changes in Ewan's IFSP and wanted us to push the envelope of possibility for him. She was determined to give Ewan a big thrust forward into the next developmental stage. She was neither unrealistic in what she wanted to see Ewan accomplish in the next year, nor was she generic in her approach to the laundry list of delays in front of us. Very specifically, she wanted Ewan to see a medical geneticist and a pediatric neurologist in order to rule out a whole textbook list of conditions and genetic disorders. She also wanted us to push for using more sign language and pictures in his life and to force Ewan to use these by ignoring his hand-over-hand actions. It was with these resolutions that we met with Ewan's new team of therapists. It was time to re-examine Ewan's list of goals and set the bar even higher.

~

Since we had moved, Ewan and I both had to adjust to an entirely new group of therapists. For speech, we had shifted gears from a young and perky therapist to an older school-based therapist who was working part-time in early intervention. She was highly recommended, and we eagerly awaited the progress that had been started with the first therapist. Before long, though, we noticed that this therapist was not achieving the kind of progress we had seen just a few months earlier. Initially, it was very difficult to get Ewan's attention in therapy, and, to be fair, some therapists are better at handling the inattentive child than others. I think this new therapist was too used to working with older children who dutifully sat in their chairs practicing articulation drills. Ewan was not a sit and attend kind of child, though. He was more like Lance Armstrong on the final leg of the Tour de France. Ewan needed to be in constant motion because in moving, he understood all the mysteries of life. He could process better and faster while moving from room to room. While his other therapists ran from room to room in an effort to engage him, this particular one patiently waited for Ewan to return to his room and therapy. And more often than not, she waited alone.

His new occupational and developmental therapists were amazing. Ewan's first occupational therapist had a highly intelligent 'clinical' personality that did not always translate into an easy relationship. His new occupational therapist was more practical than clinical and laughed more than she did anything else. The new developmental therapist was more reserved, but she inherently 'got' Ewan. Both of them jumped right in to the mix and each of them pushed Ewan in various ways. The OT brought fun with her every single visit. She taught him that therapy wasn't just enduring a 60 minute hand-over-hand session. She showed us both how therapy and fun should complement each other in every way and in every session. The OT also showed Anthony how to make that roughhouse bonding time more therapeutic for son and father. Ewan loved it when his father would hold him up high in the air and pretend to let him drop, catching him in a giant of hug of giggles. The only thing she raised her eyebrows at was when Ewan displayed that textbook picture of the Moro Reflex, that exaggerated startle that had been with him since his birth. At the age of 22 months, that reflex should have been just a memory from his infancy.

Though her time with us would be brief, the developmental therapist would come to have the most influence on the developmental trajectory of Ewan's life. While she was there to teach Ewan play skills, she too could see the potential for communication as Ewan soaked up new signs every day and appeared to be looking for something more substantial than signs and pictures. It was this developmental therapist that would suggest an appointment with an augmentative and alternative communication (AAC) specialist who would change our lives forever. But like most professionals in the world of special needs, there was a waiting list a mile and a year long, and we wouldn't meet this influential powerhouse for months to come.

As winter gave way to spring, we attempted to push Ewan out of his solitary hibernation and patterns of routine. Ewan was happy as could be when left alone to play with his trains and execute his *plan*. It was tempting to avoid rocking the boat. Life was easier when he was in good spirits. Yet the doctor and all our therapists told us to keep pushing our way in and changing the play and the plan. Every time we pushed our way in, Ewan pushed us back out. The trains were his Utopia. Trains were predictable, people are not. In an attempt to avoid Utopia, we took drastic measures. As flowers bloomed and green returned to the fields and lawns, we found ourselves pushing away from that locomotive siren song and taking therapy out into the great outdoors. Eventually, a physical therapist was even brought in to help Ewan navigate the playground and uneven landscape. We took therapy to the local parks and playgrounds because while plastic stepping stones are great, they are a far cry from the rugged irregularity of a rolling field. Yet it wasn't easy, and therapy was equally difficult inside as it was outside. In those early days, therapy generally went well, but like anyone, Ewan had his 'off' days. There were days where he pushed away from us to run and hide from these unwelcome intruders. There were weeks where he left us all and slid back into the quiet embrace of solitude. He would often play, or as his doctor had said, perseverate, on his trains or a new toy that a therapist would bring with her focusing intently only on that thing. Some days therapists would arrive during an unexpected nap for Ewan, and he would wake to find himself being pushed in ways he wasn't ready for. Much of the time his therapists followed his lead, as he would refuse to bend in any way. Often, it truly was 'his way or the highway.' Despite having some fantastic therapists who were willing to follow Ewan throughout the house, his attention span was very limited at that time. He would flit from activity to activity like a feather in the wind. For the child whose life revolved around a mix of routine and impulsion, he would often find himself frustrated at his therapist's attempts to govern and regulate activities and play. He would meltdown at these efforts to organize his disorganization or block his impulsivity and would refuse to participate. There were many days that Ewan would run from the door knowing that yet another therapist waited with her bag of toys on the other side of the threshold. At times early intervention seemed like a life line, and at times I felt that it was an intrusive nuisance. Week after week, therapists traipsed through my front door like it was Times Square, and week after week they left me with a summary sheet of each visit always ending with the phrase, "Ewan continues to need therapy." I began to wonder if the day would ever come when someone would say, "Ewan no longer needs therapy. He's done it, he's figured it out and now he's moving on with life."

    For all his needs and for all the set-backs, I was convinced the answer lay outside the safety of our four walls. It would be a theme we would come back to time and time again. In my childhood, I could always be found out-of-doors. Most of my time was spent on the back of a horse or a bicycle and playing with the multitude of animals on our farm. One of my greatest childhood memories was the time we had three of our Labradors simultaneously deliver three different sets of puppies. There is nothing like having 48 puppies nipping at your six year old heels across the summer grass. Mother Nature was the source of my childhood imagination, and as I grew into an adult, it became my church and source of inspiration. When times are toughest, I'm often found wondering outside looking for answers. There was no menagerie to lure Ewan outside, and nature did not pull at his soul the same way it did mine. Ewan preferred to stay in the shelter of the house focusing on his trains. Yet I wanted Ewan to experience the thrill of a grass-stained childhood, so we continued to push Ewan outside the comfort of house and home. I couldn't let the safety of his routines prevent him from experiencing and connecting to something greater. Even worse, we didn't want his life to become so entrenched in rehabilitation and therapy sessions that we missed childhood. While we may have been on the express train to rehab, it was up to Anthony and I to stop the train once in a while and see the landscape we were rushing past. It was up to us to help Ewan see the beauty of a twisted old oak tree. We had to show him the magic of a thousand white dandelion wisps gliding through the air. He had to know the song of a hundred robins was more melodic than any sound a train could make. The world of dirt, bugs, leaves, wind and water needed to awaken some intrinsic piece of his conscience. Something that, once awakened, would continue to exert a gravitational force upon his soul—day in and day out begging to be heard.

  The clinic cannot hold a candle to that of nature's playground. There will be times in Ewan's life when he needs to find balance, and he will not have access to therapy equipment and specialized therapists. He must use that which is all around him at all times in order to right himself. What better equalizer than the natural world? Wind and water cling to the skin and calm the mind in a way that sensory equipment cannot hope to replicate. If Ewan is going to connect more to the world of things than of people, at the very least, he needs to find comfort in the arms of the flora and fauna found only in the countryside. Ewan must find peace in more than just a cathedral, and he must learn to trust in the wide open spaces of the world. If the contact of my eyes is too great, then surely he can stare endlessly into the depths of the sky and rivers searching for the peace and order he needs. Our goal of leaving the house was about so much more than just going to the grocery store. When the obsessions become too great and when the demands of therapy inundate every hour, we push Ewan out into the arms of Mother Nature, whether he likes it or not.

Chapter Six

A Word, an Identity

    As the colors of the earth burst forth in blooms and blades of spring grass, so too did Ewan's unease. The restlessness and agitation of his infancy returned, and once again, Ewan seemed uncomfortable in his own skin. He began to gouge his abdomen with his nails 'til he bled and clawed at his clothes as if they were made of thorns. He was distracted and irritated, prone to gasping and grunting throughout the day. When we bathed him at night, he emerged from the water, no matter how tepid, with skin that looked flayed and burned as if he were allergic to the water. It was as if his own skin had rejected him, leaving him exposed and vulnerable to the world. His therapists suggested we try some sensory diets and a brushing protocol, Wilbarger's Protocol, along with something called joint compression in an effort to comfort his sensitivities. It boiled down to giving Ewan access to movement, brushing him with a soft surgical brush, and pushing his joints together in a Lego-like fashion. It appeared to work for a short time until the gouge marks on his stomach became infected and rapidly spread over his skin like wildfire. From that point on, keeping clothes on Ewan was next to impossible. Here was my Sisyphean task from now until forever. After several doctor visits and a tube of antibiotic ointment, an uneasy truce between skin and boy was formed, even if that truce didn't extend to clothing. It was about this time that Ewan developed an obsessive need for fleece blankets. He would wrap his half-naked self in a cocoon of fleece, start sucking his thumb, and slowly calm himself in an out of control world.

    While we worked to brush and compress Ewan towards an equilibrium, his hair had grown into something last seen with Rapunzel's beautiful tresses. Ewan was born with a head full of dark hair, and as it had grown out, it was replaced with lighter shades of chestnut and golden blonde. My father's gift of inky darkness was a fleeting blessing found only in the moments of his infancy. I had unsuccessfully tried to cut Ewan's hair myself while he slept or was distracted by his trains, and I was tired of week-long haircut marathons. His second birthday was coming up, and I didn't have the energy to cut it before the big day. While grocery shopping in town one day, we came across a new hair salon just for kids, replete with airplane seats and videos for distraction. Anthony and I thought surely, if there was a place for Ewan to get his first haircut, this had to be it. So we made an appointment and crossed our fingers.

The afternoon of this momentous first haircut turned out to be a scheduling nightmare. Earlier in the day, his doctor had ordered an impromptu hearing test in the off chance that all this delay and solitude was a symptom of hearing damage. The hearing test did not go well. Ewan was not thrilled with strangers sticking unfamiliar objects in his ear canal as I held his arms down. We didn't get to complete all the testing, just enough to know that hearing problems were not the issue at hand. We left the hospital to grab a quick bite and then headed off to the hair extravaganza hoping for better luck at the next appointment.

We arrived a bit early hoping that Ewan would have time to explore the indoor playground in the waiting room before he endured the metallic snip of the scissors and the constant hum of the clippers. Yet luck wasn't with us that day, as the previous appointment had cancelled and I had to prematurely pry a movement focused Ewan off the playground and into an airplane prison of immobility. It did not start well, and it did not end well. He screamed and cried and fought against every aspect of the experience. He was in tears, and I was sweating bullets from holding him down all while trying to prevent a scissor attack by an overwhelmed hairstylist. When at last I said, "Enough, just stop. He can't take anymore," Ewan had already retreated far into the recesses of his mind. I picked him up and freed him from that prison to let him move and find himself once again. After I paid for a haircut gone awry and left a generous tip for the deafening screams still reverberating around the building, I found Ewan rocking and trembling in the corner of the playground. As I picked him up to comfort him in my arms, it became apparent my touch was the last thing he wanted or needed. His shrieks of pain and fear could probably be heard miles away. Every single head in the parking lot turned our way, with a single thought displayed upon their suspicious faces: what had I done to this child to create such heartbreaking wails of anguish and pain? My face was a burning shade of shame as hot tears of failure fell down my cheeks. Almost nine months after the Japanese restaurant fiasco, I was still wrestling with how to be this child's mother.

We drove home to seek the safety and comfort of the trains. But that day, not even Thomas and his friends could calm the storm. The tempest raged for hours and hours until at last, darkness settled and Ewan fell into an exhausted and troubled sleep. I was at a loss of how to help my son through even the most mundane of activities. My every instinct was spurned and rejected by a child that grew more complicated by the day. All the therapy, day in and day out, had not helped him one iota in his despair. Every sign I knew couldn't break through the barriers he had constructed. There was no way to tell him that it was going to be ok. There was no way to comfort him in his pain and fear. I was powerless in the face of such overwhelming and unnamed forces. Despite early intervention and despite what we had learned about Ewan, it still wasn't enough to change the quality of his life.

I was determined to make some kind of impact on his life in a positive way. I bent over backwards to learn what I could in therapy and began taking photos of people and places to help Ewan deal with the flow of life outside our home. For his second birthday, I wanted to give him something I knew he would notice and care about: a beautiful home-made Thomas the Train birthday cake. I spent every waking minute for two days before his birthday planning a party he would be interested in. There were Thomas cups, Thomas plates, Thomas napkins, and Thomas balloons. It was as if Britt Allcroft had blown up in my dining room. Sometime around 1 a.m. the night before, I put the finishing touches on his cake. My hands were cramped into claw-like shapes after hours of piping tiny colored stars onto a train-shaped dessert. This time, Ewan noticed the party and saw the bigger picture, but I think I had a little blue train to thank for that. We all chipped in again to buy him yet another big Thomas train set. There were Thomas DVDs and Thomas whistles, Thomas sheets and Thomas pajamas. He was surrounded by his heart's greatest desire. While he was still in constant movement, he was happily ripping paper as he did so. Every picture of him with family that day was more like a 'quick, grab him and snap the picture' kind of shot. At first glance at old photos, he appears to be posing with various relatives. Upon closer inspection, you can see him tilting away, and an adult's biceps flexing as they held Ewan still for the 3.2 seconds it took to take the picture. We were forever chasing Ewan through life, hoping to teach him something along the way.

Weeks later, in the heat of the summer sun and in an advanced state of pregnancy, I found myself chasing Ewan across a hospital parking lot towards a neurology clinic. For so long now, I had been waiting to hear something, anything, that would help me understand my son. There had to be something we could offer Ewan that would lessen his fear of the world. The specter of uncertainty had held us captive long enough as I thought I was ready to name the unnamed.

That June afternoon, I had to go alone. Anthony was working and couldn't take the time off, so it was just Ewan and I. There was a ton of paperwork that we had to fill out in the waiting room. The room was full of children and adults in various stages of disorder and dysfunction, the kind found only in a neurologist's office. The reality of such deviation was frightening. Truly, I was not prepared to face any of this, despite my desperation. With a two year old who needed to be in constant motion, I filled out most of the paperwork while acting as goalie, trying to keep Ewan contained within the waiting room area. It was not easy for me with that enormous pregnant belly to match his boundless energy. Hands full of paperwork, I labored to keep up with the sign language Ewan needed to understand the situation. With hands for sign, hands for filling out medical information, and hands to keep Ewan from fleeing the building, I was exhausted within a few short minutes of arriving in that office. Trying to keep your two year old from bouncing off the walls or running out of the office while wracking your brain for the month and year that this child first did everything is extremely frustrating. Especially when some of those 'firsts' haven't happened yet, and you know they should have. A terrifying weariness seeped into every cell and bone of my body as I prepared myself to hear the words I knew this doctor would utter in just under an hour.

Meeting the neurologist was certainly interesting. I don't know how many neurologists you have met in your life, but they tend to be, as a whole, a bit *different*. I don't know what it is, but it seems like most of the neurologists I have met throughout the years tend to be all in their head, if you know what I mean. Our first neurologist was a kindly bald guy with that distinct 'neurologist' personality, but he spent a long time with us. While the doctor and I talked, Ewan ran his hand along the wall around and around, having some secret conversation with the green paint. Ewan was not interested in our dialogue, and he could not be bribed to participate in play with any of the toys the doctor had brought with him. The neurologist brought up issues that I hadn't thought of yet and at the same time made me feel better about others. The language and sounds we heard coming from Ewan that day was what the neurologist described as jargon. He had concerns that Ewan's language issues were very complex. He emphasized the need for an alternative form of communicating for Ewan, and pushed for more sign language and pictures and therapy. More therapy sounded a bit daunting, since we were already up to our eyeballs in therapists, therapy products, and acronyms. He was worried about things like encephalopathy and aphasia, but his biggest concern was a different A word. The neurologist finally said the word that had been floating in around our life for the past two years. This was autism.

I knew, of course. I had heard the terms fleeting eye contact, delay, social emotional testing, sensory dysfunction, and self-regulation problems enough to know it probably really was autism. Thinking it and knowing it and hearing it from a specialist wearing a white coat are all very different things, though. At the end of the appointment, we ambled across the bubbling, hot asphalt, my shoes sticking to the tar. Each step weighed on my mind and my heart. In the busy Indy traffic, I drove through a veil of tears, even though this had been sitting in the back of my mind for over a year. This word, *autism*, now confirmed, had changed everything. Before there was delay and suspicion, now it was concrete. Once again, I thought of Ewan in school playing with other children. I thought of Ewan in junior high with a girlfriend. I thought of Ewan playing baseball and football in high school and going to prom. I thought of Ewan going to college, meeting his future wife, starting a career and a family. Was that still going to happen for him? Why did it matter so much to me? There are millions of people that don't do any of those things in life and are still blissfully happy. It felt like Ewan was being denied the choice of such things. It was as if free will had just been stolen from him.

I thought of how different Ewan's life would be from Skye's. Her life would be filled with parties and people, his with objects and things. She would start school again come August, now all caught up in every subject, and she would begin a journey towards independence and autonomy. My hand fell and caressed my swollen, tight skin. I thought about this unborn child and the odyssey he or she might begin in but a few weeks time. My gaze shifted to the boy in the backseat, and I couldn't help but wonder, where would Ewan's path take him?

I met Anthony at my sister's house where he was outside playing basketball in the dying light of the afternoon sun. With every bounce of that ball I saw a life I thought we had tick away. The warmth of the sun may have been pouring down on us, but I was cold to the very depths of my soul. An emotional spectrum was pulling me under, but when I told Anthony, he didn't seem all that shocked or upset. While I was thinking of Ewan in various life stages and living at home with us forever, Anthony just kind of brushed it off. At the same time, I'm not sure he truly accepted it, as I think he was half-hoping this would all just go away on its own. That Ewan would somehow grow out of it. In a week or a month or a year, somehow things would all just come together for him. Men and women react differently to these things. I've learned throughout the past few years that women need to talk about this, hash it out, figure it out, understand every detail and aspect—and then talk about it again. Men, on the other hand, just want to fix it. There's no need to talk about it, just fix it. Only this was something that could not be fixed. It cannot be worked out with a simple plan. It cannot be solved in a few weeks. This is for life. That's the part that weighs on the minds and shoulders of mothers. This is the part that fathers cannot bear to face.

April 2010

I often liken the journey to understanding and accepting autism as the path Dorothy took along the yellow brick road. Frank L. Baum's children's story has been analyzed for having political implications in Dorothy's struggles—yet I look less for the political implications and more for the journey of the heart and soul.

The moment someone, anyone, says to you "I think your child has autism," life changes. In the blink of an eye a whirlwind of emotions sweeps you off your feet, and Dorothy's magical Midwestern tornado comes to mind. The world spins out of control as the tornado leads you towards Oz. It's a tornado of emotions and thoughts that swirl through your mind and heart until you feel like Dorothy landing in a strange world surrounded by strange people. You see your old life flash by, you see the life you thought you had flash on by. You wake up disoriented and lost in a strange, new world.

If you're lucky, you meet that special someone, that Glinda, that Good Witch of the North as soon as you wake up. Your Glinda might be a friend, a neighbor, an educator, a therapist, or another caregiver who's been down the yellow brick road before. But even if there is a Glinda in your life, you may still walk the yellow brick road alone at times. It's a journey we all must make toward the Emerald City of acceptance and understanding, and how we get there is different for everyone.

The first few steps along the yellow brick road is much like walking underwater—slow, unsure, and under pressure. It's almost as if the clock starts ticking as soon as those words are uttered. You want to do something, but you don't know what. Hitting something seems like a good idea. Crying your eyes blind seems like a good idea. Blame—for yourself and everyone else—feels like a good way to start. Those you thought you knew and loved are all different, and some are gone. Friends you thought you had will drift away as your thoughts and actions are consumed with all things autism. The family that was your rock now slips away as they can't understand the child, the disorder, or you. Like Dorothy, you walk the yellow brick road to the Emerald City, but unlike Dorothy, you often walk alone—at least in the beginning.

The word ignites a fire in your soul, though, and you hear the call to arms, that siren song buried deep in the instincts of motherhood and fatherhood. Only, this time around, your instincts seem all wrong. What works for other children doesn't work for this one. The yellow brick road gets twisted and confused, and the Emerald City is never further away than at that moment. You spend all your waking time either with the child or looking up information about autism. You become an expert 'Googler' and have read every article and snippet on the web. You collect books about autism like a buyer for Barnes and Noble. Every magazine with the headline 'Autism' on the front page graces your coffee table. You DVR every show having anything remotely to do with autism. You live, eat, and breathe all things autism. Your every word becomes centered around it, your every thought hinges on it. You know the clock is ticking, and you have thrown yourself into trying to stop the second hand from moving.

Then comes the epiphany. The moment of amazement and wonder. The first time you connect with your child. The first time you get a glimpse of his soul. The first time you actually understand his world and his life. The light bulb goes off and things start to fall into place. You realize that you walk with others on that yellow brick road. You meet other families, therapists, and educators who become your lifeline. Therapy starts to make sense, goals get achieved, and the clock seems to slow down. The rush and urgency seems to decelerate, and in that moment life makes sense. Purpose and understanding seep into your life in ways that others can only wonder at. The direction your life has gone in will amaze you.

You'll look back to that life before the yellow brick road, and you'll see how much richer your life is now than it ever has been. You begin to thank the powers that be for putting this child in your life.

We all walk the yellow brick road. At times we walk it alone, and other times we it walk together. You meet the Scarecrow—only this time you seek to understand the brain rather than to have one. You meet the Tinman—only this time you learn that your heart grows with each step you take. You meet the Cowardly Lion—only this time you learn to have courage enough for both you and your child. The yellow brick road takes you to a life once feared and later understood. On the yellow brick road you find confidence and determination. You find purpose and a will to do more. You find your faith and hope restored.

The stress of the diagnosis and the stress of our financial situation sat upon our shoulders like a ten ton boulder. The tips from Anthony's job were sporadic, but our bills and groceries continued despite the income fluctuations. I was heavy with the last weeks of pregnancy, and the hot July air could be seen rising and swirling from the asphalt. We were watching my niece and nephew one afternoon when Anthony and I just snapped from all the hardships. He was making taco salads, and in my pregnant state, I was starving every minute of every hour. It felt like there was never enough food in those days. Anthony's face fell as he said, "Oh crap, I don't think we have enough taco shells for everyone."

I couldn't take it anymore. I was hungry and tired and wanted just one thing to go right. In my practically hypoglycemic state, there was no rational response, and there was nothing Anthony could say to make me calm down. In one of the worst fights we have ever had in our entire marriage, I slapped him straight across the face with my right hand. He was stunned. I was stunned. A barrage of curses and accusations flew back and forth between us. In that one moment, every trouble over the past few months was blamed on each other. In tears, I took off in the car headed nowhere in particular. Once again, I found myself wondering what would happen if I just kept driving. I found some crackers in the car and slowly chewed them as I drove around the Indiana countryside. Eating something helped me return to my reasonable, rational self again, and I thought, "What the Hell am I doing?" Thirty minutes earlier my car couldn't get far enough away, and now it couldn't get home fast enough. All we had was each other, and I was desperate to make amends. Anthony must have thought the same thing because I could see him pacing in the garage, tears in his eyes as well. After a long embrace and a thousand apologies, we added another vow to our marriage. We promised to always buy an excess of taco shells for as long as we both shall live.

A few days later, Anthony and I walked in to the Ob-Gyn for my last check up before this new baby was to grace the world with its presence. The doc could tell I was a little frazzled, moreso than I normally was, and asked what had happened. I told him Ewan had just been diagnosed with autism and the rest of life was a tumultuous mess. We talked about my fears in bringing this new child into a world so out of control. Our previous 'so whats' of having another child like Ewan seemed much more frightening in the light of a post-autism world. Our doctor just smiled and said in his calm, reassuring manner that first, life was always going to be a tumultuous mess and what really matter was how we handled it. He then confessed that, he too, had a son who seemed to be much like Ewan. He took my hands in his own and said, "You know, you can walk through any physics or math department on any university campus and find about 12 autistics working alongside everyone else. I think Ewan's going to get through this, and you'll be surprised at everything he can and will do in his life." Here was the physics reference again, and all I could hope was that when Ewan did go to college, he'd choose something a little less enigmatic to major in than quantum physics.

The very next week we found ourselves at the hospital eager to have a baby right when my knight in shining armor Ob was on vacation. I was induced that evening. The staff expected it to be the next day before anything happened, and thus the Ob on call left for home that night. In the middle of the night, contractions began to come faster and stronger, and the anesthesiologist was none too happy about putting in an epidural at three in the morning. At first the epidural was too strong, and I couldn't breathe. The irritated anesthesiologist was then called back in to adjust it. He was even more perturbed the second time around, and in his agitation he backed the epidural's effectiveness down to zilch. One minute I could barely feel my chest, and in the next minute the pain of labor surged through every nerve in my body. The pain swept over me, and I was left with a useless catheter in my back as the contractions swept over my unprepared body. By five in the morning the baby was definitely on his way to meeting everyone. Everyone except the doctor, that is. My substitute doctor was driving from his house 20 minutes away, and the nurses were yelling, "No pushing, stop pushing, just hold it in and breath—you can't have this baby yet, the doctor is not here!"

Hmmm, yeah, I'm pretty sure that the baby did not get this memo. It was coming out, doctor or not. As I lay there writhing in pain, trying like Hell not to push and pleading with God to defy the laws of physics for my doctor's vehicle, my husband promptly passed out. As he lay on the floor, nature continued her frantic pace. Just when I thought, that's it, forget the doctor—these nurses are getting a quick promotion, in walked the young doc. In reflection, I'm sure that yelling "Where the Hell have you been?" probably wasn't the best way to start a conversation, but I don't think anyone will begrudge a woman in labor an expletive or two. The doctor barely had time to get a good look at the situation before he managed to catch the newly born baby. My husband woke just in time to see his second son come into the world. At 5:30 a.m., we held Vaughn Anthony in our arms.

The second Vaughn was given to me, I began to make comparisons. While Ewan had his eyes wide open the minute he took his first breath of air, Vaughn had his firmly shut. We turned the lights down low, but still, Vaughn could barely be coaxed to crack an eyelid. Much later, when he finally revealed the beauty of his deep blue orbs, they were unfocused and sleepy from the trauma of birth. And with that, Vaughn Anthony fell asleep.

I wasn't allowed to leave the hospital for another day, and Anthony set up camp on the couch next to me. Our newborn was much like any other. At only a few hours old, nature folded him into the rhythm and timing of newborn life. Ewan and Skye stayed with Aunt Heather while mommy and daddy luxuriated in the glow of parenthood. That night a glowingly proud Anthony went in for a short serving shift, telling every table and customer in sight about his new son. One table took a napkin, wrote "Congratulations on your new son," signed it and gave him a $100 tip. While the hundred dollars went to pay for bills and food, the napkin remains in Vaughn's baby book, a prize possession to remind us how fortunate we really are. That night, Anthony snuck back into our room and slept next to his son on the couch. Over the next 24 hours, we took turns cuddling the sleeping newborn and enjoyed making as much noise as we cared to, not startling him one bit. Vaughn could tune out all that Ewan couldn't. The world was a quiet, pleasant place to be for this new baby.

Vaughn's presence in our life was a little unsettling for Ewan. We came home and placed the newborn in a bassinet right next to me on the couch. The first thing Ewan did was notice the change in his environment. This mewling, sniffling bundle of blankets was a mysteriously attractive force for Ewan. For once, he showed a curiosity about something other than his trains. And for the boy whose universe revolved around the safety of his trains, this brother created a significant wobble in his orbit around the inanimate. This brother, only days old, was already reaching Ewan in ways no one else could. We would lay Vaughn down on a blanket in front of the couch and watch as Ewan built his train tracks around his brother. Before Ewan could only build in straight lines across the house, and now, for whatever reason, his tracks turned to circles with his brother always in the middle. The bond between brothers started the day we brought Vaughn home and placed him inside Ewan's solar system. To this day, they gravitate around each other as they attract and repel as only brothers can.

As we slowly adjusted to being a family of five, we learned how to fit this new addition in among the mix of therapists and doctor visits. For the next several years, Vaughn would become a fixture in Ewan's therapy, often unwittingly. We missed only three days of therapy when Vaughn was born. As soon as humanly possible, we threw ourselves back into the routine. Vaughn and I sat through sensory shaving cream experiments, sign language bombardments, and a host of games and puzzles. At the end of every chart, next to the part where it mentioned Ewan continued to need therapy, it always read, "Mom present and participated throughout." Now that homeschooling had given way to the freedom of summer, Skye joined in. When Anthony was home, we all squeezed into Ewan's room for therapy. It was then that therapy, and the course of Ewan's life, became a family affair.

Two months later, we packed the entire family into the car and took Ewan to yet another specialist, this time a medical geneticist. By then, Vaughn was developing and slowly opening our eyes to all the things that made Ewan different. Things we couldn't just attribute to Ewan being a boy. With a new baby in tow, our family crammed itself into a small examination room where Ewan went up and down and up and down, on and off the examination table over and over the entire time we were in the room. He made little contact with the doctor as he was much too obsessed with the table. Ewan then had to be examined by the entire team; psychologist, speech therapist, and occupational therapist. Ewan was fairly difficult that day. I couldn't get him to interact with the speech therapist at all, and he was not about to engage in testing of any kind with the OT. I remember a butterfly ornament hanging in the corner slowly twisting in the sun. This is what caught Ewan's eye, and this is what he focused on for the rest of the time. We tried to get him to say butterfly or have any kind of communication exchange, but it wasn't meant to be that day; all he saw was the light and shadow playing out on the butterfly as it twisted in the air.

The team spent a lot of time talking to us about Ewan's future. While the neurologist spent a lot of time observing Ewan and putting a name to each of the eccentricities I thought was 'just Ewan,' this team was able to light a fire in our hearts. In the room where the butterfly twisted and swirled, they told us that if we couldn't get Ewan to communicate with others, he would end up in a non-verbal classroom later in life. They pushed us to explore more than just the world of verbal speech. This group could see that I wanted Ewan to speak more than anything, but they could also see how well Ewan was doing with sign language. At the time he had approximately 100 signs that he used in therapy, and somehow they knew that there was more just waiting to come out. When I mentioned that his developmental therapist had suggested something called an augmentative communication evaluation with some specialist on the east side of Indy, the doctor exclaimed, "Oh, I know Debbie! Now that's what we want to see; we need to push the envelope with this kid and see all that he can do with someone like this AAC specialist in his corner." When I told him it would still be several months before we could get in to see this communication guru, he did his best to speed that process up. We left that visit with explicit instructions to increase the signs, increase the pictures, and to see the AAC specialist as fast as possible. He, too, used the 'A' word with us but also ran tests for any genetic disorders that might explain the whole enchilada, specifically Sotos Syndrome, which often presents with autistic-like characteristics and an overgrowth of the head. Ewan had a rather large head, and movie quotes from *So I Married An Axe Murderer* come to mind here. With that syndrome in question, we sat through several months of waiting until those results came back. At the time, only three or four labs in the United States did testing for Sotos, so there was plenty of time to wait. But in the end, Ewan did not have any genetic markers that would explain where the issues had come from. No Fragile

X, no Sotos, no quirky DNA patterns of any kind. Ewan was Ewan, and Ewan was autistic.

Chapter Seven

I Want a Name

After meeting with both the medical geneticist and the pediatric neurologist, we knew that it was time to re-vamp Ewan's therapy plan and the overall way we approached life. Ewan and I couldn't handle many more haircut disasters. What had started out as a simple list of getting out of the house and learning to speak was now getting ready to become something much more complex. It was more than communicating the here and now, I had to learn how to prepare Ewan for all the befores and afters of life. We needed to help Ewan find balance in a world of extremes. He could not live life ruled by out of control emotions and the need for, or aversion to, sensory input. By this time, I was starting to learn the lingo and unscramble the host of acronyms that follows the path of those with special needs. I had thrown myself into understanding every part of autism. My yellow brick road was full of tests, evaluations, eligibility criteria, and scores, scores and more scores. Seeing the results in black and white in a medical chart tends to change your entire perspective, and from the day the 'A' word was mentioned, a bigger picture of Ewan's future emerged. There is nothing like seeing your child's development graphed across the page with some of those skills hovering at the zero mark. The pain at seeing the gulf widen between your child's actual age and his skill level cannot be described in words. But I didn't have the time to wallow in self-pity and pain, now was the time for action. With the help of our new specialists and pediatrician, my sister the OT, and the internet, I now started to understand the exhaustive list of needs and began to push for more complex goals. I now wanted to see Ewan engage in purposeful play and to be able to play and interact both in the home and out at the park. We needed to improve Ewan's attention span and help him learn how to follow directions. In some ways, I wanted the simple things like being able to recognize himself in a mirror (which surprisingly isn't all that simple), and in other ways, I wanted more complex goals like developing self-regulation. And, above all else, I wanted him to call me 'mama.'

Over the past year Ewan had attempted to call his father 'da' and even tried to call to his sister with 'ky,' but for me, there was nothing. The one person Ewan clung to like glue didn't have a name, and I was more than a little indignant about it all. Every therapist who came to the house was working on this goal—each one of them spent day after day pushing Ewan to identify me with words or even a sign. This exercise completely confounded him, and it was as if Ewan viewed me as an extension of himself, something that needed no name. I was part and parcel of his existence—and much of the time he would use me as a tool to get what he wanted. He would put his hand on mine and take me to what he wanted—milk, food, blankets—but he wouldn't name me, and he rarely named the objects. He was using sign language, but his first instinct was always to put his hand on mine. It was several months later when I decided to sleep in one day and let daddy take over. About 20 minutes into my blissful reprieve, Anthony came rushing into the room and yelled, "He did it! He said mama!" At first, I was irate that he had applied this sacred name to my husband, but then Ewan came bursting in the room with the word on his lips as his eyes searched frantically for ME. Finally, here was something I could check off our list of goals. I had a name.

While I was starting to understand more about autism, about how early intervention could help, and the type of goals we could implement, what I still didn't understand was that many of these goals would stay with Ewan for years to come and would follow him long after he left early intervention. 'Mama' may have come to Ewan in just a few short months, but the rest of his inner dialogue would take much longer to uncover.

With a new list of goals and a new diagnosis, it was time to re-evaluate Ewan's team. After too many 'off' days and weeks with his new speech therapist, we opted to find a better fit. Sometimes I wonder if I gave up too early on some of his therapists. It's not easy to fire someone that comes into your home several times a week. And, it is very difficult to leave the comfort of someone you do know for the unknown next person to walk into your life. But making this particular change was the best thing that could've happened to Ewan. We switched to the only other therapist that served our area—one that others, including my sister, had not always liked. We took a huge leap of faith in switching to this new therapist, but looking back, she was the right person at the right time. She was able to engage Ewan in ways no else had up to that point. Sure, he had tolerated hand-over-hand activities before as others taught him signs, play, and fine motor skills, but she was able to actively engage him in a way that led to interactive exchanges between the two. All of a sudden it was no longer a one-way street of shoving information at Ewan. Now we had a two way exchange and a meeting of the minds. Now we were seeing the beginning of reciprocity. And she didn't once have to chase him down—he gravitated toward her like a moth to the flame.

       This new progress seemed to come all at the same time. First came a name for all the sleepless nights and all the factors that equaled Ewan. Hearing the diagnosis was hard, but I no longer felt I was grasping at straws. Autism is anything but concrete, but here was something my mind could grasp and begin to understand. Here was something I could read about, talk to others about, and find our place within the world of autism spectrum disorders. As hard as it is to hear those words, it's even harder to hear and say the words, 'we don't know what is wrong.' Speech, OT, and DT were able to push Ewan forward through signs, sensory techniques, and play-based therapy. Ewan always led the direction of the sessions no matter how hard they each tried to shape their hours together. Around that time, we lost one of our favorite team members to a new job. Losing this therapist was very difficult because she had been so good at understanding and explaining Ewan to me. She may not have always made huge breakthroughs with Ewan, but out of all these early therapists, she understood how he thought. She was the one who suggested an augmentative communication evaluation before anyone else, even the speech therapists. She may have been in our home to work on cognitive and social / emotional goals and play skills, but that DT evolved into a tremendous source of information about child development and the meaning behind the actions for me. I regretted losing her, but I will never forget the impact she had on all our lives in the time she was there.

       By then it was October, and the aisles of every store were filled with witches and pumpkins. I simply adore Halloween. Even though I rarely dress up myself, there is something magical about seeing your children flex their imaginative muscles and embrace the cloak of disguise. Plus, there's candy. Now that Ewan was getting old enough to traipse through the neighborhood, candy bucket in hand, I wanted him to love Halloween as much as I. We spent a lot of time and energy into turning a green pair of sweatpants and face paint into a successful Hulk experience. Therapy visits focused on the sensory experience of the face paint, the language of 'Trick or Treat,' and the social expectations of ringing a doorbell and not going in and getting comfortable on some stranger's couch. Candy is cool, hanging out in their living room is not. We bought pumpkins to decorate, and every candle on the counter radiated fall with every molecule. We even succeeded in getting Ewan to verbalize 'kin' for pumpkin that year. One day on a trip to the store, I noticed Ewan would yell out 'kin!' every so often. After tuning in to what he was doing, I noticed he had memorized which houses had pumpkins along the way. Every now and then, he would give us a peek at the inner-workings of his mind, and it would simply astound us. Because he was quiet so often it was hard to figure out what he knew. Later, while cleaning the house I stumbled across a plastic blue handle. I mused aloud, "I wonder what this goes to?" Not expecting anyone to answer, I went on cleaning and vacuuming. Then I felt a tugging on my pants, and when I turned around I saw Ewan holding up a box to a bingo toy machine. That little blue plastic handle went right there on the box to crank out the winning numbers for future bingo operators. Right at that moment, I promised myself to never underestimate his abilities no matter what he did or didn't say.

For all the preparation that went into Halloween, I'd love to say that it was a resounding success. The reality of it, though, was not quite so easy. The work in therapy was not enough to prepare Ewan for the chaos of such a unique day in our life. One minute we were a normal family, and the next Skye had transformed into a spritely witch with a broomstick and bucket. With the setting of the sun, the world had gone crazy, and Ewan's eyes widened in fear. His costume was a homemade, sensory-friendly Hulk costume with green sweatpants and purple ripped shorts sewn on top. These sweats weren't part of his overall plan to traverse about the house half-naked, though, and the phrase "Don't make me angry" came to mind as I pushed his arms and legs into the costume. With his blood boiling, I took the next step and tried to apply the green make-up to his face. It didn't matter how many times we had practiced in therapy, Ewan wanted no part of this transformation and screamed in frustration. For a second, I thought he might actually rip his shirt and pants off in a character study of Bruce Banner's fierce fury. We ended up going to a large neighborhood filled with giggling costumed children running in all directions. Porches and sidewalks were decorated with skeletons, fog machines, and eerie lights swirling around the ground. Vaughn, dressed as an identical infant Hulk, merely yawned at the macabre scenes before him. Skye, on the other hand, ran from house to house collecting candy like it was oxygen. By the end of the night though, Ewan lost his grip on reality and had given himself over to the radioactive Hulk character he portrayed. For whatever reason, he was past angry and boiled over into a volcanic-style meltdown.

That quiet, calm physicist Bruce Banner had left the building. For all the practice with make-up and costumes, I still could not communicate with Ewan about the meaning and purpose behind such traditions.

~

In an effort to give Ewan every opportunity to express his thoughts and to understand ours, we found ourselves driving halfway across Indiana for the long awaited evaluation with the augmentative communication specialist. It's ironic how much hope I placed in a visit that I honestly didn't even know anything about. I didn't really understand augmentative communication at the time, other than I knew that it included sign language and pictures to communicate with. I wondered if she was some type of sign language guru that was going to teach us both hundreds of new signs or if she was going to show us something altogether different. But what I did know was that she offered us something no one else had been able to up to that point. She offered us hope that there *was* something to help Ewan in ways that we hadn't been able to up 'til then.

We showed up at her house for the evaluation not knowing what to expect, but certainly not expecting her to place an $8,000 computer in front of Ewan. She started low tech with almost toy-like devices you had to program with your own voice and slide pre-made sheets of symbols into, depending on the vocabulary need. Then she stepped up to more symbols and more buttons but still on the low tech end of the scale. Next, she offered him an electronic device that seemed a little more high tech with a touch screen and computerized pictures that Ewan could touch. This device, called a Dynavox Mighty Mo, still required you to record your own voice for each word and phrase represented on the screen, but one would no longer have to carry around tons of paper inserts for any occasion that might pop up. This device had it all stored in its memory like a portable human brain and mouth. She had Ewan try different brands of devices as she went from a Dynavox MT4 which Ewan absolutely loved, to a series of other high tech devices, traveling up and down the technology scale from the lowest to the highest technology had to offer. Whatever device Debbie put in front of him, Ewan instantly responded to the novelty of the techy gadget. Here was a puzzle that would take him years to solve—this was not some generic toy that he could figure out in 37 seconds, this was something much more than that. He was mesmerized by the possibility of what each new window could offer him, and for the first time we had his full and undivided attention.

Within just a few minutes of exploring one of the high tech devices Debbie had plunked under his nose, Ewan used it to communicate the following life altering exchange: "I…want…pancakes." My husband and I both held our breaths and looked at each other in complete shock and awe. For the first time in his short life, our son had told us what he wanted. Before this marvelous discovery, we always had to guess, not knowing if we were truly right or if he merely settled for what we gave him, never truly knowing if we had given him his heart's desire. Tears streamed down my face as I shouted, "For the love of all that is holy, Anthony, get in the car and go get him some pancakes! There's a McDonald's right down the road, go!" I watched with joy and unspeakable wonder as my son entered a world filled with thoughts, ideas, and sentences. We had found the connection we'd been so desperate to see. Hope had come to us in an $8,000 square box of miraculous technology. It would take many months and several reports before our very own device would find its way to our doorstep. Leaving that evaluation without this piece of hope in our hands was heartbreaking. Yet our gaze had never been more focused in those moments after that evaluation. Come Hell or high water, that boy was going to have a communication device of his own.

While this miraculous breakthrough was occurring and we were welcoming our new addition into the family fold, the rest of life slowly seemed to be falling apart. With the good comes the bad, and while we had plenty to be thankful for, we were facing some of the most desperate times financially. Raising a family with only my husband working as a server was impossible. Those days when Anthony came home with just five dollars was happening more and more often. I needed to be out working, but with so much happening with Ewan—the doctor appointments which now seemed to be coming more and more often, the therapy appointments which had just been increased, and the new word for the orbit of our lives—going to work seemed absurd. Facing an ever decreasing bank account and a list of exponentially growing bills, we were facing some impossible decisions. I could go to work and we could claw ourselves out of the financial sinkhole we were in, but we were terrified of what would happen to Ewan. At this point, we knew the value of therapy and hated to miss one minute of it for fear of somehow losing all that we had gained. We knew we had to put Ewan first, but every night it tore our heart out to see everything else fall to pieces. Miraculously, our marriage was holding together despite our dwindling bank account. We may have been poor as dirt, but we still had each other. Rather than pushing us apart, this experience fused our hearts together forever. If we were going to drown, we were going to drown hand in hand.

It was in the darkest of those days that we made a choice to leave Indiana and go back to our hometown in Illinois where we both grew up, hoping to find a better life for us all, not just Ewan. Even I was at the point of wanting to go back, which says a lot about my level of desperation. I was worried that the demons of the past would catch up with us. One late night, Anthony and I sat at the kitchen table staring at a pile of bills, none of them part of the U.S. currency system. He grabbed my hand and said, "Lisha, it won't be the same this time. Life will be different this time around, I promise you. I'm not the same man I was then."

"It's that town, Anthony. There's a lot buried in there; are we sure we want to go digging it all back up? Can you handle what we may find there?"

"What lies in that damn town is nothing compared to what's sitting on this table in front of us. We haven't got much choice here," he said.

With my head in my hands, I drew in a ragged breath and said, "Ok. Let's go home."

His answering smile showed his relief and excitement, "It'll be different this time, I promise. It's just us now."

The decision to move back was not easy, but it really was our only option. While Ewan's needs were still our priority, we also had to balance paying rent, buying food and gas, and all the other necessities of life with what *he needed*. There was no point to all this focus on communication if he asked for milk and we had none to give. We were tired of struggling and wanted to wake up in the morning without feeling defeated before the first foot even hit the floor. My husband was offered a job managing a restaurant back in our old hometown, and without knowing what services would be like for Ewan, we took it. Hoping to move forward in our lives, we both wanted to find a community where we belonged, all of us. We had no other choice at that point but to move in another direction. It meant leaving my mother and my sister behind in Indy, but we were desperate to breathe again. We took the last of the money in our bank account and rented a U-Haul. It meant going back to a town full of demons and ghosts. For Anthony, the heart of addiction lives in that town and going back meant putting us all in the zip code of habit and need. For me, going back reminded me of every minute of my father's life and death and of

Anthony's addictions. That zip code was so much more than just a quaint college town. The red brick house on the hill where I watched my father die called out with a reminder of his last breaths. I was scared to go back, and I was terrified to stay. Left with no other choices, though, we said goodbye to everything in Indiana and said hello to the past and present in Illinois. Within a few weeks, we had boxed up our house and watched our lives take the fork in the road.

But as our possessions were slowly boxed up into a thousand containers and our living space evolved into a warehouse, Ewan's stress level hit catastrophic levels. This was the child that could not handle transitions and change of any kind, the child who hated leaving the safety of his house, and now his asylum had been turned upside down. Nothing was where it was supposed to be, in fact, it looked as if his life had disappeared completely. We kept his room unboxed until the day of the move, but we had everything else ready to throw out the door the moment the U-Haul truck showed up. It was in that last week in Indiana, that we saw the depth of his despair and how hard life could truly be for someone with autism. In his frustration and fear and pain, he lashed out at his own body, scratching and picking at his stomach and chest 'til he bled. The scratches quickly became infected, and not only did we have a traumatized Ewan, we also had a staph infection that spread like wildfire over his skin. One of the last nights in the house, I went to get Ewan ready for a bath, and I found him in the kitchen just staring at the light. No amount of calling his name (which didn't make him turn anyway), tapping his shoulder, or waving my hand in front of his face could take his unrelenting gaze from that light. Unsure if he was having a seizure or not, we ended up taking him to the ER, where they promptly sent us home with nothing more than a "Call your specialists tomorrow and ask *them* about it" kind of response. Our call to the medical geneticist who had been so helpful before ended with a script for an anti-psychotic to help Ewan make it through the trauma of moving. There's no more humbling act of motherhood than to accept and administer such a powerful medication. Loading the syringe with the cloudy liquid and giving my two and a half year old son an anti-psychotic medication was almost more than I could bear. It was all too much for Anthony. He broke down at this point and realized that there was something very wrong. For the first time, Anthony seemed to grasp the uncertainty of his son's development and wept. In that week, Anthony took in the pain of two years worth of an emotional spectrum: uncertainty, fear, confusion and acceptance. We both felt that it wasn't fair—we shouldn't have to medicate a child so young with medications so strong, and as the drug worked its way through his veins, I questioned everything I had ever done with this child. This drug-induced slumber felt overwhelmingly like a failure. Despite my fears, though, it was the only thing that allowed him some measure of peace from the inner turmoil he'd been fighting those previous few days. With a sedated two and a half year old son and a stressed out family, we left behind a life to begin anew. Having failed to make it in the big city, we headed back to our old hometown in Illinois hoping to find more than just demons and ghosts residing there. We were homeward bound.

Chapter Eight

You Can Always Go Home

In 1986, my mother and father packed us up in the family car to look at a house in another town. We had lived out in the country in an old white farmhouse in a tiny town in central Illinois almost my whole life, and now my parents were dragging us toward a bigger town just south of us. I was not excited about this prospect of moving. I liked my life in that old white farmhouse in the country, and as small as the town is, the friendships and comforts of home were great. I was in sixth grade, my sister was a sophomore in high school, and the last thing either of us wanted was to uproot and start over in a new town. My dad was working at an office job in that bigger town, though, and the house directly next to the business was for sale. Lazy, small town summers riding my bike around town were replaced with a bigger town that lived and died by the university schedule of fall and spring semesters. One fall day in the late afternoon, we found ourselves driving down to see the red brick house on the hill. A house we would call home for the next 15 years. A house where I would see life turn to death and breath turn to silence.

When we bought the house, it had stood empty for many years. Built back when they knew how to build a house to stand through the ravages of time, the brick and mortar had seen many families come and go. The empty house sat silently in stasis, waiting for the heart and soul of someone to bring it back to life. The minute we first walked in, the red brick house on the hill shook itself awake and the very walls began to pulse with each step of our feet. The hot water heat elements gurgled to life, water rushing through its veins once again wrapping a family in its warmth. Gazing at the strong walls and big yard, my parents fell in love with that house. We moved in right before Christmas and our first act in our new home was to decorate a tree in celebration of a new life.

The red brick house on the hill became a silent spectator in our lives, quietly standing by as our family grew and watching over us as we expanded from just my parents and my sister to include a fleet of trucks and cars my father owned. The circle drive held the weight of visitors, dates and friends who came to the house year after year. The big white barn safeguarded the different animals we raised. The fields and acres of grass cringed as I terrorized the landscape with a 1986 Honda scooter. The brick and mortar casually observed the infamous yearly Easter egg hunt where my sister and I fought over the Golden Egg in the yard, even in high school. The flowers painted a colorful canvas while the vegetable gardens sustained us through the long, hot summer months. The white garage at the bottom of the drive practically burst at the seams with spare parts and tools. The red brick house on the hill welcomed prom dates that came and went year after year. The giant hall closet at the top of the stairs folded me in its embrace through endless hide and seek games. The fireplace in the living room kept a watchful eye out on the parties that raged on in my parent's absence. The red brick house on the hill was there for the good times and the bad, a resolute force shaping our lives day after day after day. This house has become a symbol of so many things to me over the years. It was a refuge from the storms that swirled around us, both financial and meteorological. It was home.

  We moved to the red brick house on the hill because my dad had started working in the office of a trucking company. Before, he'd been on the road for most of my life, and now, he was in an office just across the street from our house. Before we'd moved, we lived in that old white farmhouse deep in the country. When I think of that house, I think of my mother, as she was the constant force in our lives while dad was out working. For most of my life in that old white farmhouse, we were poor, really, really poor. The kind of poor that one winter it actually snowed *inside* the house. Much of life was about survival: survival through the lean times, survival through the awful winter storms of the '70s and '80s, and survival without dad much of the time as he was out on the road. My mother can be extraordinarily resourceful, especially when pushed to the wall, and in those times of survival she turned our house into a veritable grocery store. She raised chickens for eggs, grew fruit trees in the back for apples, and had a giant garden where she grew and then canned every vegetable known to the Midwest growing season. She was the one who chopped the firewood, fed the horses, made our clothes and fixed the front porch. The old white farmhouse was *all mom*. The red brick house on the hill was *all dad*. It was a little flashier, a lot sturdier, and my dad was always in it, in the beginning anyway. It seemed as if the two simply couldn't exist without the other. The heart and soul of that house and our family was always my father.

Now that dad was home all the time, it was an almost miraculous feeling to pop into his office after school and see him every day. While he was making more money, it didn't always translate to a free and easy lifestyle. My dad was horrible with finances and couldn't balance a checkbook no matter how hard he worked. With more money came bigger bills. He was larger than life in every way possible and rejected the conventionality of a typical life. My dad did what he wanted when he wanted and not a minute sooner. Rules simply did not exist for him—except for one. With an accountant he might avoid the occasional taxes, but he could not escape death. After a few years, dad had to go back out on the road in order to keep one step ahead of the avalanche. The red brick house on the hill was a little lonelier without dad, and we'd wait in the living room to hear the slightest hint of him coming down the road. My dog Wilbur, a black Chinese Shar-Pei, would sit at the front window just staring out into the night waiting for dad to come home. The windows of the house would tremble with joy as my father's jake brake announced his arrival back home. The brake lights of his semi truck illuminating the driveway like an airport runway. In my father's absence, the clock ticked a little slower, and in his arrival, the rhythm and measure of life returned.

I've often wondered if that red brick house on the hill is cursed, exacting some toll for the warmth and shelter. The house giveth and the house taketh away. Not long after we moved in, several of our dogs died mysteriously. Years later, I would lose another pup to a mysterious cancerous death. Then, when I was a sophomore in college, my father, the very picture of health and strength, was diagnosed with Hodgkin's disease. If our hometown held the heart of addiction for Anthony, that red brick house on the hill was the heart of sickness for me. In the beginning, it was full of hope. By the end, the feeling of death permeated every surface. There are a thousand other memories I have of that house, but the only one I can see now is my father sitting in his oversized recliner struggling to take his last breaths. The circle drive forever after empty, all his cars and trucks sold off. The big white barn forever after uninhabited, the horses reminded us too much of dad. The garage forever after bereft of tools and junk, no one was there to put it back together again. I think of that red brick house on the hill and suddenly there is not enough oxygen in the world to fill my lungs. My father is all I see. He was without a doubt, the glue that held everything together. Watching that big bear of a man slowly shrink to half his size was more than a child should ever have to bear witness to. In some ways he was bigger than life, at every turn he threw all in, even if he ended up with a losing hand. It was all or nothing with him, and while he couldn't manage money to save his life, he taught me more about family than anyone or anything else. He was the man who would drop everything if you needed him, and many times, he did just that. With my father, family came above all else, above cars and trucks and travels. Family was first.

     My dad came from a big, bustling family with a family home much like Grand Central Station, among parents and siblings who hold true to the 'family first' motto, dropping it all to be ready for any cry for help. And there are always cries for help. People are always coming and going in his parent's house. At any time of the day or night, I think my grandparents, Phillip and Rosalie, are standing by on call to receive visitors and solve problems. No phone call or invitation necessary, their door is truly always open. And for the most part, it's easy to be yourself in that house, because every person is so radically different from the next. The Hart house is a potpourri of humanity with interests flowing in a thousand different directions all hours of the day. It is somewhat hectic and vaguely chaotic in my grandparent's house. Yet in some ways, this pandemonium provides some measure of comfort. It wouldn't be their house with the relentless procession of people and problems. I think the very nexus of human dilemma comes from those four walls. With so many feet traveling through, it is inevitable that their troubles come along as well. Sitting at their simple kitchen table drinking coffee stronger than most Turks are accustomed to, every trouble known to mankind has traipsed through my grandma and grandpa's door and sat down to sip a cup of Joe with them. Life is messy at their house, yet they wouldn't have it any other way.

     For many years during my childhood, we lived in the same town as my grandparents, and my dad would haul us over there every Saturday and Sunday and some days after school. He too would pull up a chair, grab a cup of coffee and make himself comfortable. He liked a busy life, and I doubt my father would have ever settled for Gwen Stefani's "Simple Kind of Life." He often created the many whirlwinds we were swept up in, and it was not unusual to wake up on a Saturday morning at home in Illinois and by nightfall find myself falling asleep in Tennessee. He was never a schedule kind of guy. If he wanted to go somewhere we went. If he wanted to look at a new car or truck two states over, we went. And when he really got a bee in his bonnet to eat at a restaurant in downtown Nashville, we went. He suffered from a wanderlust greater than Columbus and Magellan combined. I grew up amidst the chaos and found a way to survive and thrive through it all. I doubt combat medics have seen as much action as I. My mother, on the other hand, was like a fragile dandelion swept away by the hurricane. She is an only child that grew up in a quiet, sterile environment where the soles of shoes never touched living room carpet. Her parents and upbringing couldn't have been more different than my dad's. Where dads was messy and lived in, hers was spotless and orderly. It had to have been downright painful at times for my mom to visit my dad's family and for him to visit hers. My paternal grandparents' house could have a litter of puppies in the kitchen, and my maternal grandparents' house was a like a museum. Polar extremes are closer than these two families. Imagine my holidays, if you will. We'd get up early and drive two hours to see my mom's family, Bob and Pauline (the Branham's), and walk through the pristine silent calm of their home and then drive off to end the day at the Hart's, where nothing is silent. We went from one end of the spectrum to the other. People emerging from sensory deprivation chambers had an easier time than we did. The Branhams are the quiet of the night, and the Harts are the harsh sunlight at noon. I can't imagine my life without these two extremes, and I can't even imagine Ewan having to endure the disparate holidays like I did.

  As different as my sets of grandparents are, all of them grew up in some part of rural Illinois. In Illinois, there's Chicago, and then there's the rest of the state, and the roots to my family tree are decidedly downstate. None of us are metropolitan by any stretch of the word. My fear of more than three lanes of traffic is likely a part of my DNA structure. Both sets of grandparents are the products of the Depression, and like so many their age, they saved everything. For the Branhams, it was the basement full of every box, carton and instructional manual to any item ever purchased in their 60 years of marriage. For the Harts, it was the garage *and* basement that you could barely squeeze through. They were each a *Hoarders* episode in the making. Yet that is where the similarities end. The Branhams, with their small family, were able to afford the other brick house on the hill and spent most every Saturday afternoon at a mall in the Dillard's store. Where our brick house on the hill was full of warmth and life, theirs was still and quiet. The Harts, with their busting-at-the-seams household and animal menagerie, spent most every other day at Rural

King. If the heart of our house was my father, then surely the heart of his parent's house was his mother. The world could end in flames and destruction and she would still be sitting at the kitchen table calmly drinking a cup of coffee.

My Grandmother Pauline was physically handicapped by years of abuse from rheumatoid arthritis, and both her hobby and professional goal in life was to spend 80% of her income on clothing. Her exercise came from walking the department stores on coupon days. My Grandmother Rosalie remained much more physically active, though, and devoted much of her life to the status of her backyard plant kingdom. My grandfathers, both Phillip and Bob, were math and science wizards. My Grandpa Phil was about an hour shy of graduating from the University of Illinois with a degree in Chemistry when circumstances led him away from college and towards a job supporting his family. He worked as a chemist his whole life at a local factory. My Grandpa Bob is a unique fellow. He graduated high school but never had the means to go to college. One day after the war, he found himself with a wife and needing a job, so he walked into the nearest engineering firm and drew his way into a job. He worked the rest of his life as a draftsman with no formal education whatsoever.

When I think about the family history of chemists and engineers, I wonder about where autism fits into our family tree. I am drawn back to my two grandfathers, especially to my Grandpa Bob. His father's tale is even stranger. His father, Bert, was a mathematical genius that only had a high school education but apparently walked through life like some modern day Ramanujan. As a young child he was never given a name by his family. Born in the rural wild of Illinois, it wasn't 'til a teacher took him under her wing and nicknamed him Bird for the sounds he used to make that he finally had a name. Bird grew into Bert, and Bert grew into a man with a highly mathematical mind. My great grandfather went off to war, though, and was exposed to mustard gas. After discharge, he was left disabled and wheezing. He couldn't work after that and he died before I was born, so I have no memory of Bert, though my grandfather speaks of him often. After Ewan was diagnosed with autism, I thought of Bert as I wonder if he, too, was like Ewan. Was he autistic as well, and was this the reason his family didn't bond with him enough to even give him a name? I joke around that my Grandpa Bob has that prevalent syndrome so often found in families with autistic children: 'Engineer Syndrome.' He most certainly displays a great number of autistic tendencies and characteristics, and were he growing up today, he would likely have been diagnosed with Asperger's. In the case of my son, it's easy to see where the spectrum has landed throughout the generations of genetic code.

As for my father, well, he also had some tendencies. There is a story my grandmother always told us about dad. He was an avid reader his whole life, and by his whole life I do mean from a very young child. Apparently he waltzed into kindergarten and spent much of his time looking at books. When questioned by his teacher as to why he spent so much time looking at books, he simply responded, "To read them, of course." Scoffing, she didn't believe for a second that this kindergartner had taught himself to read. Unconvinced, she questioned him about the book he was holding, and it wasn't until he correctly answered every question that her jaw dropped as she realized that not only could he read, but he could read quite well. Hearing this story now, I can recognize it for what it is: hyperlexia. But hearing the story growing up, it tended to put my dad up on a pedestal where only gods and giants resided. He was simply cool.

Spread out between both families, there are autistic tendencies left and right. Uncles who fit the Asperger profile like the DSM-IV was written about them and cousins who display issues with the wider spectrum abound. Upon finding out about Ewan's diagnosis, both Anthony and I began a life-long journey to discovering our own autistic traits and those that run through our families. Social awkwardness, inflexibility, obsessive personalities, sensory issues disguised as personality quirks—the entire spectrum is there lurking throughout the generations. Reading about autism for the first time, I began to understand a little more about myself and my family. I can remember hiding in my mother's shirt as a child when introduced to new people. No amount of coaxing could coerce me into looking people in the eye. Everyone thought I was merely shy, or backward, as older generations sometimes refer to it. Even now, I find eye contact uncomfortable and far from instinctual. My husband, who is generally thought of as a social butterfly, tends to put on an 'act' everywhere he goes, stepping into the role everyone is comfortable seeing him in. Yet social situations can leave him sweating bullets and fighting an overwhelming nausea. His obsessive need for movement and music seems much more rational, having lived with Ewan all these years. Even his addictions make more sense in the filter of an autistic-like lens. The plant and the bottle soothing his frayed and over-stimulated nerves in a way nothing else could.

Tendencies or not, though, our families have weathered a few storms along the way. By the time my father was diagnosed with cancer, the disease had already spread far and wide throughout his immune system. Cancer may have been on the radar long before that day, but he ignored the signs and symptoms 'til it was far too late. I remember the day I found out my dad had cancer. At the time I was down at Southern Illinois University when I got the phone call explaining why dad was suddenly sick all the time. The guy who never got sick was getting ready to travel right through the heart of disease processes. He was given a timeline of measured breaths that he fought so hard to broaden. His sheer stubborn tenacity to live would be the only thing to get him through round after round of chemo, bottle after bottle of pills, and through one God awful bone marrow transplant. He had a family to support and a business to run, and, by God, cancer wasn't going to beat him. He continued to work and was on the road a lot because he was in the trucking business. Since my dad wanted us to all stay in touch even though I was three hours to the south and my sister lived way down south in Texas, he decided to install a 1-800 number for the house. I was the only kid on the planet whose dad was willing to pay for a toll free line just so that his children could call him anytime, anywhere, for absolutely any reason. In those early days, he was so confident he was going to beat cancer that it was hard to believe otherwise. I was so wrapped up in my own life then and deeply entrenched in the selfishness of youth that I failed to see the fragility of life until it was too late. I was in love and loving every second of it.

My then college boyfriend, Anthony, and I started seeing each other on my 19th birthday before I had transferred to SIU. That night a friend of mine, Stacy, and I found ourselves out and about looking for something to do and settled on a party where her current boyfriend, Brent, happened to be. Brent, also my eighth grade ex-boyfriend, was on leave from the military for a week and staying at his cousin, Anthony's, house. Despite the hustle and bustle of a university, our hometown was and is a small town. What can I say? Everyone knows everyone. We all went to high school together, and we had known each other since junior high when I had dated said ex-boyfriend. Laughing around a small kitchen table on a third floor apartment, we celebrated the night away. Somehow, my birthday celebration ended up being a walk through a moonlit cemetery at midnight. Grabbing Anthony, we walked though the dark hand in hand. I had no idea then that my fingers were entwined in the hands of my future husband.

I had just walked away from a serious relationship and wasn't looking for another one that night. When he kissed me though, something struck me about the innocent hesitancy of his lips. There is something endearing about a man who is nervous and unsure of himself, and there is something worth protecting in that insecurity. For whatever reason, I have always wanted to care and protect this man from himself and from the troubles of the world, even when he willingly opens the door to misfortune. Maybe it is his story, maybe it is the endless depth of his eyes, maybe it is the easy laughter on his lips. The night I grabbed his hand, I never wanted to let go even when I thought I hated him and everything to do with him.

When we started dating, he had just gotten in trouble with the law for possession of marijuana. It sounds like nothing or something depending on your point of view, and in reality, it was not the worst thing that could've happened to someone. Yet, in those days I had no idea what I was getting myself into. He was an enticing mix of bad boy, insecurity and laughter. He did what he wanted, free from limitations I so often felt. He was independent in ways I had never even imagined for someone so young. He had basically grown up on his own; he was the parent his parents had never been. At 15, he was autonomous and self-governing, left to raise himself. At 18, I was woefully dependent on my parents. In some ways I envied him such independence, and in other ways, I had a relationship with my parents he couldn't even dream of. We were so different, but from the very beginning, we succumbed to the magnetic attraction before us. He had drawn me in, and I couldn't walk away. Not yet, anyway.

Anthony was completely unencumbered by the rules of life and the law. He flaunted his devil-may-care attitude at every opportunity, pushing his luck this way and that way. Me and my 'plan' for life couldn't have been more different. We were young, though, and his zest for life was irresistible. My birthday was in July, and by August I was moving to Carbondale for school. I took the train home or drove three hours back as often as I could just to see him. The weekdays dragged on until Friday afternoon hit when I could fly off on the highway or the tracks to see the man I was falling in love with. Practically giddy with excitement and craving his touch and his laugh, I would rush into his arms and his bed where we would spend the majority of our time. If my father hadn't been ill in those days, I wouldn't have found a good enough reason to leave that bed for days at a time. The only thing that would drive me from his arms was the desire to see my family, especially my dad. Had I known his days were numbered, maybe I would've rushed home to see him instead of Anthony. But I didn't know. I thought my dad would live forever *and a day*. In my youth and immaturity, I sought out my own pleasures and selfishly held on to Anthony every minute I could. Sunday nights always came too soon, though, and the three hour solitary drive home in the unwelcome dark was downright depressing. By Halloween, we'd had enough of the short-lived weekends, and I had convinced him to come down to Carbondale and start school there too come spring semester. No more long, lonely weeks, we could spend every waking minute with each other, something I'm not sure he really wanted.

    The problem came the second week in the second semester of school. Anthony and I were shoved violently into adulthood when a course of antibiotics during winter break had collided with my birth control pills and created something just shy of a miracle. For much of my life I had been told I wouldn't have children, and I used birth control pills more to regulate volatile female hormones rather than as protection from unwanted pregnancy. So when I began to experience reverse peristalsis on a daily basis, I was more inclined to believe I had contracted some rare South American virus from the biology lab than I was to believe it was due to pregnancy. It wasn't until health services uncovered the mysterious source of my nauseated stomach that I found out I was expecting. I'm fairly sure I surprised the nurse on duty that day. Rather than walking in and having to explain to some unmarried college student that her life was suddenly and irrevocably altered and deal with tears of "Why me!" she was faced with an unmarried college student whose whole face lit up at the very idea of motherhood. Thinking I would never hear the name 'mother' from any child, I stood both awed and amazed at the change my life had suddenly taken. I was positively giddy and couldn't stop laughing and smiling at that poor unsuspecting nurse who was probably silently wondering about the validity of a mental health exam in addition to those prenatal vitamins.

    Anthony and I were both very young, and the depths of our immaturity flooded every moment of our life. While I may have been happy as a clam with the arrival of impending motherhood, he was reduced to a downtrodden shadow of his former self at the idea of becoming a father so soon in adulthood. Anthony and I come from two very different families. My mother and father had been married for almost 30 years, and his parents had divorced when he was only six. His parents, both teenage statistics of pregnancy and marriage, had not lived happily ever after. It's not my story to tell, but needless to say, my husband felt the noose of parenthood pull him away from a fun and fancy free lifestyle he had envisioned to be the exact opposite of what his parents had lived through. I could see the despair and hopelessness in his eyes while my own glittered with joy and anticipation. In my immaturity, I believed this baby would reform the bad boy into a responsible, devoted father. Yet I didn't understand just how great his fear of such an ordinary life truly was. He was firmly entrenched in doing what he wanted, when he wanted to do it. And part of what he wanted to do was drink and smoke pot. What had been just teenage rebellion a few months earlier now looked much more like dependency cloaked in the habit of laughter. I had no idea what addiction looked like, and I had no idea what kind of hold the bottle and that little green plant would hold over his life for years to come. In the beginning, it wasn't a big deal. We were young, with a lifetime ahead of us and the invincibility of youth a striking delusion. Now that we were bringing a child into this world, this small matter became the great divide that would pull us apart.

We didn't last long together as a couple after that. I wanted what he could not give. Unused to rules and limitations, he couldn't see anything other than the noose of adulthood tightening across his throat. Unable to give me what I needed, I held the door open while he walked through it. We went our separate ways, both with broken hearts and enough anger to power a Tunguska-like event in Illinois.

Pregnant, alone and undeterred, I moved back to the red brick house on the hill to finish college in my hometown. Back at home, I could help take care of my dad, who would continue to gain and lose ground in the battle against cancer over the next few years. I found out quickly that I was going to have a daughter, and we all experienced a slight twinge of sadness in that one moment. With my father so ill with cancer, there had been much hope that this child would be a boy bearing my last name, the family name, Hart. My dad and his childless brother were the last men born to my grandparents to carry the name Hart, and much expectation went into the thought of an unexpected boy to continue carrying on the name. Yet God has a way of giving you what you need when you need it, and He knew I wasn't quite ready for a boy like Ewan, not yet, anyway. The day my daughter, Skye, was born, my mother was by my side and my father was on the road out in Oklahoma. Upon hearing that contractions had begun, he dropped everything in Tulsa and drove straight back home to welcome his first grandchild, Skye Hart, into the world. From that day forward, both Skye and I would carry the name Hart no matter what. From the first moment my father first met his grandchild, she was wrapped around his heart and mine as well.

      But it wasn't always so easy for my parents to handle the news that their college age daughter was going to witness the miracle of motherhood. And to be fair, my delivery of such news stands as a rather infamous incident in my family's history. My sister and my friend, Stacy, came down for the weekend, and I told them both over a slice of pizza about my impending motherhood. As we struggled for a way to tell my parents the news, we settled on humor and sarcasm and found ourselves at a local Hallmark kiosk where I created my very own special 'Hey mom and dad' announcement. I then forced my sister to hand-deliver the greeting card that said so eloquently, "Congratulations! Your baby is having a baby!" I'm not sure Hallmark has ever borne witness to such a gut-wrenching reaction in all of greeting card history. My dad was bitter and angry; my mother pushed to that dangerous silent range of acrimonious fury. Despite their reaction, I remained blissfully and delusionally happy about defying modern medical expectations of my fertility, and I continue to owe my sister for her act of courage or lunacy, depending on how you look at it. But in that first moment of holding a granddaughter in their arms, I knew the anger had drained away and was replaced with a religious devotion usually only seen with saints and miracles. She was the most perfect baby, sculpted lips and ivory translucent skin. After a brief spell of mixed up days and nights, she settled into a quiet and thoughtful life. Quite the dramatically different experience from what I would see with Ewan.

      In the meantime, I continued down the path of a single parent and college student. I missed a few days of class and then plowed right back into it, taking my newborn with me to class sometimes. Skye was such a flexible baby, content to be in my arms anywhere I decided to take her. For a single mother, I had been blessed with a miracle child that was everything I needed her to be. I had not spoken to her dad, though, since we last left each other in Carbondale. Skye was around three months of age before he even found out her name. I saw him once a few months later when Skye and I walked into a store just as he was leaving. There's no more difficult act than to walk away from something you want nothing more than to run like Hell towards. My sister had always said Anthony was just a rebound guy—someone I had dated after a long relationship had broken up. Rather than bouncing back to life through him though, I continued to flounder in my self-righteous anger. I both hated him and loved him in equal measure.

When Skye was about six months old, love overpowered hate for a short time when Anthony walked back into our lives. As delusional and idiotic as it sounds, I missed him. He has a charisma to him that I find unavoidable. There is something magnetic about the two of us. We have that ability to both attract and repel in ways that only magnets can do. Get it right, and we can't be separated. Hit it wrong, and we couldn't get far enough away from each other. Wanting to see both me and his daughter, he gave it another shot at a life together. He thought he was ready to settle down into the tedious life of a young father. I tried to put away my anger, and he tried to move past the guilt and attractions of youth. I asked him to put away the self-medication of the leaf and the bottle, and he asked me to forget the past. We may have loved each other, but guilt and blame and addiction was no way to build a life. With every mistake and relapse, blame and anger spilled forth from my lips while immaturity and selfishness fell from his own. We may have a magnetic attraction, but this was like watching a car accident in slow motion. We quickly realized we couldn't make it work and again went our separate ways. It would be several years 'til we'd see him again.

I picked myself back up and moved Skye and I back home. She was an infant and had no recollection of her parent's idiocy. She continued to be doted over by grandma and grandpa. My father, this giant bear of a man, could be found at any given time, gleefully jiggling a baby in his arms with a pink diaper bag draped over his shoulder. Sometimes I would have class, and he would need to make a delivery, so he strapped a car seat in that 18 wheeler and drove on down the road. My sister had given birth to a son, Brody, just a few weeks after Skye had come into our life, and it would not be unheard of to see my dad toting around these babies like he was Jean Piaget. The man loved children and had a boundless energy to bounce them, swing them, and giggle with them. He willingly watched episode after episode of mindless cartoons. Skye and Brody grew up on his knee and bounced around his shoulders like he was a circus ride. My daughter may not have had a father in her life, but she had one Hell of a grandpa.

In the meantime, my father's battle with cancer would rage for years. At times it seemed he could subdue the disease, and at others the cancer would drive him to his knees. Every time we surfaced the cancerous waters, thinking land was in sight, the malignancy would pull us back into the deepest depths of despair. I hate cancer. I absolutely hate everything to do with it. The disinfectant smell of the hospitals, the sounds of respirators and the alarms, the vomiting and the hair loss, the clean rooms and procedures, I hate it all. The cancer amplified to catastrophic levels from one end of his body to the other, his lungs a casualty in the war. No amount of chemo in the world could stop this unbridled and unchecked growth. Our last great hope was the bone marrow transplant. He threw everything into this one treatment and bet it all. For eight weeks, my father became a prisoner in a clean room. To prepare for eight weeks of eight square feet of living space, we packed a van full of books to read, movies to watch, and even a CB radio for my dad to communicate with the outside world. Loaded down with diversions, my mom and dad drove two states away to a VA hospital in Nashville one weekend right before Father's Day. As they made the five and a half hour trip to Nashville, my dad got sick. With no immune system to fight off even the slightest of illnesses, my dad was practically septic by the time they pulled into the hotel parking lot that night. In their haste to get checked-in they forgot to lock the doors. Sometime that night, someone stole every single belonging from the van in the hotel parking lot. With only one pair of underwear and a toothbrush from the hotel gift shop, my father took the first step in one of the longest journeys of his life. And he had to do it alone. My mother had to get back to work and could only drive down on the weekends, while I juggled running the family business with single parenthood and graduate school. And I'd do it all over again, if I knew it would save his life.

For eight weeks, the prisoner paced that tiny hospital room. Having found a replacement for his stolen CB radio, in his boredom and isolation, he surfed the wavelengths of 40 different channels. Across the radio frequencies, he connected to people across the country and the world. In those moments, he was no longer a cancer patient, and he was no longer a prisoner to eight square feet of clean space. He was a traveler once again, freed from the cancerous chains and bound only by the powers of lights and space. Once the radio was turned off, my father slowly transformed into the prisoner again, forced to succumb to the will of marrow and blood.

    The bone marrow transplant reduced him to ash as the cancer was burned out of its hiding places. He was left with no protection, exposed to the world and forced to live at its mercy, and the world was without mercy in those days. His hair fell out again while the sores in his mouth and throat kept him from eating anything. His skin was pale and fragile. My father was a fraction of the man who had walked in the door, but all the pain and sores and vomit were worth it. The cancer was gone. On his birthday, after six weeks of clean rooms and a host of antibiotics, antivirals, and antifungals, we picked my father up at the end of the bone marrow transplant and brought him home cancer free. We all thought the worst was behind us and an entire lifetime waited before us. Back home, mom and I tried to reconstruct our own version of a clean room in the red brick house on the hill. Skye and I moved to a small place in town, but we went home every day so I could help dad continue to run the family business. Having a three year old in a clean room wasn't the easiest of situations. Masks, breathing machines, and hand washing became our new normal. My skin was raw from the antiseptic as I vacillated between being my dad's business partner and his nurse. In between phone calls and faxes, I gave him breathing treatment after breathing treatment, and watched his hands tremble from the effects of the drugs. Hour after hour, the drone of the nebulizer was constantly reverberating through the rooms of the red brick house. Sometimes I still hear the monotonous hum of that machine in my sleep.

    By October, my mother was starting to worry again. She is a nurse and the nurse inside her *knew* something was wrong. A yellow cast had spread across my father's skin. Yet dad continued to remain so positive about the success of the transplant that my mother could only wonder at the contradiction. That Halloween, mom and I took Skye out trick-or-treating while dad stayed in the safety of the house. A prisoner to a larger cell, but a prisoner nonetheless, he kept his CB radio firmly by his side so that we could update him on the door to door progress of his favorite fairy princess. Afterwards, Skye flounced back into the red brick house covered in yards of tulle and chocolate, washed her hands and then jumped on grandpa's lap to share her good fortune.

By Christmas Eve, mom and dad found themselves at the VA hospital again for a check-up. Only this time, there was no good news, only devastation. The transplant had failed. The cancer was back and threatening every cell in his body. The doctors told my dad his only option was to try chemotherapy again. That night my parents left the hospital more tired than they'd ever been. This was a war he just couldn't win.

Back on chemotherapy and high doses of prednisone, we watched as my normally jovial father turned inward. The prednisone affected more than just his appetite; he was grouchy and obsessed with his only hope of freedom: his CB equipment. Cancer had taken everything from him but his sense of wanderlust. Late one snowy night, my father decided to drive three hours to Chicago to pick up a piece of radio equipment. My mother begged him not to leave and to just think about what he was doing. He was angry and he was determined, and in that moment, the lure of the road was too great. He left. In the middle of the night he came back to find my mom worried sick and still crying. Realizing that the prednisone was turning him into someone none of us knew, he said enough and stopped taking it. Without the prednisone on his side, the breathing troubles built up until one dreary February day he ended up back at the VA hospital to have the oceans of liquid drawn off his lungs. That night, while my mom hunched into a small chair of the hospital room, my father patted a side of his bed and made room for the love of his life. Hours later a surly nurse came in, found my mother and father curled up together and promptly threw my mother out to the chairs of the waiting room. Before my father was discharged the next morning, the doctors walked in to tell him that the chemotherapy was failing him. He was dying. I imagine it was at that moment when my father decided not to die in a hospital room with rules, regulations, and bitchy nurses. I imagine it was then that he decided if he was going to die a prisoner, it would be surrounded by family within the comforting walls of the red brick house on the hill.

Stunned with the news that the end was coming, my mother and father made the two hour drive home with the weight of a lifetime on their shoulders. It was then that a Trace Adkins song came on the radio. "The Rest of Mine" played from the speakers, telling the tale of a man so in love with his wife that he promises to love her 'til his last dying breath.

Irritated, my mother turned the volume down as she said, "I hate this song."

My father reached back over and turned the dial back up again, as he said, "Listen. Just listen." In his own way and in his own time, he was accepting his own death.

That Wednesday night, I sat down in the living room with my parents as my father, for the first time ever, admitted that he wasn't going to live through this. We didn't know how long he had left, weeks or months, but we knew the road before us led to only one place. In the dark hours of a cold, winter evening my father planned for his death and his funeral. On Thursday, dad called in his accountant who told my mother exactly what to do with the life insurance money she would inherit. He reassured my father that she would have enough to pay the house off and still have enough left over to make her life comfortable. On Friday, my mom left work on family leave as she prepared for the journey in front of us all. By Friday night, my sister had arrived from her new home in Arkansas. On Saturday, hospice was called in and they brought breathing machines, morphine, and practically set up a hospital in the center of our house because my father refused to die a prisoner in an eight by eight hospital room.

On Sunday morning, I slept in late, exhausted from the previous few days. It was around 9 a.m. when my phone rang. My uncle Bryan had been staying up with my father through the last few sleepless nights and it was his deep voice on the other end of the line, "Alicia?"

With a raspy voice, I replied, "Yeah, it's me. Is everything ok?"

"You need to come home. Your dad is getting worse. Can you come right now?"

Jumping out of bed, I put my clothes on while holding the phone up with my shoulder, I replied, "I'm on the way right now, be there in about 10 minutes."

Our days and weeks of life had dissolved into minutes and hours. With fear coursing through my veins, I drove towards home. The heart of the red brick house had always moved in synchronicity with my father's heart. Parking in the circle drive, I didn't know what to expect. Standing on the threshold of the doorway, I waited to find the courage to go in. I stared at the red door and paused. Putting my hand on the cool metal, I could feel the pulse of our home slowly fading. Opening the door, I knew that when his heart stopped, so too, would the heart of this house.

I found my dad on the hospital bed brought just the day before with his family gathered around him. Every minute of every hour in the last day of his life was spent keeping him as comfortable as possible while cancer held him in its cruel embrace. Comfort wasn't always possible, though, and with each breath came pain. It took every muscle in his body just to draw in a single breath. We rubbed his back continuously trying to relax the overworked muscles, but even then, his only solace was the morphine. Having had his morphine earlier that morning, we were helplessly left to watch him drown in a sea of air as his lungs filled again with fluid. Shifting his weight from side to side, he fought to relax on the crinkly plastic covering and the stiff white sheets. That bed was made for death, not peace. In his last moment of strength and refusing our help, he stood up on his swollen legs and heavily walked away from that inflexible mattress towards his favorite oversized leather recliner. Falling into his chair, he lay weak and gasping for breath. Every one of those breaths infused with the gurgling sound of a drowning man. The red brick house on the hill silently watched him as he fought for every second on a cold and gray Valentine's Day. There was no celebrating that day, no candy hearts or chocolate, only the suffocating sounds of a dying man. While everyone else was surrounded by the smell of milk chocolate, we were asphyxiated by the sickly sweet smell of death and morphine. In the last moments of my father's life, he vacillated between sanity and delirium, not always knowing where he was. Lost and confused, he walked between two worlds in those last few hours. Sometimes he would walk back to us and he would know me again. Minutes later, he would move toward the next life, and I was a stranger at his deathbed. He knew death was coming, yet he never looked scared, his expression more tired than fearful. By 11:30 that morning he was asking for more morphine. His skin was sallow and his eyes were fixed in a blank stare, the openmouthed expression a result of his exhaustion. Needing a moment to myself, I walked in to the kitchen to make a glass of instant ice tea. In the next room, my mother whispered to him, "It's ok to go now."

With that act of acquiescence, my father whispered back, "Turn it off."

My mom reached over his laboring chest and turned off the oxygen machine. Holding his wife's hand, he drew in one last, ragged breath. Stirring my tea, the spoon clinked against the edges of the glass over and over as I stared down into the swirling mix. It was then my uncle Bryan came to my side, put his hand over my own and quietly said, "He's gone." My dad had left us to find a life without the warmth of the sun. My father had loved my mother and us all 'til his last dying breath. The red brick house on the hill dropped her comforting arms with the last beat of my father's heart. When *his* heart stopped, so too, did the heart of the house. When my father's soul fled his body, so too, did the soul of our house. And when my father died, the red brick house on the hill died with him.

~

Those minutes and hours after my father died left me practically catatonic. I couldn't move, I couldn't speak, I couldn't think. All I could see was my dad. I could see him, I could touch him, but he wasn't there. Never again would he comfort me, never again would he make the daily call to talk about absolutely nothing, never again would he drop everything to be by my side. Never again would my daughter sit on his knee and pull at his beard. I lost a father, and Skye lost a father figure. He was gone, and I had to learn to walk through life unable to reach out for his hand. His death left a black hole in our family. In the beginning, we clung to each other as gravity pulled us together. My mother and my dad's family were for a short time even able to hug each other freely. My mother clung to us all for support in those days. If I was catatonic, she was defeated and desolate and completely without hope. When my father died, my mother's world completely shattered. It wasn't until the third night after my father's death that she and I began to think of a life after death. It was 11 p.m. at night, and when I mentioned my need for a chocolate milkshake she said, "Well, why don't we go get one? Let's go out and get one at Steak n' Shake."

I cautiously replied, "Mom, are you sure? I mean, it's really late, maybe we should just wait until tomorrow."

Already looking for her shoes and her keys, she firmly said, "No, we're going now. This is something your dad would have done and so we will too. Come on Skye, you want a milkshake, don't you?"

Skye had been curled up next to me on the couch, about to fall asleep, and when her grandmother said, 'milkshake,' she jumped up and said, "Yep!" and ran to the door. With a smile, I followed close behind as my mother swept Skye up in her arms and the two of them giggled their way out the door. Halfway through our impromptu trip, the 'check engine' light came on and we reluctantly headed back to the house. Undaunted by engine failure, we simply jumped in the van and headed back out the driveway. At the end of the drive we suddenly heard a buzzing sound. Thinking our luck was doomed by a second engine failure episode, we stopped to solve the source of such a mysterious sound. Finally, I found my dad's pager jammed between the seats. We looked down at the screen to see a row of zeros. This had been our family message to dad when we needed him to call home. In that singular moment, at the end of our driveway at midnight, we knew without a shadow of a doubt that this was dad's way of saying, "It's okay. Everything is going to be *okay*." We knew there was hope, even when the ache of loss soaked through every thought since then.

  My mother and father had a long and loving marriage—my father fell in love with her long red hair and she with his rebel without a cause attitude and Elvis hair. In the beginning she clung to my father, and when he left to work out on the road, she clung to my sister and I, yet we knew when dad got back home the world revolved around him. But he was like that. His personality was so powerful that he tended to eclipse everything else in life. The sun and the moon and the stars were gone and that aching loss creates a dark depression that settles over her every year from Christmas through Valentine's Day. It's as if she relives that cancerous war every year. I think even now, 12 years later, that aching shadow looms over her head. I know it looms over mine when I least expect it.

  My mother is a survivor, though, even if she doesn't always believe it. When I think of my mother, I am reminded of three women. The first woman lived in the old white farmhouse, and she was a survivor. She was the woman who grew her own foods and made her own clothes. She was the woman standing by the front door everyday when I got off the bus. The second woman lived in the red brick house on the hill, and as her children grew, she went back to school and became a nurse. For the first time in her entire life, she was independent and bringing home her own paycheck. It was then she would care for her first and greatest patient, her dying husband. Her paycheck became so much more than a symbolic need for autonomy. The third woman now lives in a log cabin buried deep in the woods. A few months after my father's death, she shrank back to the insecure and introverted child of her past. She relied on everyone else for her happiness, afraid she would never find her own again.

  My mother suffers from that disorder called 'Only Child Raised in a Museum Syndrome' and can be both equally self-involved and co-dependent. She hates it when people talk about only children as selfish creatures, but it's not really a selfishness that describes her. My mother can be a very giving and caring person even if it doesn't always come off that way. In some ways, my mother has problems with empathy and theory of mind, something often attributed to people with autism. She has a hard time thinking of what someone else is experiencing, especially if it is not something she has lived through herself. She has lived through cancer, she can understand that pain. She has not lived through autism and has no ability to put a frame of reference or perspective to the situation. She may have sympathy, but I'm not sure that empathy always comes easy to her. She is a nurse, and at times she is too clinical both in profession and life. At times, I wish she would put aside the clinic and embrace her emotional side. Yet after my father's death, to embrace the emotion is to embrace the pain of loss, and that is not a place she's willing to go anymore. Not to paint too bleak a picture, my mother can be a very loving individual, and when all is right in the world, she has one of the biggest and brightest smiles on earth. When dad died we spent several days without an affectionate grin or the sound of laughter on our lips. My mom and I found ourselves in the drive-up at the local McDonald's when we saw a college kid in his pajama pants walk across the parking lot, trip, and then spill his orange juice all over the person in front of him. In the gloom of grief and heartache, we grabbed the one chance at laughter we'd seen in several days. In a shower of orange juice, we laughed 'til tears of a different kind flowed down our cheeks. In that moment, we knew life would go on whether we willed it to or not. But when my father died, mom needed someone to cling to as she always had, and she turned from him to me and Skye. For many months, she relied on me as she had my father. And while I am my father's daughter, I can never be him.

  When my father died, I sort of lost all touch with reality. I did all manner of stupid things, and most of these exploits are a book in and of themselves. I floundered in every way, not really knowing what I wanted but feeling some urge to live as much as I could as fast as I could. Grief is a greedy creature, and I indulged in every craving. If life was so short, then I couldn't run fast enough to Anthony. I had tried to feed the anger and denial long enough. I could either live alone in my indignation or I could twist outrage into passion and find a family. One evening I found myself at a party where Anthony was sitting across the room. Our sets of friends looked at the situation as if one of us might go Chernobyl at any minute and were inconspicuously looking for acceptable duck and cover spots throughout the apartment. No one moved, no one breathed for the span of about 30 seconds 'til we both just simply said, "Hello."

Hello turned into how are you, how are you turned into I'm sorry about your father, and I'm sorry about your father turned into I love you, let's get married. Call it grief, call it loneliness, call it what you will, we ended up together and found ourselves planning a wedding in a few months time. After a certain amount of doubtful astonishment that Anthony and I were giving it yet another go, my mother grew excited about this change. It gave her something to focus on, something other than grief, and it gave her hope that Skye would have a father she deserved.

We put our grief away and planned a wedding. In honor of my father's heritage, our vows would be exchanged amidst a flurry of plaid, kilts and bagpipes. My dad had not always been into his ancestry, and it wasn't until a short time before Skye was born that we began to explore our past. Maybe it was because of the cancer, but it seemed important to him to learn more about his past. I and my history degree gleefully jumped into the deep end of the library and ferreted out every root and branch of a genealogical family tree. Soon after, we found ourselves driving to Scottish and Irish festivals. When Skye was born and I chose to name her after the Isle of Skye, my dad seemed to embrace his heritage even further, toting his young grandchild to and fro among the bagpipes and caber tosses. On my wedding day, it just felt right to add that flavor of history and past to our ceremony. If I couldn't have my father standing by my side, then surely I could claim a thousand years of roots as my support system. Standing before me in a kilt, Anthony promised not to let the addictions back in our life and I promised to look toward the future. The wedding, a beautiful sight to behold, had began and ended in only a few hours. The marriage, however, had just started. When the kilts were put away and the bagpiper played his last song, we were left with the same baggage all the grief had overshadowed. Anthony and I were both still very immature and reckless, and my anger over his previous desertions couldn't be ignored. Month after month, wedded bliss turned to frustration and loneliness. Anthony retreated away from Skye and I, leaving us with every excuse to feed his habits. He turned away from his wife and turned towards that mistress of addiction. Nothing I did could take him away from the grip that mistress held over him. Eventually, the habits of the past, patio furniture, and Chinese food would do us in, and I filed for divorce just shy of our first year anniversary.

Yet again, I found myself going back home. It's a recurrent theme in the early years of my life. Maybe I was spoiled, maybe I ran away just when things got hard. Maybe I should have tried harder to make my marriage and my independence last. Maybe I should've fought that mistress of addiction, but she was far stronger than I and held Anthony firmly in her grasp. Losing my husband and my life to this other lover was too much for me. Clearly, I was not enough for him. Clearly, this mistress held his fascination and interest in ways I never could. Losing my husband to this other love was devastating so I ran back home, Skye in tow. I hope what my daughter remembers about her mother's ridiculous actions is that you can always go home. *Should* you go home is entirely a different matter. This time, my mother sealed her heart against Anthony and rejected everything to do with him. He tried to remain a part of Skye's life, and neither my mother nor I made it easy for him. Still angry over the habits and chicken with snow peas, visiting Skye in my mother's home was like visiting Death Row for him. No one welcomed him in the door with a smile. I resented Anthony in every way possible, for things he had done and for things he hadn't. I took the grief I should have had for my father a year before and placed it all on his shoulders.

Grief was still a greedy creature, and I fed it with every ounce of pain and resentment I had. I made a decision to move away and find my way into a medical school program over in Indianapolis, even if I had to bribe the admissions officer. I couldn't get away from that town fast enough. Still running away from my problems, I wanted some distance between myself and Anthony. I wanted to run away from that red brick house on the hill and never come back. My mother decided to pack up, sell the house, and move, too. The family home was empty without dad. There were no fleets of cars and trucks in the driveway, no more brake lights to illuminate the darkness. The windows would never again rattle and shake with his arrival. The heart of the house had stopped one cold and gray Valentine's Day. It was with some relief that we packed up our life and put that empty house and those memories behind us. As I was packing boxes and preparing to say goodbye to Anthony and my hometown once and for all, I was suddenly struck with the most irrational fear. For all the ups and downs, immaturity and stupidity, I still loved that man. But I couldn't figure out for the life of me why we couldn't make it work, and I couldn't see how to remove this mistress from our life. I couldn't see why the habits were so hard to put down. In a conversation about Skye and I moving away, we ended up realizing how permanent this was, and the gulf between us shrank to nothing. For once, he finally saw what the addictions and recklessness had cost him. We knew this was a mistake, but the bags were packed, the house was sold, and there was no going back now. He and I stood in the driveway watching the moving van pull away, leaving nothing but the quiet memory of a former life. He grabbed my hand as we stood there and said, "I can't believe you're leaving. I don't want you to go. Not now." I was running away again but this time with the full knowledge of all that I was leaving behind.

I looked at him and replied, "Anthony, if we are going down this road again, your life has to change. I don't want your life. I don't want your parents' life. I never have. I can't travel that path, I can't. And I can't stay here. This house, all I see is my dad in that chair gasping for breath. This town, all I see is the years of mistakes and drugs and arguments. Skye and I are leaving. We'll be waiting for you in Indiana, but only if we come first, above all else. It has to be family first, Anthony."

Tears in both our eyes, he said, "You think I don't want that? I do, Lisha, but it's not that easy. You're going to move two hours away, and if we do this, I'll be there soon, too. I'll be away from my family, my friends, everything. You're taking me away from everyone and everything I have here in this town. You'll be all that I have left."

I looked away, "I've always been here, Anthony."

"No you haven't," he said quietly. "When things get tough, you leave. I can't promise perfection, Lisha, but can you promise me you aren't going to run again when life gets hard?"

"Anthony, I know this problem isn't going away magically, I'm not stupid. But are you being honest with yourself, with me? You are walking away from this town to be with me. I can't come back here again. I can't be in this place again."

He sighed, "I don't want to be in this place again, no wife, no child. But when life gets rough and ugly, you shut me out, you have every single time. It seems we stop being friends and then I'm left with nothing. I move to Indy, Lisha, and you'll be my only friend. I can't take it again if you leave."

"I don't think I can either, Anthony."

"Look, all I want, all I've ever wanted is to wake up next to you every morning. I have never stopped loving you. Never. Not when I left the first time, not when you walked away every single time after that and not even when I signed those damned divorce papers. Give me a chance to make this right, give me some time. I want my family back. I want my wife back. God, Lisha, all I want is a normal life."

"I know. It's all I want, too," I said, and with one long hug goodbye, I left the love of my life standing in the driveway at the red brick house on the hill.

We continued to hash out our problems and see each other quietly, unknown to anyone else. It seemed a secret I couldn't share; it seemed too ridiculous to say that we refused to give up. I just couldn't say to my family, to my friends, to anyone at all, that I couldn't stay away from him. I couldn't justify to anyone *why* I still loved him, and I couldn't explain the absurdity of it all. Sometimes you don't choose who you fall in love with, sometimes you just do. I still don't know if I can explain all the reasons why I can't live without Anthony. It defies reason or explanation. I love his laughter, I love his practicality, I even love his childish behavior. I love him for everything he is, even when I want to chuck a plate of snow peas at his head. I've stopped denying that I will always love him, regardless of the arguments and disagreements and irrespective of what has happened in the past. We stopped reliving ancient history and now live only in the moment. From that point on, the new argument busting phrase for us has become, "Why you gotta bring up old shit?" Which is, of course, said in a ridiculous tone of voice that leaves us laughing rather than fighting. For whatever reason, call it divine intervention, but we knew without a doubt that we could make it work this time. I don't know why it had taken five long years for us to figure out what most people do in a few short months. We realized that all the reasons not to be together couldn't keep us apart and just accepted it. Anthony spent the next few months giving up the last of his habits, leaving his mistress behind. We hoped that for once he could lay down the urges and dependencies of his life. The first few steps toward a life free from such addictions were not easy for him. In the tiny apartment he lived in, he gave up that little leaf and sweated it out in every way possible. Anyone who says pot isn't addictive hasn't watched someone give up the one thing that every cell in his body calls out for. Addiction is addiction no matter the form it takes. He lost weight, he was nauseated, he was a shaky, nervous mess. And he was finally walking away from it for Skye and I. Moving away from our hometown, we were finally leaving the ghosts of the past behind us.

We had planned to slowly bring everyone around to the epiphany we'd just experienced because for just once, we wanted to try being together without judgment and opinion from everyone else about how wrong we were for each other. This plan to slowly enlighten friends and family about our relationship epiphany came to a crashing halt the day I found out I was pregnant. We not only had to bring everyone up to speed on our relationship, we also had to tell them that we were bringing a new life into the world. I think creating peace in the Middle East might have been easier.

My mother reacted as if I told her I was joining a Satanic cult intent on murdering the President. My sister thought I was certifiable, and my best friend at the time would've been less hurt had I slipped a poisonous viper into her shower. We had managed to piss off every single person who had ever loved us. Mercury's atmosphere was more hospitable than the air around my mother and I. In telling her, I think I lost her forever. She'll never look at me the same again, and she'll never forgive me for what she sees as a selfish abandonment. She can never forgive Anthony, and while I can move forward and see the future, she cannot and can only see the destruction of the past. She looked at this new baby and this remarriage as an unwelcomed guest into what she believed to be her only hope of happiness without my dad. For my mother, with this child came not joy and the promise of a new life, but the depression and misery and the reminder of a life lost. When I asked her blessing to name my son Terrill, she plainly said she would prefer I didn't. The mere thought of this child bearing the name Terrill was too much for her. I would have to settle on something else.

It was in this tumultuous climate of stress that Ewan Terrill was born into the world. While Anthony and I held him with welcomed arms and an open heart, others pushed away and resented his presence. His life symbolized different things to different people. To some, he was a mistake. To others, he was exasperation. To Anthony and I, he was and always will be a revelation of love, of devotion, and of passion. He has surpassed my father as the familial glue for my nuclear family. Rather than spinning our tempestuous relationship into a full-fledged Category 5 hurricane of destructive force, he holds us together with a gravitational force that defies Newtonian dynamics.

The same cannot be said for my extended family. In a way autism has become an excuse to push us apart and keep each other at arm's length. My husband's family is quite large, and Ewan's story is just one of many for them. My husband is an odd duck at times because while he may love his parents, siblings, and grandparents, he doesn't often show it. He hates talking on the phone, and he thinks one time a year at holidays is more than enough family together time to be with his parents, grandparents, siblings, and cousins. My husband has never been a man of gestures. He doesn't send flowers, and he doesn't write gushing notes of devotion. But he tells me he loves me every single chance he gets. Sometimes his family has relied on Anthony to do, to reach, to make an effort, but that's not always who he is. Sometimes you just have to accept that he loves you despite what he doesn't do. Yet I know Anthony and I can equally share the blame for the lack of a close relationship between his family and ours. I am a tough customer, not always willing to roll out the red carpet for just anyone. Between his lack of communication skills and my lack of congenial hospitality, we've created a wide gulf between his parents and our house. A gulf that only widened when Ewan was diagnosed with autism. His family has two children with autism or autistic-like conditions already in it, and I think they fell into the trap of believing the myth that all children with autism are alike. Apples cannot be compared to oranges, and Ewan is not his cousins, their lives are not his, nor is that family's journey ours. While they feel a certain comfort around the other children, I think Ewan's way of defying expectations also confuses them. I've often wondered if they think he is not autistic enough or simply not autistic at all. Either way, I cannot blame autism alone for the reasons that gulf exists between us. It is what it is, and autism has not made it any better.

My mother-in-law seems somewhat uncomfortable around both Ewan and I. I remember a time when she volunteered to take all my children out to Dairy Queen one night, and she came back much sooner than expected. Ewan had entered Krakatoan Meltdown Mode right there in Dairy Queen, and she immediately brought him back home. I'm not saying it was the wrong thing to do, certainly he was much calmer back at home. But I wondered if it was because she knew home was safe or because she didn't *know* what to do with him? After that incident we noticed Ewan was invited out less and less. All of our children spent less time with this grandmother. Our children are not close to my husband's families—partly because Anthony is so passive about calling and keeping in touch, partly because of me and to some degree, partly because of autism. Moving back to our hometown, we may have lived close together geographically speaking, but we were basically worlds apart. My husband wouldn't ask for help, and for the most part it was not always offered. On one hand Anthony's mother distanced herself from Ewan, and on the other she embraced autism by creating a very successful motorcycle run specifically for the cause of raising money for those with autism. She has almost single handedly created an unmatched fundraiser in that rural area of Illinois that doesn't always have the luxury of expansive golf outings or large autism walks. She may not know Ewan very well, but I think this is her way of trying to be a meaningful part of his life. As he gets older and more independent, I hope that they can have a relationship that exists outside of Anthony and I's dysfunction and free of our own prejudices.

As for my own family, the bonds of genetics are not always enough to keep us together. The chaos and constant stream of complications in Ewan's early life fit right into the atmosphere at the Hart household. My grandparents, aunts, and cousins all gathered around to help when we needed it. They could care less about the communication devices, the diaper changes, the food issues. They embraced the sticky mess that it was without hesitation. After my father died I became very close to them in ways I didn't think I ever would or could amidst the constant crowd and clamor. They were often the only ones Anthony and I could turn to for help, and they willingly dropped it all to meet us for doctor appointments, to lend an extra set of hands, and to give us the breaks we so often needed. Then I went back to school, and for awhile we drifted apart simply because class schedules and therapy demands left us little time to ourselves. And then it really all fell apart. My aunt had been battling brain cancer for years. She had horrifically been diagnosed at the same time my father was diagnosed with Hodgkin's disease. My grandparents watched not one, but two, children wither away under the weight of a cancerous nightmare. They had watched my father die and had to turn their gaze upon their daughter, knowing her time left on this earth, too, was limited to numbered breaths. If I hate cancer, I know they'd like to fire bomb it back to the depths of Hell from which it came. When my aunt died, I couldn't face another second of grief. I fled from that house like a refugee. I regret letting grief and death push me away, but for the sake of my own mental health, I couldn't think about death anymore. It would be several years before I could walk back into that house and not feel pain. I wish I had been strong enough to push past death, but I wasn't, and for my weakness, I've lost a significant part of my family. Although I know, even with the distance and history between us, I could still call them tonight at midnight and ask for help. And I know they'd still drop everything to do it.

My other grandparents are a different story altogether. They have remained a consistent yet somewhat distant part of my life. They did not understand Ewan and could not always grasp the journey we were on. They are from a different generation, and being isolated from a large family, I'm not sure how much they could fathom about walking a mile in our shoes. But they came to every birthday party, found the most sought-after holiday gift items, and called every week to check on us. They had a continuous presence in our life, even if they could not physically keep up. With my grandmother's physical handicap, the option of watching my children overnight was not possible, so they didn't bond with them in that way. But that is not to say they didn't bond, in fact, the opposite is true. The one role they fulfilled better than anything was to provide Skye with an outlet that only a sibling truly needs: a special time just for her. A time without her brothers, a time without therapy and doctor visits, a time without autism and a time where she came before anyone or anything else. Bob and Pauline took Skye on shopping trips several times a year where the spotlight shone only on her. She was, for that weekend, spoiled rotten and showered with all the things that Anthony and I couldn't always give her. My grandparents had created a program better suited for Skye than any siblings-only program, they founded the Skye Shopping Extravaganza Weekend and engaged in a retail therapy more fun than any counseling session. They couldn't really keep up with Ewan and Vaughn, though. The boys moved at a speed their bodies couldn't keep pace with. We had to settle for them watching and waving from the sidelines as the boys ran around for Easter egg hunts and opened presents. As Ewan's situation became more complex over the years, they understood less and less about how complicated our life was. Yet they continued to plug away and showed up for every party and holiday determined to connect in the only way they knew how. My grandmother passed away last year and another sun eclipsed from our lives. The one at every party and every holiday is now just an empty chair. My grandfather, who is now living with advanced Alzheimer's, does not always recognize me and does not remember my boys. But he does remember Skye. Those weekends spent together have somehow forged a link between the memories of the past and the realities of today that have so many times been lost to the disease. The day my grandmother passed from the earth, I think part of my grandfather's spirit fled with hers. He hasn't been the same since. Each passing year, my childhood slips from my fingers as time seizes upon the ephemeral lives of my family. Years from now, the only ones left will be my sister and I.

  My sister and I are an interesting pair. Heather has been with us from the very beginning of Ewan's life and continues to be in all our lives today. She is a constant force and has overtaken my dad's job of making daily phone calls just to chat. She was there to alert us to the problems and she's been there with advice ever since. It's not perfect between us, we're sisters, and life is never perfect for sisters. Our oldest children, Skye and Brody, are close in age which can breed an air of competition. Her daughter, Bella, creates her own gravitational pull with a bigger than life philosophy—she is the sun which all the planets must revolve around. It is truly her way or the highway. Her husband, Dennis, is a bit spectrummy himself, and it wasn't until the Temple Grandin movie came out that he started to question this part of his character. I think at times he sees parts of himself in Ewan. Heather is a therapist, which can be both a good thing and a bad thing. Sometimes I want the sister and not the therapist, and other days I want the therapist but not the sister. I know at times she has to think I overindulge Ewan, giving into his routines and sensory issues. Yet that's the therapist talking, not the sister. She has teenage children now, and my rambunctious noise makers are often too much excitement for her quiet corner of the universe. We lead very different lives, with different goals and different income brackets. She is a Republican, and I am not. She has the annoying habit of talking when I talk—but then again I have the same annoying habit, so we probably just irritate each other. Yet with sisters you take the good with the bad, the disagreements with the laughter, and the pain with the joy—sisters ride through the averages past the highs and lows. We have to, because at the end of the day when our mother ages and passes from this life, we'll be all that's left from our childhood. No father left to anchor us, we are left wondering how life would have turned out had he lived through cancer.

  I often think of what my father would do if he were here right now. What would my dad think of Ewan and how would he handle the world of autism? Would it scare him and intimidate him away, or would he simply embrace Ewan for who he is? I cannot know for sure, of course, but I like to believe that he would pick Ewan up and bounce him on his knee just like the Occupational Therapist told him to. I like to think he would've demanded to meet Ewan's long line of doctors and hear it straight from them. I like to think he would've read every book on autism just to understand Ewan's perspective in life. I like to think he wouldn't have batted an eye about taking Ewan out on the road with him, replete with picture schedules and communication devices. And when I miss him the most, I can just imagine the conversations between Ewan's inquisitive mind and my father's endless knowledge of useless factoids. My dad would've loved this kid.

Through it all, my mother has remained somewhat detached from the situation. When Anthony and I moved back to Illinois, I think something permanently broke between us all. It's not that we don't love each other, she's my mother, for crying out loud. I know that despite our ups and downs, she will always be there for me. She may be mad and terse as our conversations devolve into one word answers, yet I know under all the anger she'll always love me. But this new woman before me now is not the one I grew up with. The woman I grew up with lived in the old white farmhouse and in the red brick house on the hill. The woman I don't truly know anymore lives in the log cabin deep in the woods. Death and loss has left its scar upon my mother's psyche and changed her into someone I don't always understand. With her not willing to forgive Anthony and me not willing to forsake the bonds of marriage, we are in the midst of an impasse. Even now, I wonder if she waits for him to leave again and for me to run home. But the red brick house on the hill stands empty. I've nowhere to run home to, even if I wanted to. Home is where Anthony is. Home is where my children are. Home is in our hearts now.

I often think that I am much like the woman who lived in the old white farmhouse. I'm in survival mode, making things work because I have to. Resourceful and resolute, I am the house and the woman all in one. As strong as I may seem though, I still wait to hear a comforting word from my mother. Over the years, I've done my part to keep my life private as my mother is a nurse and she would just as soon 'fix' the problems rather than merely lend a listening and compassionate ear. I have enough professionals in my life trying to fix things and I don't need another one. What I want is a mother to listen and say all those things mothers say to their children to encourage and galvanize them through the forthcoming rough seas. Maybe she thinks I'm confident enough I don't need to hear it. Maybe she doesn't know the words to say. Yet in every conversation, I wait to hear her say how proud she is of me and whether she thinks I'm a good mother or not. To my knowledge, mom has never picked up a book on autism to learn more about what it is or to help understand Ewan. She has not gone out of her way to learn about autism. I wonder if this is because she thinks Ewan is well cared for by two dedicated parents or if it is merely something she cannot face. I know that she cares and that she does indeed worry about Ewan and all my children, but it's not always enough to overcome all the other baggage and issues that we have between us. Conversations can be difficult and superficial most days, but I cling to what I have because it's all that I have. With the passing of my father, that black hole has left the two of us with a disintegrated and chaotic orbit. The family I had, the family I grew up thinking would always be there through thick and thin, doesn't really exist anymore. So I have simply created a new one. My heart used to live in the red brick house on the hill. Now my heart and faith reside in the four walls surrounding my husband, my daughter, and my sons, wherever that may be.

Chapter Nine

Sweet Home Illinois

When we arrived in Illinois right before Thanksgiving in 2004, I had no idea where we were going to live and I had no idea what life had in store for Ewan, or any of us for that matter. Our hometown is a rural college town that is about 45 miles away from the nearest shopping mall or Target. Anthony and I both grew up in this little academic enclave, and we looked forward to starting over and raising our kids in a town where we grew up with most everybody. My husband had picked out our apartment when he had interviewed for the job, so I hadn't even seen the place we would spend the next three years of our life. I was simply happy to be in a place we could afford with a steady income for my husband. While my mother-in-law watched the children, we were able to unload a full U-Haul in record time thanks to Anthony's large family. That night, one of my closest friends helped me unpack every single box so that when my children woke up the next morning, we could start a new routine with a familiarity of the home we had just left. In the early morning light, I walked down to the nearest phone booth to call early intervention. It was time to set up an appointment with a new service coordinator and find out if my son would even qualify for anything at all in this new system of care.

To my surprise, a former high school classmate ended up being my son's new service coordinator. Already, I was beginning to feel better about having uprooted us all to our hometown. There's something comforting about going through such tremendous change with a familiar face. Our new service coordinator, Beth, would be with us 'til we transitioned out of early intervention and long after that as I watched her family grow over the years. With early intervention comes a host of people in your house—some of them you tolerate, some of them you love, and some of them you can't wait to kick out the door. Beth was a Godsend for us, helping us navigate through the maze of new laws and rules and therapists with grace and laughter. She supported us through ups and downs and through every ridiculous request I sent her way.

As Beth scheduled a series of appointments for us to meet and start early intervention services in our new home, Anthony and I celebrated Thanksgiving and our anniversary in the simplest way possible. We had spent every last dime in getting to the new apartment and we were broke. With his new job, Anthony was driving back and forth for training at a restaurant 45 miles away. In the frigid weeks before Christmas, the children and I watched the snow slowly start to fall as we waited every night for Anthony to come home. With Christmas so close and our bank account so low, we scraped every penny we had and sold anything of value we owned in order to buy a few Christmas presents. Ewan and Vaughn didn't really know or understand that Santa was supposed to bring them heaps of presents. But Skye did. Skye actually had figured out the Santa ruse two years earlier, and she knew it would be her father and I letting her down if she woke to an empty tree. Anthony and I weren't about to let that happen. We couldn't get her a lot, but we could get her the one thing she had asked for time and time again. Thanks to Amazon.com and free shipping, she woke up on December 25th to see the giant wooden horse barn she had so desperately wanted.

When Christmas passed, the press of our bills seemed a little less as Anthony was now getting a steady paycheck. We celebrated New Year's by taking the entire family to one of our favorite restaurants in the next town over. We pulled up to a cramped Mexican restaurant to see the place packed to the gills with hungry diners. The restaurant was still festively decorated with an animatronic Santa Claus at the front doors and sparkling multi-colored lights on every surface. The moving and speaking Santa Claus completely freaked Ewan out and he entered full-fledged meltdown mode right then and there. Somehow we managed to pry his fingertips off the doorframe and find a seat. We were seated next to a middle aged couple who was none too happy about our calamitous arrival. As Ewan struggled and fought against everything to do with this restaurant, I threw every sign I knew at him, hoping he would understand that everything would be ok. The couple to our side continued to stare in disapproval at the scene unfolding at my table. The wife said, a little too loudly, "Why don't they just leave? If I were that mother, I'd spank that boy right here and now!"

Realizing that Ewan needed a break and that I needed to leave before I was arrested for assault and battery, we headed out to the car to regroup for a few minutes. While Ewan played with his trains in the quiet of the dark backseat, the disapproving couple walked by the car. Still talking about what horrible parents we were for raising such an unruly child, the man said, "Did you see that mom using sign language? Clearly there's something wrong with that kid."

The wife replied, "I don't care if he's deaf, he still needed a good spanking." I watched them get in their car and leave only the faint red glow of their brake lights in the darkness. Sighing deeply, I glanced back at Ewan who was calm and happy now that he was distanced from the lights and chaos of the restaurant. Would I ever learn to be a good mother to him and would strangers like this ever know how hard it was for either of us to get through each day? Resolving to make the best of what we had, we crammed a few trains in our pockets and headed back inside.

Determined to make the most of the time left with early intervention, Beth came back to the house for more paperwork and therapist suggestions. Because Ewan was getting older everyday and gaining on that magical three year old number when early intervention so cruelly ends, Beth immediately scheduled a transition meeting for us. Now that we had moved to Illinois and started the process, we were already having to think about leaving the comforting arms of early intervention altogether. The transition coordinator came into my home and explained the world of life after early intervention. I was scared to death at the very thought of leaving such a program and starting all over again with the schools.

Early intervention is a little like a cocoon. It's this protective sphere of comfort and reassurance that shields parents from the worst the world has to offer. For the most part, everyone is kind and supportive, like some hovering grandmotherly figure in your life. The institution as a whole may have debilitating problems with funding and over-bloated bureaucracies, but those who find their way into your home quickly take up residence in your heart. For it is in those early months and years that you hear the most difficult news and are challenged in every aspect of your life. It is with this close knit group that most of us find out the true nature of our child's disabilities and find ourselves starting a long journey toward adulthood beginning from hearth and home. If you are lucky enough to have experienced the joy of early intervention in natural environments, then you know that we are spared having to sit in yet another waiting room purgatory for just a few years. Talk of having to leave the comfort of early intervention and leaving the sanctity and comfortable embrace of home was terrifying. Hearing that early intervention offered what was medically necessary while life after early intervention, i.e. life in the school district, offered Ewan only what was educationally necessary put fear in my heart and ice in my veins. To me, it was as if they were giving up on him. Saying to me, to Ewan, and to my family, that we'll only do what we have to gnawed at my conscience and pushed me to keep up the inhumane pace we had been running for the past year. Now was no time to be complaisant about the gains he had made, now was the time to reach out and touch the stars.

In those early days of early intervention, Ewan and I were blessed with some truly fantastic therapists in our home—therapists who defied the laws of physics and kept pace with my expectations. When we first moved back to our hometown, we were required to pick new therapists, and I, not knowing anything about any of these people, happened to pick our next speech therapist by sheer chance. The service coordinator said she was really perky and young but very intelligent, and I was immediately reminded of our first speech therapist. So I took a chance and picked Stacey Vitale to lead my son through the maze of language and sign and upcoming communication devices. I knew she'd either sink or swim, and it was with profound joy that I watched my son and my family fall in love with her.

It's hard to describe Stacey. On one hand, she has the personality of a cheerleader, both bubbly and vivacious, finding laughter easy on her lips. On the other hand, she has a depth that surprises you, given her outward charm. She thinks about the children she works with long after she's left the session. She seeks to understand the child in front of her in ways that most clinicians choose to avoid. Stacey has this way of looking beneath the diagnosis, through the layers of disability to catch a glimpse of her patient's mind and soul. While I was wary of Stacey at first and unwilling to trust her with one of my most precious possessions, it didn't take long for me to realize she was the real deal. Through every therapist to enter Ewan's life, this was one I would gladly drop everything for to help at a moment's notice. She could call me at 3 a.m. and tell me she needed an oil change, and I'd gladly do it.

It felt like we were finally on a path that had short-term achievable goals. I could see the light at the end of the tunnel as we closed in on getting a communication device. With Stacey's guidance, Ewan was increasing the amount sign language he used and saying more and more words and small phrases every day. There were many people who cautioned us from jumping into such alternative forms of communicating, often warning us that if we relied on signs, pictures and devices, Ewan would never learn to speak on his own. Far from inhibiting his language, all the signs and pictures only facilitated more verbal speech. These were not crutches keeping him from independent communication, but rather these were a means to the end. Ewan needed a way to communicate, and sign language and pictures made the abstract world of language something his concrete brain could connect with and understand.

He was still losing words that he would begin to use, but they were becoming clearer while he did have them. As his speech became more articulate, it became obvious that Ewan was using echolalia as he would repeat short phrases over and over. Much of what he did say was very rote and scripted, and while it was amazing to hear his voice, we still waited for the kind of spontaneous thoughts that took our breath away at the augmentative communication eval those few months before. I could tell that this new team was leery of the augmentative communication suggestion we brought with us from Indiana. It's not surprising, given that, at the time, it was not something many therapists and educators *were* comfortable with. Giving a child so young something so expensive seemed like we were jumping the gun. I could tell many people wanted us to take a 'wait and see' approach with his language development. Unfortunately, I'm not a 'wait and see' kind of gal. So while they looked at the reports and catalogs with skepticism, it wouldn't be 'til we had the device in hand that Ewan would shatter all their long-held beliefs. It wasn't until his fingers connected to a technological miracle that they would believe in what a child so young could really do given the right tools at the right time. While Stacey was hesitant at first to believe in the power of this new technology, she was willing to take a chance and follow Ewan into a new future for him, for children like him, and for an entire community.

In the months before Ewan's trial device found its way to our door, we continued to plug away at therapy and, once again, increased the frequency of therapy and the complexity and functionality of his goals. For many of the sessions, Ewan was tuned in and focused, most especially when he was with Stacey as she seemed one of the few who could find that perfect balance between pushing him too far and letting him control the direction of the session. Yet even the legendary Stacey Vitale had days when Ewan struggled through therapy. Days when echolalia dominated the language landscape and the minutes and hours danced around the same few words. Days when he was distracted and restlessly pacing the room with a disquieted spirit. We continued to struggle with the perseverations as he hid in the shadows with his trains or whatever the item of fixation happened to be that day. No matter how many times we increased therapy, we all continued to wrestle with the inconsistency of his scattered and asynchronous skills.

In going through Ewan's old reports and early intervention materials, I came across a schedule I had made of all his activities. It resembles the screen air traffic controllers use to land planes. There were days we had therapy stacked back to back and there were days we would head out to a clinic for extra sessions while rushing back home to get the next therapist in the door. Coming back to our hometown, we also enrolled Ewan in a preschool at the local university affectionately named Lab School by all the parents. Here we could see if all the hard won goals in therapy would play out in the real world alongside his peers. Lab School was a place Skye had grown up in and one of the last few vestiges of play-based care. It is a relic of days gone by, a time when a child's only job was to play and stretch his muscles and imagination. It was the perfect place to push Ewan in handling the creativity and unpredictability of childhood.

His days became a blur of therapy, school, and doctor visits. There were concerns from the move about seizure activity, and right as we moved we were forced to find new specialists to help us tease out what was autism and what was not. And, of course, not one of those doctors was within 30 miles of home. We purchased a trampoline and a six foot long foam bean bag that Ewan used as his own personal crash pad, and when he wasn't using it, Anthony could be found napping on it. My house was not a home anymore. My house was a therapy clinic, and we were open for business 24 hours a day. In the middle of all this chaos, Anthony decided he wanted to go back to school. He was tired of all the long hours and crappy pay, and he wanted to go somewhere in life rather than to continue treading water. We were tired of being poor, and we were tired of the little options we had in life. He vowed to never go back to the days of poverty we'd seen in Indiana. In one fell swoop, my daily calendar had blown up in a cluttered mass of appointments and class times.

As Anthony embarked on a new life of college classes and work schedules, I scoured our rural area for a neurologist who could help us with Ewan. The new pediatrician we now had randomly pulled a name from his Rolodex and scheduled an appointment with a neurologist not too far from our home. After five minutes with this guy, though, I knew beyond a shadow of a doubt that none of the children to walk through his door had ever been autistic. Before we even laid eyes on the guy he ordered an EEG, but his orders didn't include any type of sedative. I held Ewan down for 45 minutes straight while he kicked and screamed and fought off my embrace. As he struggled against my arms and touch, they put each and every single electrode across his scalp and forehead. Ewan finally succumbed to the exhaustion of such an ordeal and slept for the 30 minutes they needed for the test. Then he was unceremoniously woken up, and we were pushed out and told to walk across the hospital towards the neuro's office. He blithely walked in, late, of course, to say that the EEG had come back just fine and that this looked like a normal boy to him. He scratched his head and wondered aloud why on earth this kid was in such intensive therapy. Dr. *Doubt and Disbelief* said he just couldn't believe he was autistic as he watched my son take every Hot Wheel in the office and line them up against the wall. Needless to say, he wasn't our neurologist for more than the 13 minutes it took to call and find another. He may have been a specialist, but it was never in autism. Thankfully the next neuro office we found ourselves in was one we'd keep for years to come. She is a doctor that has calmly and methodically examined all the quirks Ewan has presented over the years, from autism to aphasia to apraxia and the rest of the alphabet. And she is one of the few that has stopped to peel back the layers of Ewan's health issues and, years later, help us find the root cause to his most unusual behaviors.

The other doctor to enter our lives right at this time was not so wonderful. In fact, she was down-right horrendous. She was the spiritual leader of the doom and gloom crowd who went under the guise of a Developmental Pediatrician. She somehow managed to fit every stereotype parents of special needs children loathe and despise. She was condescending, she was rude, and she fully embraced the 'He'll never do this' philosophy. The first 15 minutes of our appointment were sheer Hell for me because I've never wanted to kick someone in the kneecaps more in my entire life. And since I had gone to this appointment alone, I knew I would likely be arrested for aggravated battery and Ewan would have to see his mother hauled off in handcuffs. After a few minutes of her diatribe, I finally cut her off and let her know that I was, indeed, not a total moron, and that I had some inkling of what was going on with my son. Once I threw out a few choice multi-syllable words, and surprisingly none of them were curse words, I think I leveled the playing field a little. Suddenly, she stopped speaking to me as if I were a Neanderthal. The appointment went somewhat smoother afterwards; however, we never went back. This physician was not someone who would do Ewan any good at all, and she certainly had no intention of following up with him. Her goal was to confirm the diagnosis and shoo us out the door to doom and gloom land. I hope in reading this, the doom and gloom crowd of medical physicians and educators learn that hope comes in an infinite supply and that possibility lurks behind every corner. In that moment I could choose to believe her or I could choose to believe in my son. I chose Ewan.

    Doctors of the doom and gloom crowd can easily destroy your momentum with just a few choice words. It's easy to get lost in their list of scores and tests, and it's easy to focus on the dis- in disability. I knew his life was worth more than any number, any score, or any number of "he'll never" statements. I was going to fill his life with "he can" statements. There was no better way to prepare this boy for a life of possibility than by giving him every tool in the toolbox. My focus shifted away from just learning to speak, learning self-regulation and learning play skills to focus on giving him every opportunity to live the life of his choosing. The day I walked out of that appointment, I chose to find another way to view autism. From that point on, I would force myself to focus on something other than just a definition in the DSM-IV. That day, we stopped fighting against it, and learned to incorporate what it meant to be autistic into every part of our life. Rather than pushing it away, we embraced the full spectrum of life. This shift became etched in stone the day his device arrived. This was the day Ewan shattered every misconception ever believed about the child with autism. The day the device came, Ewan found his voice, and it wasn't with his lips. That day I learned it wasn't about what I wanted, it was about what he needed.

    That February, a series of autism related shows were plastered across the TV screen. A new autism-related organization, Autism Speaks, was marching across every network, talking about every facet of life with autism. One afternoon Skye and I sat in front of the TV to watch a segment on siblings of children with autism. A child stood in front of the camera explaining how the world revolved around her brother while she was left to the fringes of the family. With tears in my eyes, I turned to Skye and asked her if that was how she felt about it. For so long we had been wrapped up in helping Ewan learn that we had forgotten about our daughter's quality of life. Every minute and dollar was spent helping Ewan speak and interact, and little was left for anything else. Skye thought about her answer for a minute before she slowly shrugged her shoulders and uttered that one fateful word, "Sometimes."

Not knowing how or when, but finding a balance between Ewan's needs and everyone else's became paramount to our family's well-being. It was then that we signed Skye up for ballet and hoped that she could find her confidence in something that was only for her. Skye is sometimes a quiet child, not always telling you what she wants or needs until the pressure simply explodes out of every molecule. Skye, my oldest, who I once thought was my only chance at having children, felt left out and abandoned by a mother who marvels at her existence every single day. To me, she was, is and will always be simply amazing. Graceful and artistic, she is so many things that I am not. Her capacity to accept change and life as it comes sometimes amazes and at other times confounds me. She has accepted everything that life has thrown at us with a grace and humility most adults could never handle. With the birth of Ewan, her life as an only child ended dramatically. The center of attention and joy to all who knew her suddenly took a back seat to a new baby that demanded so much more than just any old baby brother. In a way, I am glad that she had those seven years of solitude and focus because it would become the foundation of her strength and resiliency. Those years gave her what she needed to become the young woman who has a gift for seeing the world from an often unseen perspective. She has an eye for the often missed parts of life, and this has had made her into the artist and photographer that she is today. In the early days, I know it must have been incredibly challenging to be usurped by such a demanding infant. An infant who never slept, turned her mother into a frantic zombie for nine months, and seemed ever so much more interested in the window blinds than in her. No ordinary brother, he would not stare in adoration at her but rather focus the intensity of his gaze upon the ceiling fan above her head.

Early on in Ewan's life, doctor appointments and therapy visits became an everyday staple. I often wonder how she looked at this constant parade of travelers waltzing in and out of the house every day of the week. Was it an intrusion or was it interesting? Not only was this brother's life a focus for her parents, but it was also the star to every therapy visit in our living room. Sometimes she would watch and participate in therapy and at others she would simply go about her life as if the fourth speech path in two years to walk through the door was no cause for concern or celebration. Often, she would find Ewan playing with her Gameboy as he had recently discovered the joy of a square pixilated screen. As a mother in the trenches, it's hard for me to remember much of these early days other than creating a master schedule of therapy and appointments that rivaled the D-Day Normandy attack plan. I was on autopilot many days, and so much of that time is a blur of cleaning before the therapists arrived, sitting to watch the therapy unfold as if my life depended on everything these experts did, and then spending the next few hours practicing those very same techniques 'til the next therapist walked through the door. Shampoo, rinse, repeat—that was my life for three years.

In many ways, this oldest child adjusted well to a lifestyle that often to put everyone else's needs second fiddle. There were no new cars, no vacations, no big shopping trips, and not a lot of room for frivolity. We lived a very simple life in an effort to change the course of one child's developmental trajectory. I look back and think that there was little room to have made much change, and I'm unsure how much I would've done differently had I a chance to do so. It was a necessary evil for the time we lived through, and I cannot but think that we did the right thing with what we had.

The day she uttered the word, "sometimes," part of my heart shattered, and I often question if I have failed her in some way, though I was powerless to stop that which had overtaken our lives. I hope my daughter can look at her brother now, see the young man he has become, and appreciate the sacrifices that were made to give him a chance at life. I hope she can see that her strength and grace to handle what life has thrown at her amazes me every single day. I hope she can understand how her brother has shaped her personality and appreciate the advocate she has become. She is now a young woman who understands and accepts the full spectrum of the human condition. I hope that she can see just how proud I am at who she has become.

As for Vaughn, the *what ifs* of his development were catching up to us. When Vaughn was born, we immediately worried about the trajectory of his life. Would his first year be like Ewan's? Would his second? Would he ever feel the frustration of knowing what he wants without the words to scream it to the stars and sky? It quickly became apparent that Vaughn's first months of life would be nothing like his brother's. But we watched and waited for every developmental milestone, walking on eggshells when it didn't hit exactly on the mark. Just as I thought he wasn't going to sit up independently on time, he accomplished it all on his own. Just when I thought he couldn't, he would prove me wrong.

Chapter Ten

A World of Possibility

Progress surrounded us like an aura. In the weeks before the trial device found its way to my door, Stacey had been working on a variety of goals with Ewan. We had increased the use of signs with him yet again and had added a wide variety of pictures for him to use above and beyond just the basics of food and toys. We were starting to use picture schedules and Carol Gray's Social Stories ™ with more success than ever. His vocalizations had increased dramatically, yet they were neither consistent nor spontaneous. Much of it was mired in the echolalia and scripting so often used among our children. Despite the eccentricities of his language, we seemed to be plugging in the right direction. Given the right moment and the right environment, Ewan was beginning to handle more of what life threw at him. Our living room had been transformed into a sensory clinic with trampolines, giant bean bags, and, of course, the train table that continued to eclipse the importance of all the other furniture in the house. Who needs a coffee table when Sir Topham Hatt provides such interesting talking points?

It was at this point we had to take Ewan out for an evaluation at the school district. The time of transition was approaching quickly, and I knew my cocoon of safety was about to bust wide open. I was unsure of how Ewan would do in this eval. On one hand, I wanted him to show them everything he had learned over the past year and walk away with the words, "He doesn't need our services." And on the other hand, I was terrified of a life without therapy. I knew school services were going to be drastically reduced, even if Ewan did nothing but scream in the corner of the room. I also knew that without the therapy we had been blessed with, Ewan would not have made the progress that he had in such a short time. Therapy is the one thing you love to hate in your life because in one moment it is empowering, and in the next it can create a learned helplessness. While I may have embraced the advocate role for my son and was beginning to learn how to navigate the disorder and the system, I was not ready to go it alone just yet. And I was definitely alone that day we walked in for the school evaluation.

As scary as it may have seemed before walking in the door, the eval by the school was really quite simple. They expected Ewan to draw a few shapes, stack a few blocks, and interact with them. Despite all the new skills Ewan was learning, not one of them was any of the above. He still could not hold a pencil to do anything other than chuck it at your forehead, and stacking blocks was not always Ewan's forte. That day he found the blocks to be boring and not worthy of his attention. His 'plan' for having to spend time in the large, open room where the eval was held included running around like a wild animal. As for interaction, he may well have become comfortable with familiar therapists and faces, but this is a far cry from performing for strangers. He reacted to the situation by migrating to the corner of the room where he focused on the trash can lid like it held the key to the universe. And here I'd been worried Ewan wouldn't look autistic enough to get services.

His performance at the first school evaluation was enough to warrant a full case study replete with psychologists and social workers. Ewan was tested seven ways to Sunday with little language ability leaving little room for interaction with these strangers. While my son was using sign language and pictures to communicate, an evaluation relies on a child's ability to understand what is being said and to respond verbally. Without the world of words and sentences, communication that day was limited to a one-way street of information. Without conversation, those testing him couldn't engage him in any meaningful way. Without signs, words and pictures, the social interaction between Ewan and the examiner was limited and chaotic. While Ewan drifted down a creek of conversation, Anthony and I were drowned in a sea of inquiry. We were asked every conceivable question about his birth, his development, and ourselves as the privacy we had lost in early intervention grew ever greater. The amount of people that knew every facet of my life just kept growing and growing.

While we waited to hear back on our first meeting with the school district, we had bigger issues to deal with. After months of waiting and wading through stacks of paperwork, the augmentative communication device trial was getting ready to start. It was the end of March, and without a firm date of when the device would arrive by UPS, I simply decided to employ the stalker technique of staring out my window every 3.2 seconds watching for its imminent arrival. I had to restrain myself from throwing my arms around that chestnut clad parcel paladin when he graced my doorstep with a two pound agent of change. He merely backed away slowly as I laughed like a school girl waving the box over my head with unbridled joy.

It was like Christmas had come early to our house. I ripped through the packaging to extricate what I perceived to be my son's saving grace. With inhuman speed I programmed the device with his name, his favorite items, foods and people. Before I could even slap that machine down on the table to brand it ready for use, Ewan gravitated toward my side eager to see the future I held in my hands. He needed no coaxing, no bribery, no push forward; Ewan instinctively reached out for the one thing that could speak his every thought. We had found a bridge between his world and mine, and we had both taken a giant step toward the middle.

The day the device trial began I started a journal to record our progress. I wanted to document every aspect of our time with the Dynavox so that at the end I would know whether or not we were embarking on the right path. We ended up having to trial the MT4, a device that was technologically fancier than the Mighty Mo, and one that would grow with him over the next five years. The cost of the device and the hoops to jump through in order to get our own needed to be weighed against his response to it. If it became an $8,000 paperweight during our trial, then I knew we were barking up the wrong tree. I was more than a little intimidated by the skepticism surrounding its arrival. What if everyone was right, what if he was too young or we hadn't given therapy enough of a chance yet? Every doubt crept into my mind in the moments before and after the device came into our life. Even now, years later, I still wonder if Ewan would have made the progress he has without it. Regardless, I cannot deny the progress he did make with the assistance of this technology, and I could not deny what I saw unfolding before my very eyes. For months, we had worked on getting Ewan to consistently say and use the phrase "I want." Sure he could repeat it, maybe even surprise us with purposeful use during therapy, but it never came to him instinctively outside of therapy. He could not generalize the use of those simple words outside the confines of 60 minutes of rehab and into the real world. And it was with awe and amazement that I watched a two pound hunk of technological marvel help him do what hundreds of hours of therapy could not. Here is what I wrote in my journal during those fateful days.

Thursday 3/24

Received the device at 4:00pm. We programmed the personal info into the device and made a few changes. Ewan watched everything we did—VERY interested in what I was doing. Made a button that said "I like trains" and he used that and smiled at me. Then he just randomly explored the device till bedtime.

Friday 3/25

Tried to get Ewan to ask for milk but he hadn't explored the device enough yet. He 'played' with the pages and words and continued to explore the device. I made a train page with Thomas the Tank Engine characters. He explored that page a lot with obvious pleasure. He liked the family page since I put pictures of his siblings, Skye and Vaughn in. Did this ALL day. By the evening the device froze up and we couldn't use it until Saturday morning. He has completely mastered moving from page to page and back between all the pages.

Saturday 3/26

Took device with us to grandma's house. Ewan used it to talk about blocks since he was playing with blocks there. Blocks! Used phrase 'make it tall' and 'clean it up.' Asked his grandpa for a cookie and chocolate milk using the device.

Sunday 3/27

Ewan practiced using the device all day. We programmed many more pages and changed some stuff around. He asked for chocolate milk, cookies, chips with the device. He talked about trains using the train page. He likes the social page and said 'hi' and 'see you later alligator' (he really liked that). Continued to explore different pages. I programmed a Gameboy page with all his favorite game boy games and things to say like 'it's not working' or 'we need to charge the battery.' He LOVES it!

Monday 3/28

Ewan woke up and went straight to the device without so much as looking at us! He then asked for a cookie with the device. I got him a cookie and he was SO happy! Little bit later he asked for chocolate milk using the snacks and drinks page. I programmed 'I'm hungry' into the device and 'I want ice' and he started to use those immediately. Took device with us as we ran some errands. I put the MT4 on his lap while he sat in his car seat. We passed by McDonald's and he asked for fries and chicken nuggets using the device! Later that night he asked to COLOR and when I got out the supplies his face lit up. I programmed in Pizza Hut pages with video game requests and some stuff about dad and he actually said "Oh YEAH!" (Dad works at Pizza Hut) And he understood! Went to Pizza Hut but it was very busy and he got upset and wouldn't use the device while we were there.

Tuesday 3/29

Woke Ewan up for therapy but it went very badly. He was tired and therapy did not go well. He did not use the device during therapy, but did the rest of the day. He did more 'I want to color,' used to ask for food, drinks, ice, and said 'I'm hungry' using device—we've never known this before for certain!! Later that night explored all the feelings buttons. Told me each one 'I feel,' 'sad,' 'happy,' 'mad,' all of them and did facial expressions with each one. He pretended to be asleep like the person in the symbol and would say 'wake up' with the device. Wanted me to act out all emotions too and pretend to be asleep so he could use device to say 'wake up!' We have NOT been able to get Ewan to understand emotions this way before! Then he pretended to be sick after pushing 'sick' button and used a crayon as a thermometer! WOW. I gave him a real thermometer and he said, with his own voice, "OH YEAH, OH YEAH!" We did this for approximately one hour.

Wednesday 3/30

Ewan woke up for therapy and immediately used device to ask for chocolate milk and a cookie. Used device entire time during therapy! Told therapist he wanted to color using device and then used shapes and color pages to tell her what to draw and what colors to use! Explored numbers page and toys and bedroom. Used the 'my bedroom' page to tell therapist he got a new bed. Later during the day he used the device to ask for chicken nuggets, Sprite, and fries at McDonald's. At night, I told him he had to go to the Doctor's office in the morning and he went to the Doctor page and explored 'something hurts, it's my __' and used different body parts to fill in the blank. Practiced 'hello doctor' and others. Used band-aids to practice and asking using the device and listening to his heart.

Thursday 3/31

Went to doctor's office. Using the device to ask for all food products and Gameboy requests. Now saying "I want" with his natural voice as he pushes the button about 60% of the time and used to be 0. Took device into doctor visit and he used device to say 'hello Dr.' and 'something hurts it's my __' but only to play around with the doctor. We used device concerning the elevator and he told us all that he wanted to do. Used the device to say he saw cars and trucks on the skywalk at the hospital. Still talking with the device, about these cars and trucks several hours later. Took Ewan and the device to the mall. He used it to say he wanted to 'go to the car' and 'time to get the mail' (his favorite thing to do). We came home and he explored the device off and on and I think he was trying to describe seeing the elevator and the cars and trucks since he kept pushing those buttons. Used to ask for all needs.

Friday 4/1

Found the 'I want candy' button and he used it A LOT but also used device to ask for his sister's Gameboy and even told me with the device 'it won't work' and 'charge the battery' when the Gameboy stopped working. Repeatedly asked for popcorn with device. Used 'I want fire truck' then 'I want video' to ask for his favorite fire truck DVD!! WOW!! Used color and shapes page to practice as well as the numbers page. Still talking about elevator and cars and trucks he saw on Thursday.

Saturday 4/2

Used to ask for all needs. Used for talking about the weather and explored weather page. We were watching TV show where there was a volcano erupting and the falling ash looked like rain. He used his device to tell me 'It's raining.' He discovered the 'book' pages and 'I want to read a book' button. We read several books and he used device to say 'read it again' and 'turn the page' and 'the end.' Did this REPEATEDLY when we read each book—about six books and he brought them all to me SPONTANEOUSLY! Never done that before! Used the 'time to' page a lot. At night he told me 'it's dark outside,' 'it's raining,' and 'it's cold outside,' and it WAS storming!

Sunday 4/3

Used to express all needs. Used to say 'I want to color' and asked me to draw shaped, faces, and use different colors. He explored the holidays pages and told me 'Halloween' and 'Christmas.' Explored doctor page again. Explored the getting dressed page and after bath he used device to say 'I want pajamas on.'

Monday 4/4
Went to hospital and had a BAD day. After preschool he used and explored all kinds of pages. He now knows and has mastered all the screens and moving back and forth. Used device to ask where Skye and Vaughn were.

Tuesday 4/5
Went to grandma's house and used to say 'I want to go to grandma's' in the car. When we were there he asked for all needs and when he wanted to leave he used device to say 'time to go to the car' and 'time to get the mail.' Also used 'I need my blanket' and 'I like trains' in the car (we got stopped by a train on the tracks).

Wednesday 4/6
Used to express all needs and wants. Talked about weather again. Used the 'I want to call' button and then pushed 'dad!' GREAT! Asked for his cat with the device. Later asked to go to Pizza Hut and then when we were there he said 'I want Daddy' and then 'I love you!!!' Asked for video game on Pizza Hut page and ordered by using 'pizza' and 'Sprite' buttons. Later that night he played with 'something hurts' and showed me each body part. Told me repeatedly 'mom' and 'I love you!!' Used at school to say, 'it's time to get the mail.'

Thursday 4/7
In the morning he heard me say to his dad to go the store and get me some things. Ewan went to his device and used it to say 'Grocery Store' and 'I want' and then got to go with his daddy!!

While I only documented two weeks what he did at home, we were also able to document major changes in therapy with the use of the device. By the end of the second week, Stacey noted during their session he was able to use the device to request 'truck,' 'car,' and to comment using the word 'crash' repeatedly. During that session she noted that he was consistently using the phrase 'I want.' We saw him be able make the echolalia functional by repeating what the device said for him. In one fell swoop, Ewan made the connection between the power of words and how to use the echolalia to his advantage. The nonfunctional just became functional.

The way that he used language fundamentally changed in those moments with the device. Before, he used scripted or rote language or provided a one word answer to request something. Now Ewan was trying to engage me. The child who preferred to play alone suddenly stepped into the flow of conversation and engaged in the back and forth of everyday communication. He was using the device to comment, to play, and to expand his thoughts. And through it all, he repeated what the device said while learning to utilize the device as his voice and to understand the power of his own voice. The proverbial light bulb had been switched on and there was no going back now. He started with eight buttons on each screen, but he consumed vocabulary like it was air. He constantly craved more and more as he began to see a wider world open up to him. It was so reminiscent of the early stories we've all heard about Helen Keller and her joy at learning the names of things. Ewan wanted to catalog and inventory every single thing, every thought, every action, and every moment. Not only did he want to name it all, he wanted us to share in his joy. For the first time, we were seeing him display skills like joint attention (using nonverbal gestures and gazes to get someone's attention). For the first time, he was using his fingers to point in a protodeclarative manner (pointing as if to say, "Look!") and protoimperative manner (pointing as if to say, "I want that!"), all while using the device to say 'I see' or 'I want.' His gaze would flick back and forth between the world, our eyes, and his device as we became interconnected in a complex web of excitement and labels. With the help of his device, Ewan spun together a gossamer world of associations. All the skills that had been absent in infancy were now starting to surface. While he was still obsessed with the trains and video games, I could see that his brain and his heart had just made room for something else. The device became an extension of himself, so much so that he would refuse to part with it, even in sleep. We decided something so crucial to all our lives should have a name, thus, 'Talkbox' was born that week.

I was able to manipulate the device to create Social Stories ™, scripts, and schedules, so I no longer had to carry reams of binders and pictures with me wherever we went. It was all now neatly contained in his Talkbox. We saw a marked decrease in his frustration and in the frequency of meltdowns with an increase in the initiation of spontaneous language. He began to focus on things that he had completely ignored before, and all the work we had done over the months on feelings and emotions slowly began to interest Ewan. We took therapy and the device on the road in a multitude of environments, including McDonald's, where Stacey was able to observe him order his own food and respond to her questions in a busy environment. However, he still had trouble with the social side to life. While at McDonald's, he went to the Play Land, and despite having his Talkbox with him, he was unable to or uninterested in responding to, initiating things like 'hi,' or asking other children to play. He wouldn't or couldn't even say 'goodbye.' He could be prompted, and he knew where these buttons were on the device, but it was not natural to him to engage in that kind of conversation yet. We were still at the phase of discovering the world, and he had no time yet for the social nuances of the playground.

That time of discovery was a whirlwind of vocabulary. The core vocabulary did not attract his interest—all the little words that make up a sentence could not hold his focus. But oh, the fringe vocabulary. He lived, ate, and breathed the fringe. He was captivated and enthralled with the world of the specifics. Ewan could care less about the core words needed to form complete thoughts—all those high frequency words we use in a grammatically correct sentence. Pronouns and verbs and articles were meaningless and abstract. He wanted the fringe words—all the words that had a tangible and concrete meaning to him such as volcano, train, tractor, spider, and so on. His mind clung to what it could touch and fled from the smoky obscurity of the intangible. The social niceties and beauty of the core completely escaped him. Building sentences with the core vocabulary was not something he inherently wanted to do, and often we would have to rely on the use of pre-programmed phrases to get him to say a complete thought; otherwise, it could easily escalate into a series of words thrown at you as fast as the speed of thought, degrading conversation into a cacophony of nouns. It was then that all those who had been working with Ewan began to see just how much he could really do. Every misconception and myth about the young child with a high tech communication device had just been shattered. From that point on, Stacey would never again doubt what he or any other child with autism could do given the right tools. It was then that Ewan found a special place in her heart, and she in his. Together, we had cracked the language code for this child and had given him another chance at life in a neurotypical world. These early days would lead us down the right path, the path toward giving Ewan something that is so often denied children like him: an improved quality of life. He broke the stereotype of that awful little phrase, "Not a good candidate for a device." His other therapists all noted the dramatic and amazing success he was having with the device, and it was with a heavy heart and infinite sadness that we had to send that device back at the end of the trial. If you can imagine his utter and profound joy at being given the world, you can also imagine his misery and sorrow at having to give it back.

April had brought with it a flood of changes in our life. The proverbial April showers seemed more like a deluge both inside and outside. First came the device, then came everything else in life. Anthony and I went to our first IEP meeting with the local school district to find out if Ewan qualified for any services at all. The first IEP meeting when a family transitions away from early intervention is a huge let down. First, everyone at the table seems to have an agenda that is different from your own, usually dictated by budgets that you have absolutely no control over. Second, all the warm fuzzy feelings of early intervention have been washed away and replaced with people on a schedule and who are not willing to chit chat. It can be a drastic change in the amount and frequency of therapeutic services as the child transitions from early intervention to school. The expectations on the part of the family are very, very high and the budget on the school district side is very, very low. I'm not implying that everything is about the almighty dollar, but in reality, schools do not have unlimited budgets, and they are not taking care of just your child. I do sympathize with schools; I know it must be hard to walk the line between budgets and therapy, and I know how much therapy, good therapists, and good equipment can cost. Small schools have small budgets, and it makes everything that much more difficult for both sides.

There was a lot of discussion about Ewan's diagnosis and other health issues and, of course, we talked about the device. Ewan had been tested without the device, and no one in the room had actually seen the progress the rest of us were so excited about. Talkbox seemed like an illusion to everyone else at the table. I could see the face of every single person on the other side of the table. Each and every one of them, a non-believer. Each person at the table had a plan for Ewan, and our input was not necessarily needed. Their predetermined plan and checklist did not include a device, and when presented with such a deviation from the norm, so many of them simply shut down.

Stacey and I pushed what we could, but terms like 'educationally necessary' floated across the table and around the room. In that moment, I knew we could only push so far. If the division was educationally necessary versus medically necessary, then Anthony and I would seek our greatest help elsewhere. Stacey would remain Ewan's greatest source of support. There was no one before her, and there has been no one after her, who has done so much for this child. In the end, the school wanted Ewan in their developmental preschool, exposed to the rigors of an educational life and their overall plan. I refused to give up the freedom and creativity of Lab School, though, and come fall, Ewan would attend not just one preschool, but two.

April was a hard month for us all as we bore witness to not only the birth of language and the loss of control surrounding Ewan's life but something much greater than meetings and words. Our life was not just device, school, and therapy. There were bills, meals, and the repetition and routine of everyday life. At the beginning of the month, I found myself five days late and shopping for something more than just a gallon of milk. Sitting on the side of the bathtub and holding a pregnancy test in my hands, I watched the blue dye slowly fan out into a plus sign. In the midst of a full-fledged panic attack, I had no idea how to tell Anthony about this. For the first time, I was scared. Still nursing Vaughn, Anthony and I were in no way prepared to bring yet another baby into the mix. We weren't ready for such a huge change in our life, and to be honest, we couldn't afford another mouth to feed. With everything going on in our life, it didn't seem like the right time. Anthony was finally going back to get his degree, Skye was back on track with school, and Ewan just had the greatest breakthrough of his young life. I felt pulled in yet another direction, a road I wasn't sure I wanted to go down. The logistics of it was overwhelming. Here I was with a baby on my hip and a preschooler at my feet. We were going to need a van, a bigger place, and a lot more energy. For the woman who wasn't supposed to ever have children, this went past miraculous and into the ridiculous. I was sick to my stomach for more than just one reason. Walking through the aisles to get diapers for both Vaughn and Ewan, I thought, "How on earth can I handle yet another child?"

When I told Anthony, I could see my own emotions play across his face. It was like looking into a mirror. I begged him not to tell anyone, it was too early and I just couldn't handle any more reactions. After a day of hand wringing, Anthony finally shrugged off the fear and with a smile said, "It'll all work out. It always does." And with that he accepted what I still struggled with. It took me a little longer to warm to the idea of motherhood again so soon. Slowly though, I began to smile instead of frown when thinking about going from a family of five to a clan of six. Most of the time we just shook our heads and laughed at what life had thrown us. By the end of the month, I was cautiously lighthearted about it all and was able to walk through the baby aisle with a secret smile on my face. Each day left us a little more hopeful that we could handle this spontaneous moment in our life. Every morning we woke up intimated at the thought, and every evening we lay down intoxicated with the idea of a newborn. I dreamed of a girl in frilly pink dresses. I dreamed of another boy playing trains and wrestling in the living room. What mattered was the dream. I could see it. I could see a life with one more child at my feet. In that moment, it became something more than just blue dye.

One dark and rainy morning at the end of April, I woke not with intimidation or excitement, but straight up fear. The sheets were stained red and a shooting pain slashed across my stomach. There was so much blood. All I could see was red. From that day on, red will always be the color of my pain. I was losing the baby we had just found room for in our hearts. By the end of the day, Anthony and I found ourselves in a sterile emergency room. After sitting in the waiting room for an hour, they quietly led us to a dark room for an ultrasound. The only light coming from the blank screen in front of us. The tech confirmed what we already knew. But all I really knew how to do was to have a baby, not lose one. We were ushered back into an exam room where a nurse uttered the words, "I'm sorry, you've lost the baby. It's for the best. It's nature's way." Under the harsh light of fluorescent bulbs and in the arms of my husband, I wept for the baby I didn't know I wanted. The nurse slowly shut the door on our grief as the dream slipped out of our hands. Nature can be so cruel sometimes.

For two days, I curled up and tried to sleep through the grief and pain. The words "nature's way" kept repeating through my brain. There were no answers, and there was nothing I could do but think of what I had in front of me. Three children and a husband who needed me to do more than just curl up and cry every day. Before I went to sleep, Anthony kissed me on the forehead and quietly repeated, "It'll all work out. It always does." In the middle of a troubled sleep and restless night, I let the dream go and vowed to wake up and do something.

Two nights later, I got up and left the house. I found myself sitting in a hospital education room listening to an autism presentation. I was depressed and miserable and looking for something to distract me from my grief. I thought if I could just throw myself into autism, I might forget the *what ifs* of a baby I would never see. The speaker was introduced by a veteran mother of a child with autism living in the area. With a quiet, self-assurance, Anne talked about life with her son. She talked about the years of confusion and misunderstanding, she talked about the day her son was diagnosed, and she talked about their first successful hair cut in 12 years. I looked at this woman with tears in my eyes thinking, "I don't have it in me to wait 10 years for a scream-free hair cut." The last few months and days had left me bone-tired and beat down. My son had his first taste of anti-psychotic medication at the age of two and a half. He had been held down in a mix of tears and sweat through 45 minutes of electrode Hell. How could I possibly make it through almost 10 more years before I could say we, too, had our first successful hair cut? I surreptitiously tried to wipe the tears off my cheeks and listened as Anne encouraged new families to attend the support group she ran for parents of children with autism. Writing the time and date down, I wondered if I would have the courage to go to a meeting. I didn't know any other parents, and I didn't even know any other children with autism. What I did know, though, was that this stranger knew more about my life than many people in my own family. If I was going to walk in Anne's footsteps, I might as well get to know her.

April continued to rain drops of sorrow upon our house as the very next week we would find ourselves yet again in the harsh light of the ER. One afternoon Ewan had fallen asleep in the living room propped up in our recliner. As I tiptoed around the house cleaning this and that, Ewan suddenly sat straight up in a panic and clutching his throat. He was choking and turning blue right in front of my eyes. Anthony was at work so I screamed for Skye to dial 911. With Skye by my side, we talked with the 911 operator and simultaneously tried to see if he had swallowed something. With fear in his eyes and froth around his lips, Ewan looked to me for help I couldn't give him. I was helpless to stop what was happening. Right before I was ready to start CPR, Ewan miraculously started breathing on his own, taking in huge gasps of air as he fell into my lap. He lay in my arms, listless and exhausted, while I hugged him close to my chest. Skye's eyes were wide as she picked up her younger brother, keeping Vaughn from crawling on top of his brother's head. Anthony came running into the house a few minutes later as Skye had frantically called him after 911. He's always said that driving up to the house seeing ambulances and paramedics is the worst feeling he's ever experienced in our life together. For a brief moment, he was terrified Ewan had died. Running up the stairs, he felt like the stairs just wouldn't end. It was the longest flight of Anthony's life as he had no idea what lay on the other side of our door. Coming in the house though, the paramedics assured him that Ewan was fine and breathing on his own. Relief turned to worry, though, as he saw just how pale and fragile Ewan was. Just when we thought the worst was over, Ewan's arms and legs began to move of their own accord in an unnatural, convulsive movement. He was having a seizure in my arms, and for the second time, I was powerless to do a damn thing about it. The movement stopped quickly, though, and Ewan fell into a deep sleep as we rushed him to the emergency room. There was little anyone could do, and we sat in the waiting room while Ewan continued on in his deep slumber, oblivious to the world around him. Seeing me repeatedly try to rouse his limp and spiritless son again and again, Anthony put his head in his hands and cried. Through the tears he said, "What is wrong with my son?" The stress of losing a baby just days before, and now seeing his son lying pale and unresponsive in my arms was too much for my husband.

  I continued to talk to Ewan, holding his limp form next to mine and rocking back and forth in our chair repeating, "It's ok, it's ok," over and over. Whether I was saying it to my son, my husband, or to myself, I'll never know. Just when I thought he might never respond, Ewan woke up in the waiting room, and miraculously, all seemed normal once again. It was as if someone had simply flipped a switch. He rubbed his eyes a few times, sat up in my arms, and yawned. Given our last experience in an ER surrounding possible seizure activity, we knew we would simply be sent home with a note to call our neurologist the next morning. I saved everyone hours more of waiting and just decided to take Ewan home and call his neuro. We now faced a whole new round of tests and hospital visits, and we were left in the dark wondering how to communicate with a boy who had just lost his voice.

For the most part, I spent every waking minute of the next two weeks either in a hospital waiting room or talking to Dynavox and every single other person who could speed time up until we managed to get approval for the device at an unheard of pace. Maybe it was the urgency surrounding his health, or maybe it was divine intervention, but Ewan was without a device for a mere 14 days. Thanks to all the evals, reports, documentation, and support from his physicians and therapists, Ewan was now the proud of owner of his very own Talkbox. Our April showers had just given way to a flowery garden of possibility. This time, that poor UPS delivery driver didn't stand a chance—he was getting mugged by yours truly the minute he rang my doorbell. What that man may never know is that he delivered so much more than just a mere package. He delivered us hope.

April 15, 2010

So many of our children with autism struggle with language. In fact, in order to be diagnosed with autism there must be some sort of communication issue. But this can run the gamut from no language at all, to the most verbal of verbals who speaks better than most professors do. The difficult part about the communication issue is not whether or not language is present—but how the child with autism uses language. As I've watched Ewan grow and develop and move from little language to predominantly echolalia to more sophisticated and complex language, I've always thought English was never his first language.

In fact, I'm not even sure words were a part of his first language.

He speaks a language that is far more elemental and fundamental to humanity—a wordless language born of the senses and the depths of the human mind unknown but to a few of us.

It's hard to speak this language, because it's not something you say—it's something you feel, something you experience. It's not a language of the hands as in sign language. It's not a language made of complex syntax and grammar. It's not a language of sentences and fragments and adjectives. It's a language of feeling. It's a language of elation, of despair, of confusion, of love. It's a language of the wind on your skin, the water under your fingertips, the sun in your hair, and of lights and shadows.

Yet, for those in my neck of the woods, English is the language of the natives. English is spoken here, is read here, and is heard here. So a bridge must be built. The bridge from the language of the autistic to the language of the neurotypical.

Often, I meet children who have never been given the opportunity to cross this bridge. The language bridge was never offered.

Too often, I hear the words 'not a good candidate' when considering higher forms of augmentative communication systems for the child with autism. Too often, we get bogged down in those clinical and educational minefields that make us believe that some things are just beyond this child. Yet, if you never try it, you will never know for sure. There is no litmus test to say who should be offered that opportunity and who shouldn't. These children continue to defy expectations every single day. And yet every single day there is always someone who doesn't believe, someone who says no, someone denying a child hope.

I remember when Ewan was very young. The language bridge was slowly built plank by plank. Sign language gave us a few steps toward the middle. PECS ™ gave us a few more. But it wasn't until Ewan was given a high tech communication system that he finally met me in the middle. The Dynavox was just the bridge we needed to speak each other's language. I made sure his language of obsessions and sensory perceptions were programmed into the device, and he made the greatest of efforts to understand why words like 'the' and 'he' and 'want' and 'no' were so important to me. We met in the middle, and we've been there ever since.

That system, that bridge, that device was what brought us together and pushed Ewan into the language of words, sentences, fragments, verbs, adjectives, and pronouns. That bridge took Ewan from an augmented speech to a natural, verbal speech that goes straight from his mind to his lips. Language is still difficult for him, and spontaneous language is something that he continues to struggle with. Ewan is very literal in his interpretation of language. He still struggles with providing the context and background of a story—often leaving out really important information that helps me understand what he's trying to tell me. Usually I play detective and must draw the story out. He continues to struggle with the social use of language and the idea of the 'little white lie.' He still struggles with idioms and slang.

Learning to communicate with the natives has been hard for Ewan. It is a process that has taken years and will take many more before it becomes more intuitive for him. It is a process that has taken him from signs to PECS ™ to devices to natural speech and he continues to push the boundaries of possibility. Before, I waited to hear one word. Now, I write down all his profound thoughts on Facebook in the Ewanism of the Day.

I believe that for some children with autism, language is facilitated by signs, it is brought forth through PECS ™, it is made possible through a communication device. And for others we have yet to find that tool, that bridge that makes the leap from autistic language to neurotypical language. For some children, we have yet to crack the language code, and the autistic Rosetta Stone has yet to be found. But it's there, I know it is—and what it takes is ingenuity and creativity on our part to help find that tool.

If you have a child whose first language isn't English, I urge you to look for that tool. I urge you to try things that others have said aren't possible. I urge you to put the words 'not a good candidate' completely out of your mind. I've seen children who everyone else had given up on surprise the world with a touch to a device. I've seen children who defy the expectations of those who believe "he's not a good candidate" reach over and use a communication device to say, "I want juice" or "I love you" or spell "H-A-P-P-Y." These small words and phrases may not seem like much, but in reality language is made up of small steps, and what is a word and a phrase today can be a conversation tomorrow.

As Ewan learned to navigate the communication device, he began to use more and more verbal speech. The breakthrough continued and we watched in awe at what Ewan could do given the right tool. By the end of May, Ewan had to endure through a second EEG, but this time, we had the benefit of sedation *and* the device. We used the device not only as a way for him to communicate with us, but as a way for him to understand what was happening around him. I was able to program the device to include a sequence of what was going to happen, and aside from having to swallow a bitter liquid, Ewan was a calm and compliant patient. The device not only gave him a voice, but it was also changed the way he understood the world. The world was his dictionary, just waiting to be discovered.

Ewan continued to breathe in vocabulary like air, and soon he went from an eight button page set up to a 20 button page set up, ushering in a flood of new words and concepts. He continued to work on those core words that make up sentences and thoughts, but his passions remained firmly entrenched in the fringe. Earthquakes, volcanoes, spiders, and almost every part of the natural world held an intense fascination for him. He quickly expanded his obsessions from just merely trains to a whole new world of 'things,' and for many months nouns continued their hold over our life.

In the beginning, Ewan was still primarily echolalic and continued to repeat what the device said, but it was in a way that provided a first person perspective rather than the second person usage so often found in echolalic exchanges. When you say to the child with autism, "Do you want a glass a milk?" they may simply just repeat the question back at you and answer, "Do you want a glass a milk?" This goes back and forth between you and the child with the adult repeatedly saying, "No, no do YOU want a glass of milk?" until it's clear Calgon is five minutes late to the party. Often, the child may simply walk up and say out of nowhere, "You want milk?" Someone unfamiliar with the child may think he is the picture of manners and civility, but in reality, he's asking YOU to get HIM some milk. Understanding that the YOU in that question is HIM can take years. Luckily for us, Ewan was able to repeat what the device said, "I want some milk," and learn to request using the appropriate pronouns fairly quickly. Ewan had just moved from a second person perspective to living life through the first. He was no longer just a *he*. He was now an *I*.

Chapter Eleven

Building Bridges

The turmoil of the spring faded as the warmth of the summer sun burst forth from the clouds. With the sun also came a bittersweet moment. It was June, and it was almost Ewan's third birthday. So much had changed in one year, yet so much was still the same. Thomas trains still held sway in Ewan's heart despite interest in his sister's Gameboy, and I spent two days baking and decorating his second ornate train cake for the big day. It was a crucial moment in all our lives. Ewan was turning three, and a life beyond early intervention loomed before us. As dawn broke on his third birthday, our short time with early intervention ended. By sunset, we were on our own for the first time in a long time. We knew so much more about Ewan than we had at the beginning of our journey, yet we were far from knowing everything. So much of his life was still a mystery, so much just waiting to be discovered.

The first days without therapists in our living room felt awkward and lonely. With Ewan's summer birthday, we found ourselves leaving a schedule of therapy day in and day out at the house for what seemed like a chasm of oblivion. Now that early intervention was over, the endless stream of therapists traipsing in and out of my front door had come to an end. School wouldn't start until the end of August. The train to rehab had stopped in the middle of nowhere. We were too old for early intervention, and for the summer, too young for school. It was sobering to think that we would not have the same therapy for him over the summer and through the rest of life. That night I went into Ewan's room while he slept and simply stared at the son before me. What he had accomplished in such a short time was nothing shy of a miracle, but we weren't out of the woods yet. When early intervention walked into my home, I wanted the quick fix. I wanted a normal life for my son and my family. His future was no more assured that night than it was the morning he was evaluated. Tracing his cheek with my fingertip, the world seemed wide open. I sat on his bed in the dark waiting to understand where he would take this family next.

Never again would Ewan have such intense focus on his life by such a variety of disciplines. This was a fork in the road that, at the time, felt like both abandonment and freedom. While I prayed for Illinois to suddenly expand the age of early intervention services to four or five, I also felt a certain amount of relief. For a short moment, it felt like I could just be a mother and not a therapist. For a few breaths, the world could revolve around all of us and not just him. After a long glance at my sleeping son, I walked out of his room and into the future.

Life after early intervention moved at a leisurely pace. Late, lazy afternoons were spent walking down to the university campus where we watched the last rays of the sun set across the water. We were in no hurry to get anywhere that summer. Skye started ballet and found an outlet that was only for her. Three days a week, Skye built a world of her own in that second story studio. Anthony was at school or working most days and nights. With only three sessions of speech a week out at the local hospital with Stacey, therapy was not the focus of our life. We went to softball games and cookouts, spending a lot of time at the local park just breathing in the fresh air. Anthony had switched jobs so that he could go to school full-time in the fall and was home every evening now. He was now working in a group home facility for elderly special needs adults. For once, our routine looked much like anyone else's. That summer, we all sat down to dinners that Anthony cooked, and we tried to enjoy them as a family.

Now that the family dinner had returned to our home, we noticed Ewan didn't want any part of it. While he was talking more and more, he was eating less and less. The frustration from language was merely transferred to the table and untouched plates. It was overwhelming to see one piece fall into place only to watch the next dissolve in front of my eyes. We tried a few strategies to encourage Ewan to eat, but we were at a complete loss most of the time. Ewan had terrible rashes and gastrointestinal issues at the time, and we ended up consulting our pediatrician, who did a round of tests. After a preliminary result of Congenital Sucrose Isomaltose Deficiency, a rare malabsorption syndrome affecting a person's ability to digest sugar, we wondered just exactly what we were dealing with. We were given a pamphlet to a feeding clinic and wondered if it was a route we needed to explore. Feeding clinics and teams focus on helping children eat through a variety of treatment methods. A feeding clinic definitely meant more therapy. After so much intensity, Anthony and I wanted a break, but we also wanted our son to eat and sought a balance we could handle at the time. Stacey had started with some basics, but I just didn't 'get' it at the time and tried to focus on what I did understand, the device. I pushed language and communication in every way possible because it was the one thing I knew how to implement.

Stacey had just come back from a conference about picky eaters and medical issues a few months ago from a feeding team, and she highly recommended we take Ewan to see them. She talked about a speech therapist who led the team and told us we should definitely go. After a few phone calls, Stacey and Ewan's pediatrician got Ewan on the waiting list, but while we were on standby she wanted us to start some activities on our own. Stacey explained a little bit about their program called Food Chaining (copyrighted) and told us how they took foods kids liked and used them to get kids to eat foods they didn't. And with that, I went home to throw a combination of foods on Ewan's plate and wait for a phone call.

In the meantime, we continued to explore the role of Talkbox in Ewan's life. This new normal wasn't like our life in early intervention. Early intervention had been a struggle not only for the amount and type of therapy we faced, but also because of the sheer amount of challenges and frustrations felt by us all. In those earliest of days, Ewan could not communicate, we did not understand, and we were both left confused and bewildered. I couldn't see where life was going in the beginning of early intervention, and I couldn't imagine how we were going to get from point A to point B. Most of the time it was too difficult to focus on the future, and instead we merely put one foot in front of the other and continued to push forward regardless of where we were going. But when the device came towards the end of early intervention, our lives headed down the path less traveled. There was something tangible about having the device in our life. This was something we could touch, understand, and use. It wasn't just a clinical term thrown about like joint attention or social reciprocity (back and forth interactions like conversations or even peek-a-boo). Talkbox became something we could do together. I spent hours programming it, and Ewan spent every waking minute going through page after page soaking in the words and phrases. We pushed the envelope in using that device, moreso than anyone thought we could. I spent hours programming photographs, phrases, and vocabulary that would help Ewan understand life in my world. If he showed even the slightest interest in something, that 'something' went into the device as we filled up page after page with new concepts and ideas for him.

Much of the time, we blazed a trail in how kids like Ewan were using a device and in what the device could actually do. I usually made a weekly call to technical assistance attempting a great many things that weren't in the instruction manual. Most of my trickier questions were answered with a confused reply, "Well, if you happen to figure out how to do that, call us back and tell us how you did it." I looked at every facet of life and wondered how I could connect Ewan to it through this new bridge. In those days, we spent our time building bridges between his mind and ours.

Ewan's first language was not English, not even that of syllables, words, and phrases, but rather of something much more elemental. He lives in a world that we often forget about in our hectic lives. A world where the sense of touch can say more than a thousand dictionaries ever will. He lives in a world where the sense of smell provokes stronger and more intense memories than any photograph. The fact that Ewan sees so much more than I and processes it in such a foreign way to me should never be a factor in determining what he can or cannot do, so to say that his world was a ghost of this one before the emergence of language in his life is to minimize the importance of how he thinks. The syllables, words, and sentences were merely the bridge to connect his way of thinking to mine. They became a way for me to see just how different life could be from a totally unique perspective, one that's pregnant with expectation and endless possibility unfolding right before our eyes. The device became an opportunity to share the world with Ewan in more ways than just vocabulary as the bridge brought a wider world into existence.

We brought meaning to each and every aspect of life in a way he could understand. Talkbox made everything significant and exciting; the world was truly just waiting to be discovered. From that moment on, his mind and body set a pace that was hard to keep up with. He was a pioneer pushing past the edge of possibility. After the device entered our lives, it opened Ewan's eyes to everything around him. He tuned in. And when he tuned in to something, I tuned in. I tuned in to every glance, movement, posture, and hint of interest in the least little thing. If he took an interest in it, so did I. What was important to him became significant to me. What became significant to me became a clinical tool for Stacey. She created therapy session after therapy session that revolved around his interests. He was transformed from the child who only obsessed about trains to the kind of child that found wonder at every little thing in this world. Everything was exciting, and his appetite for knowledge knew no bounds. Ewan moved from obsession to obsession in those days and continues to do so even now. In those early days, though, the obsessions became my friend and comrade in arms. Together the obsessions and I managed to capture Ewan's interest and kindle a passion in his heart and a thirst for knowledge. Without these obsessions, we would've been lost for so many years. No longer a hurdle to life, the obsessions became integral to how we understood and connected with Ewan. There is beauty and elegance in all things, if we but look for it. The obsessions were the kindling I needed to spark a fire in his heart and a passion for learning. Whether it is trains, games, or weather patterns, Ewan immerses himself in all aspects of his obsession as he lives, eats, and breathes it no matter what *it* is. He is truly a master of his craft, whatever the craft happens to be.

Of course, the communication gap was still very great in those early days. Ewan still used his Talkbox, and our world had to be broken down into a series of photographs and videos in order for him to understand the bigger picture. As his expressive language (what he could say) grew, people often forgot that receptive language (what he understood) was still very confusing for Ewan. The abstractness of the English language transformed into the concrete through sign language, pictures, and his device. It was only by using all these techniques that Ewan has learned language. Through our work with Stacey and our increased understanding of how Ewan perceived the world, we continued to make miraculous progress with Ewan. Stacey continued to push Ewan by scaffolding language skills in such a way that we all learned from each other. After those pivotal moments in early intervention, life was not a one-way street of knowledge passing from my brain to his. Rather, the exchange and flow of awareness went both ways as I learned how to help him by understanding the way he processed the world around him.

We also used the device to bring order to the chaos of everyday life. While our schedule was practically normal for summer, Ewan still craved a military precision style of schedule. For someone like me who grew up in a house of unpredictability, this new adherence to a visual schedule was frustrating. In early intervention, we were prisoners in our own home. Now that Ewan was older and was leaving the house, he did so only to the tune of a rigid schedule. If the schedule said you went to the bank first, you went to the bank first even if they didn't open for another 10 minutes and you could've squeezed the trip into the post office in beforehand. We lived only by the schedule, and if it wasn't on the schedule, we didn't do it.

The more we left the house, schedule in hand, the more Ewan started to hum. It was during that summer in 2005 that the humming reached its zenith. It was like living with a stalking beehive, just waiting to burst out in a vibrating purr at any moment. Ewan was in constant motion, humming a three note tune all the while. If we had a soundtrack to our summer that year, it was surely the closed lip song stuck on repeat. Large scale industrial generators were quieter than this boy. And if it wasn't the humming that just about drove us insane, then it was surely the volume of Ewan's voice. When he found that he could speak and repeat what his device said, he continued to go about life with the volume stuck on 11. At first, we thought he was merely excited to have found his voice. But as life moved forward that July, the excitement and intensity did not lessen an inch.

Towards the end of July, we celebrated Vaughn's first birthday at the local park. It had to have been the hottest July on record that summer. We were all melting in the extreme heat, and for this child's first birthday I watched his every move like a hawk. We waited for all the signs we saw at Ewan's first birthday party. Was he looking at us? Would he turn when we called his name? Everything seemed right on schedule except for a few nagging doubts. He wasn't speaking or saying any words yet other than da-da. Just shy of his first birthday, his use of language was worrisome enough to Anthony and I that we had Stacey and a physical therapist come out and evaluate Vaughn. Stacey came to address our speech concerns, and PT came to address our pediatrician's concerns about Vaughn's obvious bow-leggedness. Stacey eased our fears about language concerns, and sure enough, within a month Vaughn started talking and hasn't stopped since. PT was genuinely concerned about the degree of bow-leggedness and encouraged us to take him to a children's orthopedic clinic for a check-up. After a visit with an orthopedist, Anthony and I were told Vaughn's legs were deformed enough to need surgery in a few years, and we were sent out of the appointment with a script for special shoes and a Denis Browne bar. It wouldn't be until after a second opinion that we were told that the bow-legged issues would work themselves out later in life, and we could donate the shoes and the bar to the nearest orthopedic museum. In the next year we would continue to watch Vaughn and try to determine what was typical development, what was atypical, and what was just modeling after his big brother. Younger siblings of a child with autism are simply different, and distinguishing between typical and atypical is complicated. This child's developmental trajectory is mysteriously enigmatic, often puzzling even the most knowledgeable professionals.

The summer passed by too quickly, and a world more demanding than the one we had just left was beginning to open up. When the summer ended, so too did our therapy vacation. At the end of early intervention, life seemed an open road of possibility. We had the device, and we had been through months of therapy and evaluations. Now was supposed to be the time where life slowed down a little. Reality is never so easy, though, and it seemed that the world came at us from every possible direction all at the same time.

While Ewan was in therapy with Stacey three times a week during the summer, it was nothing compared to the schedule I was about to set. I thought I was captain of the train in those days, and I set an unheard of pace. Ewan's day was all about going, doing, and transitioning. When August came we were bombarded first with a feeding clinic appointment, then assaulted by a rapid succession of school meetings (Ewan, Skye, and Anthony all started classes the same week) and launched into Lab School shortly thereafter. Our summer of softball games and parks and lazy afternoon walks had come to an end.

Chapter Twelve

The Creole Incident

My mother, God bless her, is not a good cook. Some part of the DNA chain that understands recipe instructions is missing from her sequence. Her equally under- and over-cooked biscuits are legendary. One time, the microwave almost exploded from an over-cooked bag of microwavable popcorn, and we very nearly became the first family in North America to file a popcorn-related damage insurance claim. Given my rather interesting childhood forays into the world of food, one would assume that I have a very limited understanding of the sheer possibilities for the human palate. One would be right. I am, for the most part, exceedingly traditional and conservative in my scope of foods and cooking. Wine and fancier spices do not often grace the ingredient lists of my favorite recipes. I grew up with parents who believed in the healing powers of meat and potatoes—even if the meat was undercooked and the potatoes considerably over. So when I met my husband many years ago, I experienced somewhat of a culture clash in regards to dining out or eating in. This is a man who willingly tries something new at restaurants time and time again, even when confronted with a meal that clearly sucked. I am the complete opposite. I find something I like at a restaurant and will continue to eat that one thing 'til the end of time. I find comfort in the continuity and repetition; he enjoys the spicier side to the unpredictability and novelty. Believe it or not, but my husband and I got a divorce once partially over Chinese food. Well, that, a new patio set, and a host of other issues, but still, the Chinese Food Incident stands as a symbol of our contradictory personalities.

My husband says that we are both Foodaholics in that we love to eat more than we do just about anything else. We'd rather eat a great meal than we would vacation in the south of France. So what does it say about me that I'd rather eat one great taco than sail the Mediterranean? Apparently, a lot. I love food. Despite my most interesting childhood meals, I look forward to breakfast, lunch, and dinner pretty much every single day. The words "Time to eat!" elicit a most mouthwatering reaction from yours truly. I simply get giddy thinking of my favorite pizza joint.

On my own personal hierarchy of needs, food comes before all else. I was the one who slapped my husband over a taco salad. In my defense, I was exceedingly pregnant and willing to eat the wood paneling if necessary, but still, I slapped him over Mexican food. Unbelievably, he did not try to divorce me after the Taco Salad Incident and instead stocks up on shells every time our meal hails from south of the border.

It is to these two 'foodies' that a child is born. First, a girl is born. A beautiful, laid back and even-tempered baby girl. An infant who turned into a toddler who turned into a preschooler who turned into a young lady who prefers vegetables and fruits to cakes and candies—quite the rarity among today's youth. Second, a boy is born. A boy that in the earliest of moments seemed as different as night to day from his sister. An infant who turned into a toddler who turned into a preschooler who turned into a boy who looked at food as if it were some sort of alien space experiment gone awry. A boy who would literally run away from the table in fear and in tears. Third, yet another boy is born. A boy who looked to big brother for direction and guidance, and upon seeing his brother scream and vomit at the table, now approaches the dining experience as one generally does the latest Hollywood horror flick. Over the years our meals have consisted of tears, tears, and more tears. Our dishes have been met with more anxiety than one might find at a dental extraction. Our love of food and rapturous euphoria over the world's best lasagna is not shared by two out of three children. Where oh where did we go wrong?

It was late August when the day of the feeding appointment finally arrived. We were all getting ready for school to start, and we were preparing for one heck of a semester of school and therapy. The whole family was there that day and once again, Anthony, Skye, Ewan, Vaughn, and I found ourselves crammed into yet another doctor's office. Anthony and I had been looking forward to this feeding appointment because we were looking for a way out of the rut we were in. After weeks of unsuccessfully putting together foods in a haphazard way, we were ready to hear something miraculous. We were tired of serving up plates of food, only to have each and every one of them rejected by our son. We walked into that clinic with very high hopes for what these people could do for Ewan and for all of us. This time around there was just as many licensed professionals in the room, and it was filled to the brim with khaki pants and big hair. Dr. Mark Fishbein, the GI doc, was there; Cheri Fraker, a speech therapist with a huge amount of red hair, sat next to him; Cheryl

Swenny, a quiet, tiny psychologist, huddled in the back; Sibyl Cox, a fiery registered dietician, was on Dr. Fishbein's other side; and finally, Chris Mogren, a muscular male nurse practitioner, tried to wrangle Ewan onto the top of the exam table. I believe there was also a reporter somehow crammed into the corner with the psychologist, and she just so happened to be doing a story on this feeding team. This 10x10 room had eight adults and three children breathing the same air and staring at each other like it was the O.K. Corral. I felt a little like the proverbial goldfish in the fishbowl. Everyone staring and judging, judging and staring—they wondered about my mental stability, and I wondered if these people were as good as they thought they were. But I knew we were here for a reason. We were here because of the sleepless nights I had spent asking myself, "What am I going to feed this child tomorrow?" So many days I had aimlessly wondered the grocery store overwhelmed by the sheer amount of foods close enough to touch but completely out of reach. All the years of vomit, reflux, gagging and tears, both his and mine, had brought us to this point. We were here because of our journey through life with a boy we rarely understood. I found myself in the middle of a three ring circus. I wanted to know that we didn't have to do this alone, and I wanted to know there was hope, even when the plate is full and the child still starves.

They asked what had brought us to the clinic that day. I took a deep breath, down to my toes, and told a story that started with the day Ewan was born…

His very first experience with nourishment began within seconds of his birth as I tried to nurse him. Those first moments were the proudest for this mother as I watched my son latch on and let his instincts take over. Nursing my veggie hippy daughter had not always been easy in the beginning. There's nothing like sore nipples to deter a new mother from enjoying the bond of breastfeeding, so it was with infinite joy that I easily and successfully nursed this boy to robust health right from the start. Ewan approached breastfeeding like he did breathing. It was a life-line he utilized for far more than just nourishment. Every ounce of worry and discomfort in his young life was put at ease through the act of nursing. And nurse I did. For such an easily disturbed infant, I nursed practically round the clock. Every sound, every light, and every touch would send this boy into a startled and agitated state that only breastfeeding could alleviate. The more he nursed, the more milk I produced until I was the envy among every dairy cow in the state of Wisconsin. I had more milk than Prairie Farms. The more he nursed, the bigger this boy became until he began to resemble the genetic offspring of the Michelin Man.

But all was not well with my ferocious young eater as the more he nursed, the more he also threw up. And for the boy who nursed round the clock, you can imagine just how much vomitus this could be. For all intents and purposes he looked the picture of health—rolls of fat and rosy red cheeks only convinced me of the superiority of my inherent milk production skills as I downplayed the importance of my reflux stained carpets. Despite my pediatrician's urging for a closer look at this vicious cycle of gastrointestinal need and rejection, I believed that all was well for my growing boy's GI system. I finally succumbed to the push for reflux medications after a particularly heinous upchuck that demolished half the pediatrician's office. Yet when the medication failed to prevent the now infamous reverse peristalsis abilities of this young lad, I decided that enough was enough and declined calls from my pediatrician to try different medications and a scope of his GI system. And I kick myself for this ridiculous lapse in judgment every single day of my life.

As my breasts maintained their status as #1 choice of infant soothers, my sanity was reaching its limit. Ewan nursed around the clock in those infant insomniac days. By the time he was six months of age, I felt like a conscripted participant in a real-life ongoing Rorschach test. I was starting to wonder if a new reality television series was secretly taping me as I moved through life much like a mindless zombie last seen in *The Night of the Living Dead*. As Ewan continued to move through life with eyes wide open, he continued to take in every part of his surroundings as if the volume was stuck on 11. Everything startled him and so many mundane things fascinated him, yet the only thing that seemed to calm him was nursing. But even that was not quite so easy. It was never a seamless and easy system of nourishment for him, and it was never a moment of peace and rest for me. Breastfeeding Ewan was much like nursing an Olympic gymnast. As much as he craved the milk, he pushed away from the intimate human contact found only in breastfeeding. Skin to skin contact, flushed with the warmth of human touch, practically repulsed Ewan. He stiffened in my arms and rejected this motherly touch. He dived in for the nourishment and comfort of the milk only to gasp and pull away as if starved of oxygen. Often he arched so severely that he would almost throw himself out of my arms. It was not exactly the most relaxing of moments between mother and infant. I remember the envy I had for the mothers and their little papoose contraptions that allowed for easy and discrete nursing in public. There wasn't a sling on the market that could hold this infant in place during a nursing session. Had I nursed in public with that boy, I likely would've ended up on the evening news for lewd and disorderly conduct. When I did end up resorting to breastfeeding in public, I generally relied on a blanket the size of a small house to cover us both.

Yet I still didn't see what I would later recognize as one giant red flag waving in the wind.

Nope, we blindly pushed on through these dark and sleepless days. I posted little notes like "This too shall pass" all across my home. My husband would open a random drawer or door and find this innocuous little phrase on some random white piece of paper. It was by this one phrase that I made it through this phase of Ewan's life without a fashionable yet reversible little white jacket.

Then came what I thought would be my saving grace, the introduction of cereal. Oh how I awaited the fateful day when I could shove some infant cereal product into this boy's greedy little tummy. I believed every single wives' tale on the street about the miraculous powers of cereal. I believed that with one little spoonful of rice cereal I would blissfully be sleeping through the night. How pitifully naïve I was. I did everything they tell you not to do. I cut holes in nipples, I tried feeding the cereal through bottles, I tried putting it on spoons, I tried just about every known way to ingest cereal orally only to find this little guy wanted absolutely nothing to do with it. My plan to fall asleep sometime before I was thirty fell apart right in front of me. I was devastated and exhausted and lost. But I clung to the one thing I did know how to do—nurse this baby—and nurse we did.

By the time Ewan was nine months of age, we were desperate to get him to experience the joy of eating, and we again tried infant cereals and infant foods. We found through sheer luck that this boy would tolerate infant rice and oatmeal cereals by adding cinnamon and nutmeg to the mix. Most other foods were met with a turned face and closed lips. He touched foods briefly but never had the desire to experiment with what we served him. He never reached out for what I ate, never really showed an interest in the world of food other than just a small handful of things. From the very beginning, his relationship with nutrition was twisted and distorted. This was a boy who wanted milk, milk, and more milk and could have happily lived life without anything else.

When Ewan started early intervention, one of the first goals we listed on our IFSP was for him to eat better. We wanted Ewan to love food as much as we did, and while we had a rather large laundry list of other things that needed our attention, we knew that without food he'd have no energy for speech therapy or anything else for that matter. Without nourishment, we'd be stuck circling the drain caught in a rut. The first OT to take on this task was, quite honestly, not one of my favorite therapists. She was odd, somewhat brusque, and truth be told, she had social issues of her own to deal with. As strange as she was, she agreed to help with some of the more difficult parts to life with food.

One of our greatest challenges at the time was going to the grocery store to actually get the food that I wanted him to eat. If I couldn't make it through a grocery store trip with this kiddo, I couldn't exactly produce anything for him to try at meals. One of our IFSP goals was to get out of the house and live life similar to any other family raising young children. So it was one day that Ewan's OT found herself helping us shop throughout the store and ended the trip at the café inside the local Wal-Mart. Grabbing what was available, she put some Cheetos in front of Ewan and a variety of dipping sauces, including hot mustard, honey, and barbecue sauce. It sounded and looked completely unappetizing to me, yet she was able to entice Ewan to try more things in this brief encounter than I had all year. A theme was starting to emerge for this toddler's palate preferences: flavor, flavor, and more flavor. Through experimenting and exploring over the next year, we were able to eventually wean Ewan off of breastfeeding and move toward table foods. By the age of two, he had a handful of foods that he would accept, including cinnamon waffles, Oreo cookies, potato chips (including barbecue), chicken nuggets, and about 60 ounces of milk a day. Clearly, he had not lost his need or love of milk products.

Early attempts at manipulating his diet included reducing the milk intake, to absolutely no avail, and introducing other kid-friendly foods like hot dogs, pizza and spaghetti. He responded to all of these things in much the same way one would to a ticking time bomb. It was as if he hated everything I loved about food and eating. I simply could not understand this part of him at all. I could 'get' the language, the sensory, the social, the behaviors, and all the other parts to autism but this. How could he forsake every ounce of comfort and joy the wide world of food held for him? How could he turn his back on this intrinsic and intuitive part of life? How could he run from everything that I held dear?

So much rejection in so short a time was just too much for me. He didn't like to be held, he didn't want to play with me, he didn't want to talk to me and now he didn't want to eat with me. It seemed as if I had given birth to someone else's child. And I fought back. I pushed myself into his comfort zone and expanded the touch he could tolerate. I pushed myself into his reverie and established a communications base in his alien world. I pushed my food agenda into his life, and by God, he was going to eat and enjoy what we ate even if I had to force it. And force him I did.

I drew a line in the sand and watched the Battle for Thermopylae unfold at my kitchen table. It wasn't for many months that I realized I was Leonidas, and Ewan had the iron will of Xerxes himself. I may have held my own for a short time, but in the end, he slaughtered my will and my resolve. The night I conceded defeat was the Night of the Shrimp Creole Incident; a night that will forever live in infamy in this family's memory.

That night, my husband had prepared a wonderful spread of spicy rice and shrimp and vegetables until my house smelled like the soul of New Orleans itself. My food loving daughter was seated at the table ready to spring on a bowl of creole like a predator of the African savannah. Even my little Vaughn, propped up in his high chair, giggled and popped rice in his mouth like it was candy. Ewan, on the other hand, looked as if the table were covered in a series of torture devices. I could see it, and I didn't care. I wanted him to eat more than anything else, so I stood my ground and forced him to eat. I held his hands down and shoved the spoon in his mouth, forcing it past his lips and teeth. The tears fell, his little body shook in desperate agony 'til he gagged and vomited it all back up. Finally, my husband put his hand on mine and whispered, "He can't do it. He just can't." Throwing the spoon across the table, I stepped back and looked at what I had just done to this child over a bowl of creole. In that moment I accepted all my failures, put my head in my hands and simply cried.

I knew without a doubt we couldn't do this on our own. We needed a life-line, and we needed it now more than ever.

I told the feeding team that we came to their office by way of three neurologists, one pediatric GI, three occupational therapists, four speech therapists, two pediatricians, and a partridge in a pear tree. They asked for a minute to confer with each other before they went further with their recommendations, and in one minute half that tiny room cleared out. I was hoping that surely, surely they had the answers, and that surely, surely I would walk out with a child that could do more than just drink milk. I came to this office proclaiming to the world, "I've been there, done that, now make my child eat."

The door opened and half the occupants filed back in. The first thing the GI doc said was that the malabsorption test result was likely an error. With such a rare syndrome and such borderline test results, it was an unlikely suspect in Ewan's feeding habits. They then pointed out that we hadn't been following the Food Chaining protocol, and that if we only did a portion of the program, it would never work. We had to make a choice of doing ALL of Food Chaining or none of it. The team discussed how skewed Ewan's diet was with so much milk in his life. With over 60 ounces of milk a day, they explained that there was little room left for food. Their simple suggestion of cut back the milk and use *all* of the Food Chaining principles, including food education, just didn't seem like a good enough answer to what we were facing. We had tried to take the milk away before, but it hadn't changed one thing. If there was a child who would simply starve himself rather than eat, it was Ewan. He just didn't care about food; he had no passion for anything on the table.

As we walked back to our car in the parking garage, I looked over at Anthony and said, "Well, what did you think of *that*?"

He shrugged his shoulders and said, "I guess I thought there would be more that they would do. It just doesn't sound like it's enough. I think the problem is so much more than just milk. What do you think?"

I thought for a minute. Stacey clearly thought these people practically walked on water. Surely her instincts couldn't be *that* wrong. I finally said, "I kind of agree. I'm disappointed that it just boils down to milk and similar foods. And what the Hell was all that talk of food education? I don't even know what that means."

Anthony shrugged his shoulders again and sighed, "Me either. Sounds a little hokey if you ask me." With no definite answers, we got in the car and drove back home.

We left the office that day with the same child we came in with, and we left this office confused and overwhelmed by what this team and by what their program, Food Chaining, had asked of us. We left this office convinced they were all a little nuts and this would never work, even if my name were Betty Crocker. We left that office thinking food education was the dumbest thing we'd ever heard of—I mean really, who needs to teach a kid about food?

As it turned out, I was the one who would be teaching Ewan about food, and he would be teaching me about living a life with food.

It wasn't until several weeks after I left the feeding clinic that Ewan happened to watch a show about agriculture. This show followed the farmer through the fields and the food to the store. It was this short, cute little program that would change the direction of Ewan's therapy and education. At the end of this tribute to the modern American apple farmer, Ewan turned to us and used his communication device to say, "I want to eat apples!" Later that day, I purchased stock in the Red Delicious futures, went to the store and stocked up on every kind of apple known to central Illinois. And I watched my son willingly eat something he willingly asked for. That epiphany was the beginning of Ewan's journey towards a life with food.

After that, I became a believer in what all those people had tried to show me a few weeks before. It was then that I bought into the program hook, line, and sinker. From that point on, I kept in constant contact with Cheri, the lead speech therapist. It was then that Cheri became my guide and my inspiration. She pushed me to be more creative and inspired by what she saw as an opportunity to learn from and to teach Ewan. This woman 'saw' so much more than just a kiddo with autism who chugged milk by the gallon. When Ewan watched that show about apples then had the resulting epiphany of actually wanting to EAT an apple, I knew Cheri's idea of food education had true merit, and we pushed this new concept into our life. Cheri believed that Ewan had no idea what was edible and what was not. She thought a thorough and systematic educational focus on the meaning and reason for food would help Ewan connect the dots between his plate and the act of eating. We had reached a moment where real progress started to happen. We started to believe in what they had tried to explain that fateful day in a tiny clinic room amidst a sea of tan pants and nametags bearing multi-syllable credentials. Over the years, Cheri and I have developed a friendship beyond the regular therapist / client relationship that often produces some of the most creative ideas for Ewan and a host of other children who benefit from her work. But it wasn't always so easy and care-free. I asked Cheri to write a synopsis of that fateful first day in clinic with us to give you the perspective from the other side of the exam table. Treating and understanding feeding aversions and picky eating can be tremendously complex. Such work is not always easy, and answers are not always readily available, no matter how desperate the situation. And we were certainly desperate that day. Desperate and tired. It seems that we, as parents, put so much hope into that one hour visit with specialists that anything short of the return of Jesus Christ makes it seem like a failure. And I was expecting a lot that day from a group of strangers who would ultimately change my life forever.

From Cheri:
Meeting Ewan
*That day in our pediatric GI/feeding team clinic started like any other, we were **busy**. We had five children to evaluate that morning. Dr. Mark Fishbein (GI doc), Sibyl Cox (dietician), Chris Mogren (nursing staff), Cheryl Swenny (psychology) and I walked into a treatment room that day and we met Ewan for the first time. Ewan was accompanied to clinic by his parents, Alicia and Anthony. We also had a visitor with us that day, Betsy Moore, a reporter from WICS News Channel 20 who was observing the team. She was writing a story about our team and, more specifically, on our therapy technique of Food Chaining.*

There were a lot of people in that little room. Alicia says that she recalls "lots of big hair (that would be me) and khaki pants." We introduced ourselves and told the family a bit about what would happen and about our approach to evaluation and treatment. In turn, they told us about Ewan's history and current treatment. When I mentioned Food Chaining programs Alicia cut me off and said, "Oh, we have tried that, it doesn't work." I could hear Betsy Moore taking notes behind me in the moment of silence after that. We all knew where we stood now, but still, I liked Alicia right away. Here in front of me was one smart, straight talking lady. I asked Alicia who was doing Food Chaining with them and how it was being done. They were not rating foods or teaching Ewan to eat. They were making the mistake that many, many people make, just focusing on eating, only combining foods. I knew there was a great deal to offer this family if they would only allow us to help them. But we needed to know and observe more. As Alicia and Anthony shared their story and their struggles, I looked into the eyes of one of the brightest little boys I have ever met. He was amazing. Yes, he had autism, but those eyes held such promise in so many ways. We started asking more specific questions and Alicia and Anthony started telling us Ewan's story starting in infancy and taking us to the present day.

Being in feeding clinic with our team, especially in the old days with Dr. Fishbein, was a fascinating process for me. Parents start talking and in my mind, it is like I am watching a painting being completed on a huge mural. I see the picture forming as they speak. I watch the child and fill in areas on that mural about risk factors, potential, learning style, strategies that might help and if there is any joy in eating each day. I watch their skills and I can see my mental image of their future swallow study in my mind. I hear things come up that I know my colleagues are processing and I can keep thinking and let them handle that part but I anticipate hearing what they will all say later. The interview process may shift suddenly if something very important is revealed. One team member may then ask many questions and we all know that discovery is at hand. I am always questioning myself to see if I am missing anything, so I am processing information on so many levels, at such a rapid pace, it is exhausting and exhilarating at the same time. The dots start to connect for each of us during the interview and observation process and I can feel the shift again as we all complete this part of the assessment. The best part is when we all get to go back in our meeting room and share our observations. It challenges me, stretches me and always reminds me of what I don't see easily. We talk and debate and share and design a treatment program and that moment really can mark the beginning of our story with a family. We just have to see if they will trust us or not.

We are all excited to help every family that comes to see us, but it may all go up in smoke. They may be relieved and trust us right away, they may cry or become angry and sometimes the door slams shut and I know they will not hear the message. We must rule out many things and assess certain areas in depth, all of which takes time and patience. Our Food Chaining programs must be implemented as a whole, each part is dependent on the other areas being addressed. Picking and choosing pieces will not result in progress. It is hard work and some families just can't face more on their "to do" list; they don't see the road ahead as a place where we can lift that burden. It is quite basic at first, we have to gather more information and sort out what is major and what is minor and get our ducks in a row. After that, we get to the fun part, the customizing and designing of a treatment program, but that only happens to families who stay with us, communicate with us and follow up.

As Alicia, Anthony, and Ewan talked with us that morning, I started designing a treatment program for Ewan. This one would take diagnostic therapy and we would need to closely follow up with Ewan as we started to implement this complex program. The team had evaluated the issues and come up with a comprehensive medical, nutritional, oral motor, sensory, learning program in one hour of contact time. I could see that Ewan was a child who had tremendous potential but I could also see the roadblocks in front of him. He had an angry belly with a hoarse vocal quality. He was loud, loud, loud and cleared his throat a lot that day. I suspected he had reflux up to the vocal cords. He was drinking a great deal of milk to put out that fire in his belly. We needed to change his diet but we had to know what was causing the fire. He needed to eat, but he simply didn't understand what fruits and vegetables were and had no strategies to unravel their mysteries. He needed to develop flexibility in his eating style; the foods he selected were uniform and simple textures. There were things to explore and learn in watching Ewan eat. I needed to know if he had too many sensations flooding his senses at the table. I needed to know if some foods frightened him or if certain textures could result in a painful feeling in his mouth. I needed to know if he smelled and sensed after-taste of foods for hours after eating. He needed to be taught about food and literally learn to eat it. Food could be a tremendous life/language teaching tool for Ewan. The family was putting tremendous effort and energy into this but it was not producing results and this was getting to be a burden. We sensed pain and discouragement that day, but we also knew that this was a family that had a great potential if we could only make them see the value of our program.

We went back into the room and we shared our recommendations with Alicia and Anthony. It was not an overwhelmingly enthusiastic response. I really did not know if they would allow us to help Ewan or not. After we finished talking to the family, I remember telling Betsy it would really be a shame if they didn't try Food Chaining the right way. I shared with her how I would treat him and told her that Ewan was a child who could really make progress but it was all in the local physician's, therapists' and parents' hands now. Dr. Fishbein shrugged his shoulders and patted me on the shoulder and said, "Time will tell, Ms. Fraker," and we went on to the next treatment room.

What we did not know that day was that this child would become a major part of all our lives and that we would carry him in our hearts. We did not know that his story would play out over the years as we helped Stacey Vitale, CCC/SLP, his local speech therapist, treat him for GERD, feeding aversion and later in the process uncover more health issues and growth challenges. Who knew that Alicia would become one of my dearest friends and that she and Stacey would become major contributors to our work in feeding therapy? We all fell in love with Ewan. He has taught us so much. That was a very important day. I can look back now and see how big of a day it was and appreciate and laugh about it now. It reminds me of one of my favorite quotes about a different kind of 'chain' from Great Expectations...

"That was a memorable day to me, for it made great changes in me. But, it is the same with any life. Imagine one selected day struck out of it, and think how different its course would have been. Pause you who read this, and think for a moment of the long chain of iron or gold, of thorns or flowers, that would never have bound you, but for the formation of the first link on one memorable day." - Charles Dickens.

Because of Ewan, a chain of gold and flowers certainly started to form that memorable day.

~Cheri Fraker

After leaving Cheri's office that day, we struggled with what she had asked of us. It seemed she asked too much of us as parents that were already overburdened with therapy, school and medical appointments. We came expecting a quick fix and left with a thick stack of papers and homework. I didn't want homework. I wanted something easy. And if there's anything I've learned about feeding aversions over the years, 'easy' is the one word that doesn't apply. There is nothing easy about a child that won't eat. There is nothing easy about crying yourself to sleep because you spend night after night thinking about what to feed this child at breakfast, lunch, and dinner the next day and the next and the next. There is nothing easy about losing your temper and forcing a child to eat, only to watch him vomit it back up.

No, 'easy' is not a word I would use to talk about feeding aversions.

If it hadn't been for that one video about apples, we might still be struggling to understand the world of the feeding aversive child. In one moment, Ewan's whole relationship with food changed. I no longer forced him to eat, but rather waited for Ewan to teach us about a life with food. From that moment on, he led and I followed. This has been happening a lot over the years since his third birthday. He pushes forward into unknown territory, and we are either left in the dust or we are scrambling to keep up. Somehow this boy always finds a way to do all the things we think he will never be able to.

Chapter Thirteen

The Education of Ewan

Just a few days after the feeding appointment, we looked toward our next big hurdle: school. Anthony was a full time student and working full time. From 6 a.m. until 8 p.m., he was usually *persona non grata*. Skye was now in fourth grade and in ballet two and sometimes three days a week after school. Vaughn was Vaughn, content to perch upon my hip from sun up to sun down. Our concerns about anything other than bow-leggedness had abated for the time being as he began an infant program at the Lab School just two days a week. And Ewan? Well, this boy was getting ready to start the autism equivalent to the Iron Man marathon.

After the device entered our lives, it opened Ewan's eyes to the full breadth of what the world could offer him. He was transformed from the child who only obsessed about trains to the kind of child that found wonder at every little thing in this world. Everything was exciting and his appetite for knowledge knew no bounds. At home and at Lab School, obsessions and curiosity were cultivated. At the developmental preschool, obsessions were starved and pushed aside while the formal art of reading, writing, and arithmetic reigned supreme. Like anything in the autism life, the journey from then to now was a bumpy road of understanding, acceptance, and trust.

Ewan was also getting ready to start more speech therapy sessions at the local university speech clinic. With few options for any other types of therapy, we simply doubled up on what we knew worked with Ewan. Two and three times a week I drove Ewan and Vaughn out for sessions with Stacey at the local hospital and the other two days a week we walked across campus to the university speech clinic. I knew very little about the university speech clinic other than it was a university and if anyone would know how to help Ewan, surely it was a group of Ph.D.'s sitting around a table. However, when it came down to it, the undergraduate and graduate students were the ones doing the one-on-one therapy with Ewan. For the most part, these were young, inexperienced, and sometimes naïve students walking into a room with a three year old boy using a communication device that cost more than their yearly tuition. We had expected them to know exactly what to do with the device, but they were just as confused as everyone else. Generally, sessions were dictated by the clipboard and monotony of choices and sequences and wh- questions. Creativity was hard to come by in those sessions as my son's life wasn't quite as important as that final, passing grade or that clinical teachable moment from Ph.D. to student. To be fair, they tried hard and most did the best they could with what little experience they had, and the set-up was more about teaching students to be future speech pathologists than it was about Ewan. My expectations, though, were high, and I quickly realized just how special Stacey was in the world of speech pathology.

When the new schedule started, I put a lot of faith into what the school system and university clinic could do for Ewan. These were supposed to be the big dogs, the big Kahunas of special needs, and if anyone could push him to the next level, surely it was them. With this transition to such highly specialized therapists and educators, Anthony and I were hoping to take a step back for once and just be normal parents. After so many years of being therapists to Ewan, we wanted nothing more than to just be mom and dad. We wanted the freedom to go to Skye's softball games and ballet recitals without having to worry about sensory issues and language demands. When Ewan was with us, I was not wholly focused on everyone in my family. I was generally in Terminator mode, looking for potential meltdown triggers and sensory issues, walking through life in a never ending reconnaissance mission. Multi-tasking was the theme of my life. Finding the peace to just sit back and enjoy the ride was outside my grasp, yet I was hopeful that the new school and clinic might give us the break we were looking for.

We were looking for normal, hoping to find it wherever we could. Normalcy meant not needing devices, special toys, or therapy gadgets with me every time we walked out the door. Normalcy meant no more clinics, specialists or therapists. We wanted to do what we wanted without having to explain anything other than, "Meet Ewan, he's three." What I didn't realize then was that we had just entered another round of the emotional spectrum parents of special needs children often feel. We were still in fix it mode, hopeful that the answers were just around the corner and some staff member had the magic wand to make it all better. The expectations we had of the staff at school and his new clinic were unfair and unrealistic, yet your heart's desires don't always make sense. As when we entered early intervention, we were hoping for yet another quick fix.

But early intervention and the school were two very different entities. While early intervention is focused on the needs of the child and the family, the school is focused on, well, the child and the school. All of a sudden, it felt as if the family had been left behind and the child had been adopted by some other entity. For all the time I spent planning and participating in therapy sessions, the school now asked me to step back and trust in their guidance and their work. It was a relief to have some time to myself, and I was ready to step back, yet it wasn't just my presence the school avoided. They neither needed nor wanted my *Ewan expertise*. I was ever so politely asked to step back and promptly shown the door. Where before I was a part of Ewan's progress and education, now I was asked to merely drop him off and go home.

Most of the staff there were not interested in exploring our understanding of Ewan, nor were they invested in this new technological bridge. Accepting this drastic change from early intervention to school would have been easier had the school been willing to accept Anthony and I as equal partners in the educational process. Yet, when the IEP checked off the autism category, they simply blindly moved forward with some predetermined plan irrespective of our opinions and beliefs. IEP meetings were not a meeting of the minds, but rather a checklist for what staff thought was appropriate. It was hard to completely let go of the reins and let someone else lead for awhile, especially when they showed little interest in the very things that had been successful in helping Ewan. It was even harder because I had no relationship with those doing the leading. With no relationship, there was no trust. In early intervention, the parents have so much control over what the goals are, who the therapists are, and how things will work. In the school setting, a parent is almost completely left out and unheard. For three years, the parent has been respected as an authority figure on the child, and at that magical 3rd birthday and a day, all of a sudden the parent has become an uneducated second fiddle. All of a sudden, the teachers know best. All of a sudden, the therapists at school know what's best. All of a sudden, the parents are left waiting on the sidewalk while the child passes hour after hour swept away in the maze of halls and classes.

There's a reason why the school / parent relationship is so difficult. There's a lot of trust that is exchanged the minute the child is dropped off outside the building, and trust is usually won, not merely handed over at the signing of an IEP. A child's teacher is assigned by someone else, a child's day is dictated by someone else, and what is taught and how it is presented is dictated by someone else. Even when the relationship between parent and school is going well, it is often an uneasy truce between the two. It's as if each party is waiting for the other shoe to drop. Either parents are being too demanding or schools aren't doing enough. The emotional process starts all over for a mother and father as they adjust to this new and alien world.

I say alien world because even though most of us living in the United States have gone to public school, special education is an entirely foreign entity. Most of us went to Kindergarten and waved goodbye to a tearful parent as we got on the bus to go to school. Many of us progressed from 1st grade through high school and went from class to class throughout the years without many problems beyond the occasional mean teacher. Yet special education isn't quite the same thing. It's an entirely different set of rules and an entirely different experience. How many parents had even heard of an IEP meeting before going to their child's first one? I know I had never even heard of IEPs and had a limited understanding of the maze of special education requirements until Ewan came into our lives.

An IEP meeting is a humbling experience, especially if it's just parents on one side and a slew of school officials on the other. I liken it to an ambush you might find in a Gary Cooper western. Anthony compares IEP meetings to court proceedings with parents as defendants and school officials as the prosecution, judge, and jury. We have two rules that we try to follow for IEP meetings, especially important ones. One: bring food. An experienced mother once told me that it's easier to catch flies with honey than vinegar, so why not bring sugar cookies? Two: at crucial meetings our side of the table is packed so that we have more people than they do or at the least, an equal amount. It sounds silly and juvenile, but we find comfort in numbers. I've had to go to IEP meetings alone, without my husband, and I would never recommend it to anyone. I'm a tough customer, and it still felt like the Spanish Inquisition had come to town. Plus, if my husband is able to go with me, it's always nice when he can squeeze my knee and silently tell me to back off and not go supernova at the table.

Needless to say, I was in for quite a shock the day that I took Ewan to his first day of developmental preschool through the school district. Up to that point, Ewan had only been attending the Lab School. This preschool was very open, very willing to listen and work through each child's needs, and the class was made up of mostly typically developing children. The setup was perfect for providing such detailed and attentive care. The Laboratory was a hands-on class for future child development / early childhood professionals with about 30 students each semester. Because of the sheer numbers of college students, each child could have very individualized care. The developmental preschool was different though. The class consisted only of children with special needs, and there were no typically developing peers in the classroom. There was one teacher, and a one-on-one aide or two and a total of eight children.

The first day I took Ewan I was expected to pretty much 'hand him over' at the door and be on my merry way. I hadn't really ever done that before. At Lab School, parents were welcome to come in and help their child transition to the classroom. They were also welcome to come in and use the observation booth's one way mirror to watch their children at any time without being seen or disrupting the class. The doors were always open, and the relationships between teacher and child always equal. I'm not sure if people ever sit and think about the enormity of literally letting go of your child's hand and placing it in someone else's. People may say I'm an overprotective parent or one of those annoying helicopter parents, but in reality, trusting another adult with the welfare and education of a three year old really is a big step. This was no five year old who could talk for himself and explain what happened. He also wasn't socially and emotionally ready for kindergarten. This was a partially verbal and echolalic three year old who was socially and emotionally delayed.

On the first day of school, Ewan took his device and walked down the hall to his classroom. Watching that little boy walk down that long hallway with his class was difficult for me. His oversized backpack made him look even smaller and younger than he was. But he made it through the day, and luckily so did mom and dad, albeit with a few more gray hairs than before.

The first week of this new preschool and speech clinic was a bit of a letdown for two parents seeking the unrealistic. It became clear very quickly that these professionals didn't have all the answers. They too, were struggling to understand Ewan just as much as Anthony and I. We were facing a group of people who had no history with Ewan, but we were also dealing with groups who had preconceived notions of what a child like Ewan should be doing. Everyone had their own opinion of what Ewan needed and how he was going to get from here to there. What they all agreed on, though, was that the device would only hold him back. The one thing that had sparked an explosion of development was simply tossed aside as they doused the fires of his passions. What each one of them failed to understand was that Ewan held the key to understanding his past, present, and future. By reaching out to the device, he was shouting to the rooftops what it was that he wanted and needed. Yet only a few of them truly listened to his cries for help.

What Ewan needed was someone who could wear many hats, someone not devoted to a single discipline. Ewan needed people who were willing to step outside of their diploma and embrace a wider world view than just pragmatics, due process, and operant conditioning. The people in his life then divided themselves into separate camps, all determined to change the tide in their favor. It was less about Ewan than it was a professional pissing contest about who knew best. If I felt pulled a million different ways, I can't imagine how confused Ewan felt. The synergy between Stacey, Ewan, and I was lost on some of these new professionals in his life.

Quickly though, we realized that the developmental preschool wasn't all that we thought it was going to be. I mistakenly assumed that since the teacher was a special education graduate, she automatically knew how to use devices like Ewan's and would be comfortable programming the device. However, the teacher found it difficult to make use of the device in the classroom and many times it sat unused on the shelf. This was the first high tech device she had ever seen. I never expected her to do all the programming for the device, I knew she simply didn't have the time. For a while, she would give me the themes they worked on in class, and I programmed pages and vocabulary words surrounding those themes. I found songs they were using in the class that week and uploaded them to the device. Yet all the programming in the world doesn't help if a device is left to collect dust on a shelf.

In the beginning, parents were to stand outside and wait for the class dismissals as the children walked to the buses or their parents, but this quickly turned into a daily exercise in futility. When the bell rang, hundreds of kindergarteners and preschoolers walked out the door to find 20 or so running buses, each engine revving and belching smoke. Ewan walked out every day to the sound of each engine idling in a discordant rhythm that echoed off the walls and trees. He was thrown into the bright sunshine and the gasoline-soaked air to search for a familiar face among the chaos. The herd of children and teachers emerging into the line of parents and cars piled up as far as the eye could see. Ewan's day ended with this chaotic and frantic note turning even good days into bad days. Every single day, he would walk out crying. Some days he would knock me over in his rush and relief to get out, and others he would be in full meltdown mode for hours after school. It was too much to get him to transition well given the chaotic environment. Eventually, we had it set up to where I could walk in and get Ewan a few minutes before dismissal, before the buses arrived, and before 200 screaming kindergarteners filled the hallways. This turned out to be a much better approach for Ewan, and it also gave me a little insight into what was happening in the classroom. Most days when I walked in to get him, the device was turned off or in a spot where Ewan couldn't reach it or even think about using it. The teacher would say he didn't really need it, but who's to say he didn't? Yet, I understood the reluctance to use such a device with a child displaying emerging language skills. I could also understand not always knowing how to incorporate such a device into the flow of the classroom environment. Certainly, it takes work, it takes time, and it takes a lot of ingenuity—but it can be done. It also takes a willingness to be open to incorporating new ideas and technology into the classroom and a good relationship between teacher and parent. A relationship I'm not sure the teacher and I always had.

    Because she hadn't been there throughout early intervention, she had no frame of reference with Ewan. She had no idea the role this device played in his life, and she had missed out on the miracle and leap of language Ewan had taken with Talkbox. She saw only the child in front of her and not the rich history of his past. All the trainings and IEP meetings in the world couldn't bring the breakthroughs of the past into the present. She saw the boy but not the journey.

Chapter Fourteen

This

A few months into the school year, I was already wondering if we had made the right choice for Ewan. Lab School was going well enough given all the demands Ewan had with scheduling therapy and preschools, but the developmental preschool was a whole different ball of wax. Lab School and the developmental preschool were two very different places with two very different philosophies. It was like spending the morning in Maria Montessori's living room and then traveling across time and country to spend the afternoon with the creators of No Child Left Behind.

Lab School is a very different type of preschool than what most parents and educators are used to today. I wish there were more preschools out there following this kind of model. In fact, I wish the educational system as a whole would embrace this kind of philosophy. It feels as if our children are being pushed to learn more material at a younger and younger age, so that reading can be mastered in kindergarten or 1st grade. Shifts in education have forced our youngest children towards worksheets and repetitive learning. The Laboratory experience is very much the opposite, though, and has greatly contributed to Ewan's passionate pursuit of knowledge. At Lab School, learning is not only fun, but children are often unaware that they are being exposed to the basics of science, math, and culture.

Basically, there are a few guiding principles. They do not use worksheets or premade materials of any kind. They use positive language supports (saying what you WANT the child to do rather than saying 'No, don't do that'). They encourage creativity in all things and in all ways. They foster independence among the children, and by that, I mean developmentally appropriate activities, such as allowing them to wash their own hands and pour their own drinks. They don't work on letters and numbers and writing as primary goals, but if a child is interested in such pursuits, they, of course, follow the child's lead and encourage it. Materials such as musical instruments, books, dress-up clothes, household items, and toys are available throughout the center. One of the best parts about the Lab School is its focus on concepts rather than worksheets.

Teachers demonstrate to the children what a concept such as carbonation is and what it looks like. They explain what absorption is and then let the children experiment. The experimentation part of Lab School fit perfectly into Ewan's way of thinking and understanding of the natural world. The focus on experimentation allowed Ewan to explore cause and effect on an elemental level, one that did not always need or require language beyond, "Wow! Do it again?" Generally, Ewan could get by with what little language he had and some choice echolalia during his time at Lab School. Through all the experiments and concepts, Ewan relied on his perception of the experience to understand it rather than using language.

I think for many children with autism, there aren't enough words in the English language to describe what he or she feels. It is an experience that requires all the senses, all the time. For the child who may see the world differently, sometimes language is wholly unnecessary for learning. I can describe water for someone who has never seen it, but to feel it is to understand it. I cannot wholly describe the slippery sensation of water on skin, it must be felt. In just an hour and 50 minutes, Ewan could sit back and simply give in to the cravings of his senses and experience all the elements of life. For once, in his therapy driven life, he could simply enjoy play and be exposed to a gaggle of other minds with no expectations that he *do* anything other than attend. In a world driven by goals and benchmarks, Lab School was a break from everything statistical. Lab School was more of a social and play experiment for Ewan than it was a rigorous academic preparatory program. Usually he cried when I made him leave rather than vice versa.

The developmental preschool was different, though. The sole purpose of this program was to prepare Ewan for kindergarten, from the academics to the rituals and routines of the public school system. This system was not one in which he could simply rely on his own voice and echolalia. While Stacey embraced the device, others turned away and clung to their traditions and clipboards. To succeed in all these therapy and academic programs, he would need access to his communication device—access that was not always provided. The problem we faced was not a lack of experts, just a lack of generalized knowledge across disciplines. Lab School was chock full of child development professionals, but they lacked the specialized knowledge to always understand Ewan. The developmental preschool was full of educational models and paradigms, yet they often forgot about the world of the typically developing child. The university speech clinic was full of research, theory and practice, but it was limited to knowledge found only on the speech language pathologist's clipboard. Stacey was often the only one to take a chance and step outside her comfort zone to see the bigger picture. While Stacey and I were willing to try something new, we were blindly groping at straws, accidentally stumbling into success.

The first full week of both preschools and two different therapy clinics left Ewan completely exhausted. That Friday, he came back from his school here, school there, therapy here, therapy there schedule and promptly fell asleep on his sister's bed. Afternoon naps were highly unusual for Ewan, and I wondered if he was coming down with some kind of virus. That day he had been quiet and sluggish, not really responding to school or therapy with any kind of excitement. That afternoon he took the longest nap he had ever taken and was just dead to the world. The background noise of the house and kitchen didn't even faze him. After three hours, I went in to check on him, calling his name and shaking his shoulder to get him ready for dinner. He finally woke up but was crying and irritable at the least little thing. He also couldn't speak. He couldn't pronunciate anything and he sounded drunk, slurring his words and using gibberish. His emotional rollercoaster continued to swing from one extreme to the other until we could get him to bed for the evening. Exhausted, he fell back asleep, still unable to speak the words that had been so clear the days and weeks before. The next morning he woke up less grouchy, but his speech was still unintelligible. If it hadn't been for the device, we would have had no idea what he wanted to say. With the use of his device, he told us, "Something hurts. It's my head." We gave him some Tylenol and about a half hour after breakfast, his speech returned as if someone had just flipped a switch. I watched him the rest of the weekend, worried the words would slip away again, but they didn't. He was back to his old self, exploring the device and his trains and games.

Not knowing what had happened, we ended up back at his neurologist's office looking for some explanations. We discussed the possibility of seizure activity, but it didn't fit the situation entirely. We were hesitant to put him on powerful seizure medications when we weren't sure seizures were even the problem. With two normal EEGs and a normal MRI, we decided to observe him for a few more weeks to see if he improved or how often these spells occurred.

Between two preschools and two speech clinics, Ewan, Vaughn, and I were in constant motion transitioning from one activity to the next. Anthony and Skye, too, were busy with their own school programs and afterschool activities: Skye finally finding the one thing she could call her own, Anthony flitting from school to work like any other undergraduate—except he had three children and a wife at home. Life was so chaotic that year, we barely saw each other coming and going. Financially speaking, our world was on an even keel. We weren't wealthy by any stretch of the imagination, but our bills were paid and our bellies full. The money motive to moving back to our hometown made sense, but I still feared the ghosts and memories of that town. Every now and then, Anthony would stay out a little longer, a little later, and I was left to wonder if the addictions of the past were coming back to haunt us. When that old mistress came calling, I would slam the door in her face while Anthony and I went back to square one. I always asked him the same question, "Is this really what you want for your life?" Every argument the same, every path coming to the same crossroads time and time again. Every time he would promise it was the last and that the days of the past were firmly left in the past. Yet every late night spent with his friends left me questioning where the road would lead us, forward or backward.

Part of the problem was stress. While finances were much better, I was worn down from constantly having to defend Ewan's needs. Pushing the envelope was a wearisome process. Anthony was deep in school and work, and I was left dealing with all of Ewan's therapy and school issues. He went to the IEP meetings with me, but Anthony was more of a warm body on our side of the table than he was his son's advocate. Anthony trusted me to make the decisions about Ewan's life, and while I was prepared to be that advocate, the stress of dealing with closed mindsets was wearing on me. My husband hates meetings of any kind. He's an action kind of guy, and a meeting dedicated to talk, talk, talk is something he considers a colossal waste of time. In the beginning, it felt like he and the staff were at the meeting simply because they were required to be—staff because they were getting paid, and Anthony because he was simply Ewan's father. He went to the therapy sessions, at times, to give me a break. Where I would go in and actively participate in sessions, Anthony often chose to sit in the waiting room, enjoying a brief moment to himself. Where he saw his participation as a distraction to therapy, I saw myself as part of it. He went to most doctor appointments with me. Yet I was the one who spoke up, commenting on Ewan's behaviors and issues, as I was the more observant person. Anthony has often said he feels as if he's been given the supporting role in a major motion picture. Ewan and I always seem to take the leading roles in this dramatic film while he's off to the side providing the comic relief. From the very beginning, Anthony has believed it is his presence that matters more than anything he could ever say.

Emotions were overwhelming then, and we dealt with them in different ways. Despite Anthony's separation from Ewan's clinical and educational needs, he, too, was dealing with his own sadness. Working in a group home facility for elderly adults with special needs, Anthony had a unique view into the future. While he might not envision his son living in a group home into adulthood, he could see where both ends of the spectrum blended together. During the day, he spent his time with the severe and profoundly disabled. Through the evening, he watched his son mature and achieve goal after goal. In the dark of the midnight hour, he considered the complexities of the human brain. The profoundly affected brain and the highly functioning mind, sharing a host of similarities, both confused and amazed him. Those he cared for in the daylight and the son he cared for by twilight each sought the calming mechanism of movement and the musical intonation of humming. With the severe and profound he cared for, humming fulfilled many things: happiness, tactile needs, and even a form of conversation. These wordless tones were an expression of love, tranquility and language. Over and over, Anthony would find one of the group home individuals humming quietly to himself in relaxation, reaching a kind of meditation only Benedictine monks find through chanting. Be that as it may, the monk is identified as a servant of God and the profoundly disabled is condemned as self-stimulatory. Eventually, my musically-inclined husband looked past the behavior and decided to hum back in response, using the high notes in order to create a harmony between the two of them. The response from that individual was unequivocal joy. Joy at maybe being understood, joy at maybe the creation of music, or joy at maybe conversing with another human being without syntax or morphology. From that day forward, Anthony never doubted that these protoconversations had meaning and value to both he and that resident. Yet he never thought to try this at home with his own son. His son was starting to use words, and it was words that he fell back upon in the nighttime hours. Day after day, he watched someone else's adult son rock and hum his way through life. Day after day, he saw his boy grown into the man. Anthony understood why Ewan found humming so soothing because it resonated with his own musical mind. The experience of working in that group home changed Anthony in more ways than any book, lecture, or support group ever could. Anthony's understanding of his son and the larger forces at play was an internal epiphany, though, and did not translate into radical changes in how he participated in IEP meetings, doctor visits, or therapy. Rather than jumping feet first into the issues of disability, he turned to school and work and left the rest up to me.

With our schedules and stress with school and Ewan, we knew that our time to have more children had passed. We were ready to make a decision on this overdue issue. The events of the previous spring still weighed on our minds. Anthony was done with the diapers and midnight feedings, ready to move on to the next phase of life, yet I clung on to the idea of motherhood and continued to wrestle with idea of moving on. Anthony and I stayed up late one night talking about the future when he said, "Lisha, I'm ready for something else in life. I want to go on vacations, and focus on more than just babies. You're my wife—for once, I'd like to focus on *that*."

"I know. I think about it too," I said as my eyes were stinging, "but it's like something is constantly pulling me toward children. I can't explain it and I can't control it. Every time you bring this up, it feels like you're asking me to give up a part of myself. I've been given the gift of motherhood and now I'll be throwing it away."

"Lisha," Anthony said as he put my head on his shoulder, "maybe it's time for you to help *other* children and not just our own. At some point, this has to end. Think about Ewan, he needs so much of your attention, and what he doesn't get goes to Vaughn and then trickles down to Skye. Think about me, I need you too. You can't keep dividing yourself in two, you know."

In my heart, I knew what my brain wasn't ready to accept. It was time to move on and focus on the children that we had. Anthony and I made the decision more permanent as he signed up for a vasectomy. Never again would we hold another newborn of our own. The miscarriage we suffered the previous April settled over my head and my heart as I mourned the loss of pregnancy and motherhood. I turned to the children in front of me and poured everything I had into their lives. The hardest moments in my life would drive me towards the red brick house on the hill, and that fall, life was certainly difficult. In times like this, the car steered itself toward the north end of town seeking the one thing I couldn't have. Sitting in the driveway, I wondered how life might've turned out had my father lived and given me a shoulder to cry on. Late one night, staring at the red brick house on the hill, I said goodbye to the children I would never have.

I took all the pain and grief from a lost motherhood and poured it into Ewan's education and therapy. I was sick and tired of facing obstacle after obstacle in his life. All the time I spent dealing with roadblocks took me away from being with my family. It was time to push the envelope again, and no amount of misguided opinion was going to keep Ewan from reaching for the stars. While my husband didn't need the books, lectures, and support group meetings—I did. I continued to read every book and research article I could find on autism. I went to lectures and continued to grill every therapist I met on every single aspect of autism. I finally found my courage and walked into one of Anne's support group meetings. I needed help, and I needed it from those who were already living the autism life. It was my first step toward finding a larger family. These were people who understood my frustration and had spent hours agonizing over every goal and benchmark on an IEP. It was through that group of (mostly) women that I truly took the leap from parent to advocate. It was then I realized that if Ewan was going to succeed, all those helping him had to collectively believe that we were all heading down the right path. It would do him no good to have his educators and clinicians on one side of the line and his parents on the other. Ewan had chosen the means for his future. He had chosen the path and we could either walk with him or let him go it alone.

We offered to bring in educational representatives of the device manufacturer to do an in-service for staff on how to use and implement the device. Stacey demonstrated how successful therapy had become since she had begun to utilize the device in every session and offered to help them recreate such success in the classroom. While Ewan's language was progressing at a miraculous rate, it was still difficult to understand and elicit spontaneous language. The device not only expanded on the length of his replies and utterances, but it also helped him understand what was being taught to him. And what better place for such an educational tool to be used than in an academic pre-kindergarten program? What many people failed to understand in those days was how difficult language continued to be for Ewan. He struggled to maintain consistency with the world of words and sentences, and he continued to lose words, although it happened far less often than it had during early intervention. The days when Ewan would wake up and 'forget' the word for common place items continued to happen. He would resort to saying 'this' over and over until I would redirect him to his device or pictures or ask him to sign what it was he wanted. By allowing Ewan unfettered access to his device, he was able to maintain a hold on the vocabulary he had already learned and avoid those lapses in memory. Even on good days, Ewan struggled with word retrieval. His frustration rose as he searched and searched for the words that were just on the tip of his tongue.

By October, Ewan had another episode of forgetting the words of common, everyday objects like milk, juice, cookies, and train. All he could do was point and say, "This, this, this." We also noticed that every time he sat down for snack or dinner he would start to cough as he drank and ate. Still wondering if he were suffering from a cold or allergy, we tried over the counter medications, but nothing seemed to alleviate the word retrieval or coughing issues. Again, it was just a short period of time before he returned to his normal activities and language. With no notion of what was causing the problems, we were simply left to ride them out.

So many barriers still stood in Ewan's way to using and understanding language like other three year olds. Ewan's English as a second language approach has generally produced a lot of miscommunication between him and all the native speakers. There have been many conversations where crucial information is missing, in the wrong part of the sentence, or given without any sense of context at all. When he was younger, it was limited to a few words such as, "Green truck! Green truck!" What he failed to tell you in that sentence was that a green truck ran a red light and almost smashed into his mother's car on the way to the speech clinic. As he has gotten older and verbal speech has become his primary form of communication, communication exchanges and conversation have improved, but still maintain a level of oddity that often leaves the listener confused. Many times we are given just bits of the information we really need, and we are left to draw out more facts and details through questions and investigative work. Unfortunately, many children do not have the patience for this and would rather roll their eyes and walk away than work so hard at making communication work.

Despite Ewan's obvious success with the device, the school was very hesitant to use it. Every day when I picked Ewan up from school, the device had sometimes not even been turned on. The staff believed that Ewan could adequately say what he needed to during his school day even though his communication was limited to short replies to questions or on echolalia to fool them into believing he was communicating. When he was evaluated the previous spring, his speech was largely absent, and his intelligibility was very poor. For the most part, his speech was very clear at this point, and what he did say seemed more appropriate than it had in the past. Having said that, it would be a mistake to describe Ewan as an independent communicator who did not need the device anymore. His answers to questions like "What color is this?" or "What animal is that?" were one word answers. The discourse at the developmental preschool was limited to yes / no, right / wrong, and closed end questions. Yet longer and more meaningful communication was still just outside of his grasp. He didn't independently and spontaneously comment on his surroundings or about life outside of the here and now. The past and the future had no meaning for him yet. He might try and tell you something that had happened right before coming to school or clinic, but it was limited to just a word or two, leaving the listener to decipher the meaning. One day before Christmas he walked into school and said, "Ding! What's that? Ding! What's that?" The teacher playfully laughed and said, "Who's at the doorbell? Is that Ewan?" Yet what she didn't know, what she couldn't know, was that Ewan was trying to communicate a scene that had unfolded right before school that afternoon. At lunch time, we ran to the store to grab some school snacks when we came across the Salvation Army bell ringer. With each ding of the bell, Ewan gravitated closer and closer to the bell ringer. He looked up at me and said, "Ding! What's that?"

I replied, "Ewan, that's his job every holiday season. He takes money to help people who need it." I then gave Ewan a dollar and showed him where to donate his money.

The bell ringer gave him a sticker and said, "Thank you," to which Ewan signed back, "You're welcome." Going to school, he approached the teacher and tried to tell her what had happened, but so much was missing from the story that the story was lost.

That same week we happened to be running late to a session with Stacey because of a train issue along the way. Ewan was still very obsessed with trains, and as a particular brand of train car paraded past us again and again, Ewan said, "Meow. A cat. Meow. A cat." Turning in my seat looking this way and that way for a stray cat, I didn't understand where he had seen this mysterious feline.

Sensing my confusing, he finally he pointed to the train and said, "Meow. A cat." As I looked up, I saw the logo of a feline face fly past on the side of the train cars.

When we got to therapy, I said, "Ewan, tell Stacey what you saw today!"

He looked up at her and said enthusiastically, "A cat!"

She took him for his word and excitedly began to talk about cats and kittens. I put the device in front of him and he independently pushed the buttons, "I saw a train!" The whole conversation suddenly shifted, and I was able to interpret the rest of the story as Ewan started making train noises around the room. If it hadn't been for the device or my witness to the events, we would have missed a crucial opportunity to communicate. He didn't always mean what he said, and the words that came out of his mouth didn't always match the situation. Yet the teacher and the school still didn't see the need for his device. They were happy with the status quo of short answers, echolalia and missed opportunities. She continued to assume that his three word utterances and his responses based on two choices were age appropriate. One day we sat down to talk about his language issues and how he was using the device in class. She confided in me that it was her opinion that all the communication coming from the device was not spontaneous, and she didn't think it should be encouraged as a means to achieve spontaneous language. The teacher then told me such continued reliance on a device would only serve as a crutch for Ewan, holding him back from taking the next step. Despite seeing far more non-functional echolalia at school than we did at home, she remained convinced the device had no place in her classroom. At home, the device was always available to Ewan; thus, the echolalia that we did see was very functional as he repeated what the device said in first person fashion. Most days, Ewan left the school building in tears, repeating the same words over and over as the frustration spilled over his lips. One day, I figured out I could track how the device was used throughout the day. I was shocked to see that Ewan used the device an average of 19 times during the two and half hours of his developmental preschool and an average of 440 times in the four hours directly after school. In one 50 minute therapy session with Stacey alone, he used the device 82 times. With the help of the device, Ewan was able to construct seven word utterances with Stacey, far more than what the preschool had reported. The device provided a visual frame of reference and boundary for things to say about given topics and sequences of conversation. When given the device, he had access to the whole English language. Without it, he was left stumbling through the dark. Day after day, I would walk in to pick Ewan up from class, and each time my heart would sink when I saw the device turned off and sitting on a shelf. I would have been infinitely happier with a dead battery and smudge prints from overuse rather than the pristine, fully-charged device we went home with every afternoon. The teacher still didn't see the need for his device, though, falling back on the belief that what Ewan said was age appropriate given his disability. Yet every day that I took Ewan to Lab School, I watched and listened to the typically developing three year olds in his class. The conversations and thoughts flowing from these children were key to helping Ewan. I listened as elaborate stories from their weekend spilled forth from their lips, a torrential downpour of thoughts and comments. These three and four year olds at my feet were not just saying words and labels, they were *conversing*. A whole world of past, present, and future expressed in every thought. The expectation that his teacher had was to compare him to other children with language delays. With such limitations, how would Ewan ever continue the progress we had started in early intervention? If we wanted to give Ewan the stars, we had to reach far past the rooftops and limitations toward a life of infinite possibility.

  Part of the problem was fear. This was an $8,000 device that no one wanted to be responsible for if the screen ended up cracked from a vigorous smack by a three year old. No matter how many times I assured everyone that the D in DME stood for *durable* medical equipment, most of his staff was afraid to touch the device. If they wouldn't touch it, they would never learn to navigate through pages and folders. Each time I brought it up, they reiterated their fears that they would somehow erase the whole thing and crash the system. Despite our assurances and despite the numerous backups we had created, there was an overriding fear to use the device in the classroom. To be fair, Ewan was likely the first child so young to own a device of that magnitude in the entire half of Illinois. Most teachers and clinicians simply had no idea what to do with it, and when faced with such novel technology, most tended to fall back on the belief that this sort of thing would only hinder his linguistical progress. The day the teacher sat down and told me she thought the device was a crutch, keeping Ewan from communicating on his own, I knew it was time to show staff the future of assistive technology. Stacey and I spent much of the Christmas break poring over AAC research in an effort to prove that this device could and would serve a purpose in Ewan's life beyond that of a crutch. Totally immersed in all things AAC, Anthony and I decided to take Ewan back to Debbie, the evaluator who helped him get his device and hear it straight from the horse's mouth.

We had exchanged a few emails before popping up on her doorstep, but even then, I think she was highly surprised by the progress Ewan had made in such a short time. During the second evaluation, Ewan was verbal and engaging. He was able to ask and answer simple questions, but as the conversation grew more difficult and the language demands expanded, Ewan reverted back to echolalia, not always understanding the language or his role in the exchange. At the end of the evaluation, Debbie confirmed our thoughts and validated our beliefs: Ewan continued to need the device to reach his potential. Without it, he would flounder in the echolalia and word retrieval issues and fall into the pit of learned helplessness. Debbie reminded us that our expectations for Ewan should always be the next step beyond. Her parting words were, "When Ewan doesn't need the device, it will be apparent. He simply won't use it anymore."

When the semester ended and Christmas approached, Ewan had another episode of severe word retrieval issues and resorted to the word 'this' for everything. He definitely still needed this device in his life. As we opened our presents in the dark wee hours of the morning, Ewan simply said excitedly over and over, "This! This!" When he opened the present with his very own Gameboy, his tone switched to awe as he slowly uttered, "Thiiiis." It was like he held a precious stone in his hand. While he got trains for presents as well, we could tell by the twinkle in his eyes *this* had just replaced *that*. Trains were still very much a part of his life, but the rest of his time was now devoted to helping a smiling pink ball inhale and swallow his enemies. When he woke up the next day, he grabbed a picture of the Gameboy box, held it up and said, "This?" The *this* issue continued to last several days, so after the holiday, we ended back up in the neurologist's office. We discussed the possibility of migraines or something more complicated. Given Ewan's lack of ability to describe any other symptoms, we were left guessing at the true nature of the problem. Worried that we were dealing with an unusual type of seizure, his doc ordered a third, longer EEG. In an attempt to rule out such issues as Landau Kleffner's (a rare seizure disorder with regressive language problems) and other seizure activity, we headed off on an early morning trip to the hospital. Once again, Ewan was hooked up to wires and electrodes, although this time he was well-prepared for the venture with Social Stories ™ and his device. We had even practiced putting on Play Doh-like electrodes in our hair the day before. That morning I didn't need to hold him down for 45 minutes 'til he fell asleep. That morning, he helped the tech put each electrode on and fell asleep all on his own. The results came back a week later, a mysterious 'normal' result for the child with such obvious issues. When the neurologist recommended seizure medication despite the normal result, Anthony put his foot down and said no. For once, he interjected his thoughts into Ewan's care and stood his ground, refusing to back down. He was working in a group home facility and saw the effects of the same medications we were being asked to trial.

Quite passionately, Anthony said, "Look, I go to work every morning and I help with the med pass, using some of these very same drugs you're talking about putting my son on. I see the effects of the drugs and how residents are either too tired to do anything or how they now have permanent damage from the meds. Their tongues stuck lolling about; I don't want this for my son. Not unless we absolutely have to. He deserves a chance to do this on his own. If he gets worse, we'll walk down that road, but not yet. Not yet."

The doctor and I looked at each other, surprised by his vehemence. "Ok," I said, happy to see Anthony taking a stand, "We'll wait. Maybe this isn't what we think it is." The doctor agreed to wait and observe Ewan a little longer before doing anything. If the problems continued or increased, we would have to go the route of medication or risk harming Ewan in an entirely different way.

Due to our concerns with Ewan's word retrieval problems and the developmental preschool's continued refusal to incorporate the device into classroom time, Anthony and I eventually scheduled an IEP dedicated to all things AAC related. We scheduled an IEP meeting for January, hoping the spring semester would be the start of something great. All of the work we had done at the hospital and at home was about to clash with the school's idea of where and what Ewan should be doing.

I don't like IEP meetings. I never have. I'm a control freak, and the last thing this control freak wants to do is sit down at a table with seven other people to discuss what *they* want to do with my son. The IEP process and school / parent relationship is skewed and abnormal. It is an adversarial relationship no matter what the huggie feeling books may try and tell you. They have *their* agenda and philosophy to protect. The other side of the table scares me. It always has. It feels like a mob hit that's about to go down—everybody eyeballing each other, everyone with their poker faces on. The minute you walk in the room, it feels like you just walked into a court room and not a meeting room. The 'we can't do that' person sitting at the table, presiding over the proceedings like a judge. The 'your child really doesn't need that' person sitting at the table, acting as prosecution. The few supporters from either side of the table, hanging out with the rest of the jury. Mom and dad at the defense table, fighting for every freedom and accommodation.

Anthony and I walked into the meeting that day fighting for Ewan's right and need to use his device. Stacey and an outside school advocate joined us in our defense. In my arms was a detailed outline of the reams of research I carried in a big white binder. The eyes on the other side of the table widened as I plunked down that five pound binder reinforcing our theory that AAC supported Ewan in every possible way. We spent the next 45 minutes discussing the difference between a crutch and a support system as I paraded article after article in front of them, dispelling the myth that we should let Ewan sink or swim in the seas of syntax and morphology. A few times Anthony had to squeeze my knee to keep me from throwing my big white binder across the table, but at the end we came to an uneasy truce. They would attempt to incorporate the device into specific parts of his day and into his speech sessions after an in-service on how to use and program the device. Anthony and I simply had to trust that this meeting would lead us all down the right path.

Chapter Fifteen

A Recipe for Success

While we fought against closed mindsets and obstacles in the school and clinic environment, at home and with Stacey we were achieving phenomenal progress. Another 'light bulb' moment happened, and our reach for the stars left us somewhere in the upper atmosphere. Cheri's Food Chaining plan was taking us places school and clinic couldn't. A program that was designed to get children to eat was doing more for Ewan's education than the school system was.

Our 'light bulb' moment of discovery started with that farm to table video. I remember when Cheri talked to us about the importance of educating Ewan about food. That day in the clinic, I thought the red-head was nutso, and Anthony thought the whole process was hokey. I asked teachers, child development professionals, dieticians, doctors, and the random person at the grocery store what in the world food education was. I was met with blank stares and no answers at all about what to do or how to do it. As always, though, Ewan tends to provide the most answers right when we need them. The things that Ewan needed were to some degree without precedent, and there wasn't a book on the planet or a class in any university that was going to show us what to do.

I've often felt that autism creates a blizzard of individuality and I refer to it often as The Snowflake Disorder. In some ways this is more relevant to me than the idea of a spectrum. Each child is as unique and distinctive as the snowflakes that fall from the sky. There is a symmetry and purpose binding them together in a frozen state of precipitation, yet there is also exceptionality among the whiteout. Autism may produce the squall, yet the child finds sanctuary in the idiosyncratic nature of his own mind and heart. He may be autistic and he may see life through an autistic lens, but his perception is his own—characteristic of only *his* personality, experiences and convictions. I know a hundred children with autism and I can find a hundred more that love trains, but only Ewan has walked a mile in his own shoes. Only Ewan has lived *his* life. Ewan is Ewan—he is wholly and utterly unique despite the fact that he shares a syndrome with thousands of other people. If Ewan was to truly succeed in anything, then our approach to helping him must be as special as he is. If you are reading this and think you want to do exactly what we have done, I urge you to rethink the notion. Guiding the child with autism is less about replicating a cookie cutter approach and more about understanding what both nature and nurture have created in the child before you. It was always about following Ewan's lead and believing that he knew himself better than anyone. It was always about observing Ewan and interpreting his reactions. It was up to us to trust that he would gravitate to the things that could help him the most. Every idea, treatment plan, and tool on the market was tweaked until it shifted into something Ewan could truly call his own. There may have been a foundation in Food Chaining or in AAC, but the house that Ewan built was of his own design. By following his lead, we discovered so much about the way *his* brain worked and how *he* saw the world. I may have had a vision for Ewan, but it was his eyes that held the key to something greater.

Once we saw the potential for Cheri's notion of food education, we decided to really give the whole idea of Food Chaining a second shot. Before when Stacey mentioned combining foods and textures that Ewan liked, I experimented with Frankenstein-like food creations and really didn't get very far. What I didn't know the first time around was how much I didn't understand about the concept of Food Chaining, and when it didn't work, I threw the proverbial baby out with the bathwater. After meeting Cheri and hearing how much more Food Chaining was than just putting two similar types of foods together in sandwich style, I realized how much work the concept was going to take. So we started very slowly with very simple strategies. Our first focus was food education. After watching Ewan's excitement about that first apple video, I called around looking for more educational materials about food, farming, and food production. Most people thought this notion of food education for a preschooler who wouldn't eat stretched the limits of creativity a little too far. But I know what I saw, and I could practically feel the spark in Ewan's mind connecting the dots together. He needed to know why to eat what I put in front of him. He needed to know it was safe to eat and that the items on his plate were actually food. I can honestly say that in most instances, Ewan did not view the food on his plate as edible. He needed to understand everything about the food we wanted him to eat before he was even willing to try a taste of it. He needed to know *why* he should eat anything we put on his plate; eating was simply not instinctual for him then.

Ewan had this tremendous fear of food. I didn't know then where this irrational fear came from, but at the time he didn't look at the act of eating as a source of comfort. He found no joy whatsoever in food. Rather, eating was more of a chore for him, and often it went far beyond that as most meals would feel more like a torture session. Day in and day out, for every snack and meal, it felt like Ewan was being forced to eat. Almost every single person I met uttered that annoying little phrase, "He'll eat when he's hungry." Ewan might end up starving and thirsty and turn toward milk or his failsafe of waffles, but he never looked at food the same way other children did. He never ran toward the table in excitement. We spent hours and hours of our time teaching Ewan about living life with food. Much of the time, food was not even present in our therapy sessions as we devoted our efforts to explain the history and culture of food in our lives rather than just sit him down at the table and force him to eat. Does it sound ridiculous? It absolutely was. Yet in Ewan's world, force has never been the answer. He has always needed to see the big picture before he could wrap his head around it and assimilate our beliefs into his.

After we put in the time to explain what food is and why he had to eat it, we then began the journey through the entire program of Food Chaining. When Cheri explained what Food Chaining really meant, she emphasized the need to not only chain similar tastes, textures, and aftertastes (Flavor Mapping) but to also use dipping (Flavor Masking) as a way to bridge old foods to new foods. She also emphasized the importance of leaving his core diet alone (Transitional Foods). Rather than remove those waffles, cookies, and milk, we should leave those alone as we slowly branched out to others through flavor mapping, flavor masking, and food education to a variety of new foods. The more I learned about Food Chaining, the more complex it all became until I wasn't sure I could do any of it. When I sat and thought about adding this huge program into what we were already doing, my brain practically shut down with the idea of doing more therapy, especially one that seemed so time consuming. Yet when Ewan had the apple video epiphany, Anthony and I couldn't deny the value of this program and tried to get creative about how and when we were going to fit this all into our already busy day.

As we thought about all the different things we were working on with speech language sessions, augmentative communication strategies, and now preschool, it became very obvious that we didn't necessarily have to dedicate a whole block of time just to Food Chaining. Anthony was working and going to school full time, so he was gone more than he was home. With Anthony being the absent chef of the house, I was left trying to do it all at home, including handling all the meals. The focus of our attention was on how to incorporate Food Chaining into what therapy he was already doing. There simply weren't enough hours in the day to focus on each little problem in Ewan's life. It was time to bring it all together and consolidate as much as possible. Given that Ewan's language skills continued to grow and need guidance, we simply asked Stacey if she could combine our sessions on language and food and AAC all into one. It took a lot of creativity and multi-tasking on both our parts, but we finally manage to weave a quilt of connections for Ewan, connections that had meaning, perspective and purpose for him. We played up to his visual and technological strengths and made a bridge between his communication device and our version of food education. We integrated Food Chaining's rating scales for taste, texture, and aftertaste. We created pages on his Dynavox to sequence the way to try new foods that prompted Ewan to look, touch, taste, chew, and eat them. The vast amount of vocabulary on the device was integrated into the bigger picture of understanding how to speak about food, how to describe it, how to understand where it came from, and why he should eat it. Our goal was for Ewan to talk about food in more ways than just good and bad. We needed to know what it was about food that he did or didn't like, and we began a long journey down the road of descriptive language. Adjectives had overtaken the place of nouns in our life. Then the process of eating was broken down into the multitude of tiny steps that we, as adults, take for granted. Whole pages of his device were dedicated to the sequences he needed to see the bigger picture before him. He couldn't go from A to Z by me just shoving food in his mouth. When Stacey presented us with a clinical goal, our first question was always, "How can we make this meaningful for him?" From that point on, percentages of delay and success ceased to have any meaning in his life. We were able to twist clinical goals and needs and into something much more functional and fun for Ewan.

It was an exciting time for all of us, as every single one of us thought we were on the right path and had faith that this would change Ewan's life. Our first few steps down this new life of creativity and function were filled with hope and excitement. We stayed in constant contact with Cheri about what Ewan was willing to taste and how he rated these foods. This communication provided even more ideas as she brought her experience to the table about where to go next with these tastes. Stacey and I then took these ideas and put them into the bigger roadmap of helping Ewan learn more about life, not just food. Our goals evolved over those months to not just get Ewan to eat but to learn more about life and to *enjoy* that life, all so Ewan could begin to trust food and learn more about himself in the process.

The work we were doing at home, clinic and school finally coalesced into real change for Ewan and for my understanding of how his brain worked. Much like the device he carried, Ewan's brain separated life into categories and themes, chunking concepts together as he deciphered the whole. We began to take the obsessions Ewan had developed over the past year to meet goals with vocabulary, social skills, feeding needs, and sensory issues all while managing to make every single activity fun. I refused to force Ewan to sit at a table and go through a checklist on someone else's clipboard. At the university speech clinic, they did just that, and it was a frustrating experience to watch Ewan deal with the methodical monotony of clipboard central. To be fair, these are undergraduate and graduate students learning to be future speech pathologists. They are young and nervous and tethered to that clipboard like it's a personal flotation device. Ewan had been working with some of the most creative, seasoned therapists the world had to offer, and it is infinitely unfair to compare apples to oranges. But if two days a week Ewan was going to be tied to a desk with an undergrad, then every other therapy and educational opportunity had to be twice as creative.

One particularly rough day at the other clinic sparked a conversation between Stacey and I about the need to move away from the table and towards something greater. The student therapists had spent session after session bringing every speech therapy catalog to life—as if the clinic room was sponsored by the Patron Saint of Therapy Tools. There they used picture cards and traditional kid board games to help Ewan understand sequencing, turn-taking, and the valuable skill of losing gracefully. The problem with all this being that Ewan was not a cards and board game kind of kid. Slouching into a chair in Stacey's office, I sighed and said, "Stacey, I've just about had it with board games and tables and clipboards. The next clipboard I see is getting chucked out the window and lit on fire. I'm done with this boy sitting at a table for 50 minutes as we check goals off a list."

In her perky and optimistic way, Stacey replied, "Ok, ok, we can start changing things around here, but you have to remember, the clinicians working with Ewan at the other clinic are *students*. They are nervous and terrified and there's a reason why that clipboard is so important. It helps them stay on track and handle goals through the session. I was just like them in college. My Lord, I can't even tell you how nervous I was the first time I walked into a session with a child."

Snorting, I couldn't imagine Stacey awkward and uncomfortable in the clinic room. Exasperated, I said, "Alright, I can accept that this is a learning experience for them, but it still doesn't mean Ewan has to sit at a table and play ho-ho dilly-o twice a week. Does he *look* like a ho-ho dilly-o kind of kid to you?" Turning to Ewan, we both watched as his eyes darted back and forth around his handheld video game, fingers punching A and B in quick succession while he and a little pink puffball dominated a pixilated landscape.

Smiling, Stacey replied, "No, he doesn't. Ok, so no board games."
"And no flashcards," I interjected.
"And no flashcards," she agreed. "What does that leave us with then?"

"All the things this kid loves. All the things that kids like him do when they aren't in therapy all day. This kid has seen more table action than a three and a half year old ever should. From now on, you are banned from using the table for more than five minutes. The table is merely a flat surface to put food items on. From now on, there is no table, Stacey."

With a slight twinge of fear in her eye, she said, "No table?"
"Nope. No table."

Stacey pursed her lips and thought for a second, "What do you suggest then?"

Grinning from ear to ear, I replied, "Bees. Ewan likes bees right now. Let's do something with bugs and bees and it cannot include a table and chairs. He also likes *Codename: Kids Next Door*."

Frowning in concentration for a few minutes Stacey was quietly thinking it through when suddenly her face lit up, "Oh! Oh! We could have a bug hunt in the hospital garden, and then I could set up a scavenger hunt with fake bees around the speech department. Oh! Let's also act out an episode of *Codename: Kids Next Door* and let Ewan solve a mystery and maybe even play some games on the computer!"

Knowing that I had sufficiently tapped into Stacey's creative center, I was about to reply when Ewan suddenly said, "Bees?" He had looked up, distracted from the video game by the mention of another one of his obsessions. We all laughed then, seeing how important it was to focus on subjects and ideas that Ewan had a passion for. The 'No Table' rule started that day and changed every aspect of Ewan's time in therapy. Later, we would find ourselves using the table again but first came the months of creativity. Our bug and bee theme took Ewan from bug hunts to bug books to silly made up bug songs. In the middle of our bee theme, Stacey brought out a box of Honeycombs and a bowl of honey as we tied the element of food into the grand scheme of things.

From apples and pumpkins to harvests and history to geography and social rituals, we managed to incorporate his obsessions with our life goals. Therapy had stopped being just a list of complex clinical goals of sequencing, pragmatics, pronoun reversal, and expanded mean length utterances. Along the way, therapy was transformed into a learning experience complete with functional life skills. Therapy sessions made the obsession *du jour* our focus and strength rather than something we fought against. Stacey and I followed his obsessions as they bounced around month to month. Freed from the restraints of school-based curriculums and standards, we were able to pursue the teachable moment in an original and imaginative way. Ewan had led us down the road to success and it was only through our willingness to trust in his approach that he flourished and thrived. Our recipe for success was one part obsession, one part education, and two parts fun.

And progress began to happen in the smallest of steps. If you are the parent of a child that doesn't eat, even the smallest of steps can seem like the largest of leaps. What one family barely noticed, we celebrated with enthusiasm. We seized upon the concept of food education like it was air and applied our recipe to every part of life. Ewan needed the world broken down and categorized, clustered together in a coherent message, and he needed some measure of control in how the message was delivered. If we had ignored Ewan's strengths and abilities and stuck to the clipboard, we would have lost him in those crucial years.

With our new, integrated approach, we noticed Ewan reaching out for foods that we had long forgotten about. His obsessions with volcanoes led to Hawaiian luaus with fruits and fruit juices. His obsessions with plants and farming led to a host of agricultural breakthroughs across the food pyramid. A brief obsession with baseball led to an increased understanding of sports and concession foods. While corn nuts weren't the most nutritional foods on the market, the sunflower seeds we chained from that were. We opened our eyes and saw so much more than just junk food and meaningless activities. We saw flavors and tastes that could be expanded into a larger repertoire of more sophisticated and healthier cuisine. Stacey and I discovered an approach to helping Ewan that relied on letting Ewan lead the sessions. Ewan began a journey towards a life with food, and we began to embrace each teachable moment as they came to us. The grocery store became our library where we went not to shop, but to explore and to learn. I began to fear the store less and less, and saw each new meal as an adventure, not a burden. Meals remained difficult, yet we were seeing Ewan find a real interest in his food. He wanted to know more about what it was and where it came from. That spring, we spent a great deal of time walking and talking. Our hometown is smack dab in the middle of the cornucopia of the Midwest, and come spring, the farmers are out in full force tilling the rich, black soil. As the farmers planted crops, so too did Ewan and I. We planted seeds that spring at home, and Stacey had Ewan growing a plant out at the hospital. Part of his clinical work was to care for and grow a plant, working through the sequences each visit. Food was more than just something that came out of a box. Food was real, fresh, and alive.

  That March, I was invited to bring in some treats to Ewan's developmental preschool for St. Patrick's Day. Even though it was St. Patrick's Day, the theme of the day was vegetable soup. The class had read a book about how to make it, and the activity was for them to make their own and then eat it as a snack. Now, I don't know too many three year olds who are dying to have vegetable soup, so the fact that they wanted to make it at all was surprising to me—especially since every veggie in the recipe came out of a can. We hadn't quite gotten to the 'can' part of food education. In Ewan's head, food was fresh from the field, and he was completely thrown off by the goo that came out of that can. It smelled and looked very different from what he had seen in the supermarket produce section. But I bit my tongue and watched as the children sat down for snack and the soup was served. The look of horror on Ewan's face as the soup was placed in front of him will forever remain etched into my brain. I'm sure my look of horror was equally unforgettable as the teacher tried to force Ewan to take a bite of it. She told the children, "In my classroom, everyone takes one bite of something new. So everyone needs to find one thing in the soup to take a bite of. There are tomatoes, corn, green beans, and peas in there." Unfortunately, we were not at the all-important part of Food Chaining that had prepared Ewan for canned tomatoes, and he was positively horrified at this unidentified floating object in his bowl. Sensing Ewan's hesitation, the teacher then proceeded to walk over to Ewan, wrap her arm around his back and attempt to shove a spoonful of soup in his mouth. To this day, I'll never understand what this was about. I've had many people try and get Ewan to eat or to force him to eat. Hell, I've been one of those people myself. I'll never understand why so many outsiders feel they have some special touch with this, holding some kind of messianic feeling about their feeding prowess. So many people have said to us, "One weekend with me and he'll eat whatever you put in front of him." If Anthony and I had a nickel for every time we heard, "When I was that age, we ate what was on our plate and we were grateful we had anything at all," we would be living easy in a condo by the beach. This teacher must have been the President and Treasurer of the I'll Get Him To Eat club because it was clear this soup was going down one way or another. Thankfully, I happened to be standing next to him and told her it was enough that he was merely at the table sitting in close proximity to such a pungent recipe. The Veggie Soup Incident signaled the end for that preschool—it just wasn't the right fit for Ewan. With just one spoonful, that experience could've set Ewan's progress back another year. Anthony and I decided that it wasn't right to push Ewan in so many directions, especially ones that didn't fit in with our worldview of how he should learn about life. Ewan continued on at Lab School and was able to make phenomenal progress with the just the one preschool rather than two.

Lab School turned out to be the right thing at the right time for Ewan. For the first time that school year, we all seemed to be working in concert together. Lab School provided the concept-based play and social exposure, while Stacey and I weaved together a holistic approach to understanding life and food through Food Chaining and teachable moments. Rather than focus on numbers, letters and academics, we provided Ewan with the foundations of intellectual curiosity, something so many children are missing these days. The device gave him the *whats* and we gave him the *why*.

Lab School was set up so that students could have hands-on practice making creative lesson plans from scratch. It is not a place where you will find worksheets, printables or Xerox copies. This preschool is about walking in with nothing and walking out with armloads of pinecone birdfeeders, original pieces of art, and the memories of almost two hours of creative play and exploration. It's a place where children still get dirty and go outside no matter what the weather. Children are exposed to the fundamental steps of the scientific method. They test hypothesis after hypothesis, watching the world play out in a series of experiments. Through observation and evaluation, children learn the boundaries of the natural world. Ewan had difficulty with the sheer amount of transition at Lab School, and he didn't always love circle time. Yet, looking at the awe etched onto his face during activity time revealed the depth of his interest and excitement in all things scientific. Through Lab School's focus on experiment and play, and our focus on expanding his knowledge base and communication skills, we all lit the fires of interest and obsession in Ewan's life. The future scientist was born.

Early intervention was about Ewan and his therapists, and Anthony and I were merely along for the ride. It was a time for them to teach me about Ewan—how to help him and how to cope with the everyday frustrations and difficulties. Life after early intervention became about Ewan and our family, and his therapists were the ones in the backseat. Each served their purpose, for without such intense services in the beginning, Ewan would never have been able to take the lead. He would still be circling around the train table lost in his solitude. Early intervention guided him into our arms and on his third birthday set us free. We took that freedom and ran with it, traveling through life with eyes wide open. The door in the darkness opened up to a world of possibility. Ewan's desire to learn, label, and investigate increased a thousand fold. His curiosity had been roused, and there was no going back now. What started out as therapy evolved into a lifestyle of passion and discovery.

We had to make a choice: either we continued down the road as therapists or transformed our role as Ewan's guides through life. Seeing the progress we had made with Food Chaining's education ingredient, we embraced a life of guidance and education. Therapy is focused on deficit and delay. Teaching is about sharing knowledge with others. We were tired of percentages, standard deviations, and evaluation scores. We wanted to embrace the intellectual curiosity that burned through Ewan's veins. It was then that Anthony and I stopped being therapists and started being teachers. Our role in Ewan's life had just taken on a new dimension.

Chapter Sixteen

A Quilt of Connections

Life felt entirely different that spring. Like a flower in spring, Ewan's development blossomed that year. Now that we had left the afternoon developmental preschool, our afternoons were free to take walks, explore concepts and Food Chaining, or simply enjoy the time doing nothing. Our new afternoon schedule allowed Ewan to just be a kid. For the child who had spent the better part of three years in intense therapy, it was a relief to see Ewan relax and be himself without lapsing into an obsessive solitude. While he still needed his quiet time, he now preferred to play in the living room or around us, rather than away from all the action.

April and May gave us the down time we needed, but they were also difficult months for Ewan as he had several days of reverting back to the 'this' issues. We had somewhat of a breakthrough, though, as Ewan tried to tell us what was going on internally. He pointed to his head and mouth and said, "Something hurts," then pointed to his eyes and cried, "Eyes are spinning." It was then he went over to his device and pushed a button that said, "This is my doctor, he helps me." Clearly Ewan was not well, but none of us knew exactly what was wrong. He was starting to choke on his drinks every now and then and rub his right eye over and over, complaining that it hurt. His doctor thought maybe he was dealing with a post-nasal drip and itchy eyes, so he put him on allergy medication, yet none of it made any difference. The doctor, who was supposed to help him, was just as stumped as we were.

As we tried to maintain a sense of routine and normalcy for Ewan on his bad days, we pushed forward and grew adventurous through the good ones. This new, more flexible schedule also gave me the time I needed to program more vocabulary and Social Stories ™ into Ewan's device. We were constantly finding new ways to connect with him through this visual medium. We signed up for Cosmeo and explored the internet looking for novel ideas to bring themes to therapy and home. The idea of thematic learning came out of his developmental preschool with their 'theme of the week' ideas; we simply explored that at home instead of at the public school. The concepts of the Lab School were brought in and used to expand on the themes. Stacey brought language, social, and food goals into that same theme, until we had covered that subject every which way possible. We took a 360 degree approach to the topic *du jour* and kindled that passion for learning.

I looked at life through his eyes and brought the sensory aspect into this holistic approach. As I tried to understand his perspective, I also wanted him to understand mine. It was time to weave together a larger quilt of connections, striking a balance between the two. This quilt had to piece together the warm, colorful patchwork of humanity and the cool, peaceful seclusion of the autism spectrum. His quilt would keep him warm in the winters of his solitude and cool him down in the intensity of his volcanic meltdowns. His experience and perception of everything suddenly mattered. Life was more than just a series of labels. Even the seasons of the year became so much more than just a definition. I uploaded sound effects to the device and brought the sounds of each season to a corresponding picture. The 'gush' of a shoe in the mud went into a visual scene for spring. The chirping of crickets on a hot summer night brought meaning to the months of July and August. The crackling of feet on a thousand dried leaves in fall made October so much more than just costumes and candy. The press of a boot on the snow created a winter with more than just Santa Claus and Christmas presents. Talkbox became an opportunity to share the world with Ewan in more ways than just vocabulary, as the bridge brought a wider world into existence.

Our focus on this new holistic approach to life and learning became a family affair. For once, we were not doing therapy. We were just living life in a purposeful way. We did things as a family more often and took walks around campus, the local parks, museums, planetariums, and bowling alleys because Ewan now found these things fun. He would continue to struggle with the sensory aspect of such ventures, but if we timed it right, provided a Social Story (TM) beforehand, and sometimes even practiced the event, Ewan was enormously successful.

Each month we perfected our approach, and before long we had a series of themes and activities that promoted our teachable moment philosophy. Like with the device, we had struck it big with this approach and were seeing tremendous gains across the board in Ewan's development. His understanding of everything around him multiplied a thousand fold, and his need to learn more intensified as well. He soaked in everything to do with the natural world; his obsessions with science began in those days and hasn't slowed since. It was fundamental to our thematic approach to consider Ewan's obsessions and let him lead the way. We began to work within and around the obsessions. We also looked back to our very first goals with early intervention and went back to the basics. We wanted Ewan to communicate, and we wanted to get out of the house. Only this time, I wanted to be out in the community away from school and clinic rooms. We wanted to do what other families did as much as possible, whenever we felt like it.

For Ewan's fourth birthday, we decided it was time to move on from the Thomas train cakes of the past. His life was about so much more than just trains now. His world expanded from track and train to include passions for video games, outer space, insects, volcanoes, and agriculture. His presents that year did include trains, but it also included more pink ball adventures for his Gameboy, binoculars, telescopes, footballs, t-balls and a chalkboard. His grandma Linda also got him his first tricycle. Just a few weeks beforehand, he had learned how to pedal his first tricycle around the playground at Lab School. Instead of participating in endless games of chase across the play yard, he was now riding around and around the circle drive with the other kids. The obsessions he had developed that past year allowed him to learn and grow. Before, his obsessions with the trains separated him from the chaos of people. Now his passions were forging unions and weaving his life into ours. The video games continued to intrude upon his free time, yet it was something he allowed Anthony, Skye, and I into. We were invited to play with him rather than pushed to the side. While the video games may not have been the best idea, it gave us another way to connect with Ewan and be a part of *his* life. When we left the house, he could, for a short time, walk away from the pixilated adventures to find interest in the real world, but this would get harder as he got older.

His passion for video games was used to our advantage as Stacey incorporated pink puffballs and computer games into sessions and clinical goals. Computer games led to educational games, and soon Ewan was learning so much more than just how to beat each level. Again, we had taken his interests and turned them into fun and functional goals. It was then that Anthony and I decided that we had sufficiently captured his attention for vocabulary through his communication device, but knowledge of all the things in this world was simply not enough. We wanted something much more substantial than just those labels. The next step was to take the obsessions and passions of his life and help him find his place in the greater community of childhood. Before he was a single mind, with one purpose and thought, divorced from mankind. Now, it was time for him to join the collective thoughts of humanity, married to the art of conversation.

Since language is about communicating with other people, I wanted to prepare Ewan for a life with other minds, thoughts and opinions. He needed to know how to stand up for himself, to speak his mind, and to resolve problems in his life all through words alone. If we wanted Ewan to truly have a life of his choosing, then he had to speak for himself, whether that was with his lips or his device. I could no longer translate for him, as the world was not waiting to hear my voice. I had to push him forward and stand back all at once. This process has been a burdensome task for Ewan, as many times he'd rather just be left alone with his obsessions. But time and time again, I've pushed him back to the world of 'others,' even knowing he might fail miserably as he reached out to these children and adults. As his mother and his guide, it has been the hardest task of all.

I often liken autism to an island. In the beginning, it's easy to want to isolate ourselves on Autism Island for our sanity and our happiness. It's ever so much easier to live with this child in a home where we can control every aspect of life. Going out into the unknown, being with other people, and doing something new is truly frightening to us. We are overwhelmed at the loss of control, and the 'what ifs' hit like a tsunami. Then we experience that light bulb moment of discovery, when the world and child suddenly make sense again. This child's brain stops being the enigmatic puzzle and the behaviors, quirks and obsessions piece together a coherent story of humanity. You meet other families and other children and adults with autism and the island dissolves into a nation. Yet those with autism long to find their citizenship in the wider world, and the obstacles they face in the process dominate the landscape. I wanted Ewan to be a part of more than just his family. I wanted him to find his place in the community. Yet the barriers to socialization loomed over us like Mt. Everest. Well if the world is our Mt. Everest, then consider me Ewan's personal Tenzig Norgay. We were finally embarking on a journey outside the safety of house and home towards a life filled with people and possibility, and we weren't coming back 'til we reached the summit.

The first place his therapists and teachers wanted to start was with eye contact. As simple as this sounded, I didn't want to start there. It seems easy enough to ask a person to look at you. Regardless, I had read far too many first-hand accounts of adults with autism describing how difficult eye contact is for them. I have pushed Ewan in a thousand different ways, but this was one thing I wanted him to give only when he felt ready for it. If the eyes are truly the windows to the soul, then he would bare that piece of himself at a time of his choosing. The pain of exposing the depths of his soul oftentimes proves too much, and I will not force this on him.

With that in mind we started small. First we added social groups at the speech clinic and slowly threw Ewan into the mix of children and conversation. Those first forays into the social world went well, yet these were small steps of parallel play, sharing, and turn-taking, things his peers had mastered much earlier. Many times, we enlisted the help of girls his age who were much more patient and sensitive to Ewan's differences. Therapy sessions turned into play dates as we sought to bring meaningful exchanges to Ewan and his peers.

In the summer of 2006, we spent much of our time exploring the outdoors, riding bikes, bowling, going to art classes, zoos, movie trips, festivals and parades, and even trying creative movement classes. Ewan loved to move, but, these classes were not easy, and he was not always successful. Anthony took Skye and Ewan bowling much of the time, and more often than not, Ewan could be found trying to run down the lane to check out the mechanics of the pin drop system. We all bought new bikes to compliment Ewan's new ability, yet Ewan and Vaughn were far more content to ride about town in the back of a bike trailer, as Anthony or I huffed and puffed our way through the streets. Art was not exactly Ewan's forté, and he retreated to a corner of the room where he could hide or spent much of his time pacing around the room. But he went, and we tried. When we failed, we learned from the experience so that we could try again.

We connected with my mother often that summer, visiting her oasis among the tress. Tramping through the woods, Ewan discovered his love of bugs that continues to this day. My mother came out of her shell and reached out to my family, all of my family, including Anthony. The wounds of the past were healing, and she was finding her way through grief with a friend from her past. Don, a former high school classmate, had connected with my mother at a reunion. Her loneliness and bitterness started to trickle away. With Don and my mother, we visited Indianapolis several times that summer, navigating the zoos and museums of the city.

The festivals and parades were difficult for Ewan as the sounds and smells and people were often overwhelming. Yet we continued to visit and explore the world of food by experiencing the joy of eating and celebrating everything from blueberries to popcorn. He started another session at the university speech clinic, and they too explored the world of food with him by focusing on the sequencing of cooking. It would be one of the most successful semesters he would have at that clinic. He didn't always eat what they made, but he was finding how much fun food could be when everyone stopped forcing him to take a bite.

It was also in June when I decided to create a website about Ewan's life. This book began all those years ago as I sat down and wrote out everything about Ewan's life and our philosophy about autism. The Autism Life was born that summer as we began to explore what it meant to be autistic. The day I created The Autism Life website, my two sets of grandparents sat down at their computers complete with a Stone Age dial up connection to read through what I had written initially about our life with Ewan. They read through every page and tried to bridge a gap in their limited understanding of what autism meant. It wasn't something they intuitively understood, but they made an effort to cross the bridge from their world to ours. My mother-in-law also orchestrated her first autism fundraiser, leaving Anthony and I to figure out how to help as many children and families as possible with $3,000. Agonizing over every penny, we did what we could with what we had. It was a start, though, and in one season, we made the leap to a larger autism community than what could be found in my living room. During that long hot summer, I took my first steps toward an advocate role for all children with autism, not just Ewan. Anthony's hope for me to find happiness helping more than just my own children was starting to take shape.

We grew as a family that summer and tried to connect with Anthony's mother through the autism fundraiser and with my mother through trips to the zoo and walks through her woods. It felt like we were finally moving past the earlier struggles to reach a better stage of our relationships. When it was just my mother and I, conversations and outings were pleasant and almost relaxed. That shade of sadness from my father's passing rarely settled over her face. In pictures and videos, she looked happy and at peace with her life. Maybe it was because she wasn't alone anymore, she had Don, even if it was a long distance relationship. When Don came to stay for an extended vacation over the 4th of July weekend, we decided it was a good time to connect with someone who might be my future step-father. That weekend, we spent one day at Indy exploring the zoo and museums yet again. The kids had a blast, and I was happy to see my mother in a better place with a companion to walk with her through the rest of her years. Still, it was hard to see this man I barely knew bounce Vaughn on his knees and carry Ewan on his shoulders. Don is a good man, but it physically hurt to know that it wasn't my father holding my sons in his arms. Skye has vague memories of her Grandpa Terrill, but my sons have nothing but a pile of photographs. Despite my sorrow, I am infinitely glad my children have someone who is willing to step into the void and be the grandpa they need.

The next day, Anthony and I were back home for the annual 4th of July parade hoping to participate in one of our hometown's more family-oriented activities. We were there for about 10 minutes when Ewan completely freaked out. I ended up taking him home while Anthony stayed behind with Skye and Vaughn. Ewan ran around the house shutting the lights off and closing the blinds, crying and pointing to his head. Wondering if he was exhausted or having a migraine, we simply just held onto each other in the dark 'til everyone else came home.

The next day Ewan's fear of the light had abated, and in the sweltering heat of a July day, Anthony decided to cool off with Skye and Ewan at the local pool. Once there, Ewan went into sensory overload, jumping up and down like a jack rabbit. As children laughingly splashed and tossed water balls back and forth, Ewan's communication skills degraded into a chaotic jumble of excitement. Ewan gravitated toward a group of older boys, and Anthony sat back to see how it would unfold. He watched as his son was shunned and ostracized for his differences by this group of boys. Not caring that he was younger, not caring that he was obviously different, that pack of boys told Ewan, "Go away stupid, leave us alone." Gathering his son into his arms, Anthony headed to the other end of the pool, hoping to find someone Ewan could play with. Stuck between his anger at such little bullies and his sadness for his son, Anthony struggled with being a father that day. Later that night, Anthony headed out on a bike ride around campus. Telling me it was just a quick ride through the university, I expected him back shortly. I knew he needed a break and time to process what had happened earlier. But when he didn't come home for several hours, I was frantically worried that he had been in an accident or worse. Calling his closest friend, Casey, I tried to track him down, but he told me Anthony hadn't been there. Looking out the window and questioning whether or not I should wake the kids, get in the car, and go look for him, Anthony leisurely rode up on his bike. I hysterically yelled down, "Where have you been? I've been worried sick about you!"

He calmly replied, "I was at Casey's, why?"

Suspicion immediately flooded my brain, "I just called him and he said he hadn't seen you. What the Hell is going on? Why are you lying to me?"

"Look, I know what you think, but seriously, I was just at Casey's house having a few drinks. That's all, Lisha, just a few drinks."

Looking for the least bit of red in his eyes or the smell of that little green plant, I asked, "Then why did Casey lie to me?"

"Lisha, who knows why Casey does what he does, but I'm telling you the God's honest truth here. I was just riding through town, saw his lights on and stopped to hang out for awhile. It's been a long day, and I just needed a break, that's all. I swear."

Still unsure if he was telling the truth or not, I stormed off to bed. Staring up at the red glow coming from my alarm clock, I wondered if the past was catching up with us. Had that pack of boys finally managed to beat Anthony back into his old addictions? Was the stress of school and work and family going to push him over the edge? Not knowing where our life might be headed, I tossed and turned all night long, hoping my husband was being honest with me and with himself. Raising Ewan wasn't easy, and if every disappointment and struggle would end in a few drinks for him, then it was going to be an alcohol-soaked life. Seeing his son fail at such a simple activity as playing at the pool was almost too much. The next morning he told me he spent the night looking through old photographs. He came across a photo of Ewan from that Halloween in Indiana. In one picture, Ewan looked straight at the camera with his costume on. There was a lost look in his eyes and a sense of confusion. In another picture, the confusion had given way to tears as his frustration reached the tipping point. Despite how hard we had worked to make him understand the holiday, it still seemed outside of his grasp. Feeling his son's struggles from the day and the photographs of the past, he broke down realizing how hard life was going to be for his son. I put my hand on his shoulder and said, "It won't always be this hard for him. It'll get better. I believe that Ewan can do anything if we but give him the right tools. I'll talk to Stacey about what we can do to help him."

Taking a deep breath, he replied, "I just hate seeing kids be mean to him. He's so damn sweet, those kids have no right being jerks to my son. If they would just give him a chance, they'd know how much fun he is."

I thought for a minute before saying, "But that's the problem, Anthony. If we don't help Ewan communicate through his device or his lips, these kids won't stick around to find out *who* he is. He'll say something that doesn't make sense and they'll run off, not caring about what he might do or might say. We have to get him in past the first few turns of conversation, we've got to find a way to hook those other kids in, rather than turn them away."

That day we decided it was time to push Ewan to the next level. There was so much more that Ewan needed to understand about life and the people in it. While Ewan was beginning to see the power of language and was going through most days labeling everything in sight, we knew there was much more at stake than just a series of definitions. It was a time to connect the dots for him and give him something beyond a series of categories on his Talkbox. Our greatest hope was to see him label, learn and *converse*. There was no point to all the experiments of life if he couldn't explain his research. The miracle of communication, in whatever form it may come in, is unbelievably complex. There is so much more to the field of linguistics than just learning how to label and categorize the world around us. Language is about communicating a thought or an idea *with someone else*. In the beginning, we wanted nothing more than to just hear Ewan speak. We prayed for just a few words from his lips. When he uttered those first words himself or through his device, we quickly realized we wanted something more than to just hear speech. We wanted to hear his innermost thoughts, opinions and beliefs. We wanted him to proclaim his passion to the world with emotion and thoughtfulness. To the everyday passerby, such feats may not seem significant, yet to the parent of a silent child, the weight of everything *not said* torments your every thought. A syllable here and a consonant there elicits a conviction that there is more to be heard and more to be shared. As much as I would like to say that language is not the end all be all of life, it is truly the one thing most parents want and need from their children. To many adults with autism, language is valued too highly by parents and neurotypicals. I can appreciate the sentiment, as there is so much more to life than just nouns, verbs, and adjectives. The person who does not speak may have much to say and may say it through many other means. Yet I cannot deny that most of my prayers have been to hear Ewan's voice or to see him eat. Watching his life unfold in a series of sentences and meals, we have borne witness to a powerful metamorphosis that has often left me, the writer, at a loss for words.

Nonetheless, words alone do not equal language. Language is far more complex and convoluted. There are hidden meanings, double meanings, little white lies, and a thousand reasons not to say what you want. Language is often about not speaking, even when you so desperately want to. Communicating is about feeling, emotion, and, at times, learning to control the passion. Language is about discourse, a flow of conversation back and forth between two minds. All very difficult circumstances for the child with autism.

For Ewan, the world of words has often been a minefield. He tends to talk around an issue as if language is a carousel of words and repetition. Conversations often have a twirling quality to them as his thoughts dance around the subject, pirouetting in and out of intelligibility. The listener struggles to connect A to B and unveil the meaning of his ramblings. The stutter he has developed over the years makes this process that much more painful. Feelings have frequently been hurt by his matter of fact approach to speech. There is no filter between brain and lips. If he thinks it, he almost always says it. Ewan always manages to say that 'one thing' that everyone else ignores like the 200 pound elephant in the room. He continues to flounder in an abstract world with his literal mind. All the core words still flutter about his mind like an elusive butterfly. And while Ewan has learned to speak, and speak quite well, the art of conversation continues to elude him.

At Lab School, where Ewan was surrounded by children, these exchanges were limited to chasing each other on the playground and playing with trains after circle time, two activities that did not always need words. Ewan excelled at those childhood games that focused on physical activity. He could run, jump, and climb with the best of them. When the running stopped and the conversations and the rules of etiquette started, Ewan would lose interest and wander off toward solitude.

At times, his intensity would intimidate other children. The child who screamed in frustration over the least little thing seemed a volatile concoction they regularly tiptoed around. Ewan is quick to tears when the world seems out of control, and in those early days he could be found crying over the least little thing. In spite of all that, his peers at Lab School turned a blind eye to his tearful misery and often attempted to comfort him themselves. When the world becomes too complex, Ewan dissolves into a puddle of tears. In many cases, this has kept Ewan from making friends as he is labeled 'that kid.' The children of Lab School, though, were often patient enough to wait out the tears and see another side of Ewan. The same cannot always be said of other children in his life. Some are understanding, and many, such the boys at the pool, are not.

While his high pitched shrieks unnerved his peers, it was his infectious smile and peals of laughter that always brought them back. I used to say that Ewan was like the character Norm from *Cheers*. He would often walk into preschool amid excited cries of, "Ewan's here! Ewan's here!" I might not have always seen Ewan sit and chatter endlessly with his friends, but they were always ready to run and giggle with him. Over the years there, he latched on to one of the girls in his classroom. She became his salvation, and he shadowed her every move. In almost every picture from his Lab School days, Ewan could be found firmly planted by her side. This is the same child I compared Ewan to when he was an infant. The daughter of my friend, she had known Ewan before they had even taken their first steps. She replaced me as his guide and would be there to mentor and calm him through his time at preschool. To this day, Ewan talks about this girl—not in an obsessive, weird way—but rather, as someone he trusted and loved. It was with her that Ewan felt comfortable enough in his own skin, to take the first successful steps toward a conversation.

As his vocabulary grew, so too did the turns in the conversation. What began with maybe one or two turns with answers to "What's your name?" or "How are you?" slowly turned into three or four turns. He didn't often initiate conversations with others unless requesting, or, in reality, demanding something. If there was one area Ewan excelled at, it was telling you what he wanted or what he didn't like. The other children at Lab School were surely aware of Ewan's likes and dislikes, as he tended to shout them from the rooftops. That boy has always been loud. Before he found his voice, his shouts and screams were deafening. After he found his voice, he continued on in that thunderous tone. He tended to talk to the other children like another adult, often using the very same phrases therapists and teachers would use with him. He was opinionated and bossy with no fear of pointing out other's mistakes. No one can say *no* like Ewan.

His need for continuity and a military precision of routine and order seemed to explode in his preschool years. The more we pushed him outside the safety of his comfort zones, the greater his need grew for schedules and patterns of predictability. We were left with approximately an hour and 50 minutes of socialization at Lab School. The minute his foot crossed the threshold of home, the winter of solitude settled over his shoulders, and he retreated back into serenity of stimming and obsessions. The stress of being with all the others of the world required an opposite yet equal reactionary need for solitude.

The harmony of life between what I wanted and what Ewan needed in those early years became much easier to achieve. He seemed able to handle the stress of socializing when limited to a mere hour and 50 minutes a day. The time at Lab School was the perfect balance of free play and structure, routine and flexibility, and individuality and collaboration. Lab School has been about creativity and fostering social emotional development in children. It has provided generations of children the foundation to living in a world of others, rather than an insistence on handwriting and reading. And if I had to do it all over again, I'd choose Lab School every single time. Ewan needed that time to develop coping skills of being with others all day long. Had we focused solely on those pre-academic skills and forsaken these crucial social emotional skills, I think the school years would have been even more difficult.

Lab School also provided Ewan with access to typically developing children that were his own age and adults. Thinking back, I believe that it was just the right mix of routine, rules, expression of creativity, and understanding of child development that Ewan really needed. He flourished there, although I know some of the college students didn't always feel as if everything was hunky dorey. I know there were difficult times at Lab School; it wasn't always easy for them. Ewan had a hard time with circle time, with all the children sitting together and being able to focus on the teachers. He also had a difficult time transitioning from free play to the more organized tasks of the day. Lab School had a lot of transitions during the hour and fifty minutes the children were there, and it really challenged Ewan. And when Ewan was thrust past his threshold, meltdowns were set in motion. Transitioning from one activity to another or one thought to another was, and is, extremely difficult for him, and staff really pushed the envelope in this part of his development. Lab School motivated him in many ways, but it also gave him an ability to practice social and language skills we had been working so hard on in therapy. Month after month Ewan began to defy all our expectations and speak more and more. While Lab School may not have known how to use the device any more than the public school, it was an environment that facilitated social exchanges that Ewan could handle independently.

  Ewan's ability to navigate the English language continued to grow that summer. The security of knowing his device was available at all times gave him the peace of mind to experiment and expand his linguistical abilities. Ewan's chalkboard birthday present got a lot of mileage that summer. Our little professor was already practicing his version of Dr. Henry Jones in the living room. Anthony and I positively cherish a short video clip we have of Ewan standing at his chalkboard, drawing wavy lines to represent his story. Line by line, Ewan explained to us why he had just smacked his brother. The emerging language coming out in front of that plastic chalkboard was a beautiful sight to behold, even if I didn't always understand it. He continued to substitute the wrong word, making conversations difficult, but oh, how he tried to tell us his thoughts. They may have been rambling and odd, but these were the thoughts running in his head, and we were finally seeing what had been hidden in his brain all these years. In explaining his smack down defense against his brother, he told us, "I was trying to look you," which really meant, 'I was trying to find you.' We continued to interpret what he was saying, and it was with great surprise that Ewan retold a story a few weeks later with perfect clarity. One night Anthony and I happened to be watching a 9/11 documentary while the boys played with their trains and toys, chasing each other around the room. A few days later the evening news came on, and the words New York and Twin Towers were spoken. Ewan popped up from his play, ran to his chalkboard and furiously began drawing his wavy lines of quasi sentences again. Pointing to the curvy streaks, he said, "Listen, this is the second tower. This is where the people were when the walls came down. There was an accident and people were hurt because of the walls. They were all yelling and crying and it came crashing down on them. That's the planes, where the planes crashed down." Anthony and I stared at each other completely shocked at what we had just witnessed. Goosebumps rose on my arms. We realized in that moment what our son was giving us. Ewan was giving us a glimpse at his thoughts. God only knows how many words he had just said in a row. The strange new world of terrorism that Ewan was born into had just become a moment he connected to through the world of words and sentences. Our quilt of connections just got a little bit bigger as life had come full circle in just a few years time.

Chapter Seventeen

The Invisible Wall

It was with that moment of explosive language that we entered the next school year. Thinking that it was time to expand his mind and his Talkbox, we went from a 20 and 30 button setup to one with 40 buttons. By expanding the vocabulary, exchanges like the 9/11 one continued to happen with more and more regularity. Ewan was finally opening up and letting us in to his world, his thoughts, and his mind. It was September, and everyone but me was in school. Anthony was still a full time student, Skye was now in fifth grade, and Ewan and Vaughn were now both at Lab School every afternoon. While they hit the books and the playground, I held it together at home thinking about my own future. Ewan was doing so well that I wondered what life might hold in the next year as Kindergarten approached. Would he be able to attend full time, allowing me to follow my own path, or would I still be attending to his needs and comforts arranging for therapy and doctor appointments? It had been a life of sacrifice up until then with me staying at home. Would I always sacrifice or would I have a chance to breathe and move forward from the stalemate I'd been in for so long?

Much like the rest of our spring and summer, Ewan continued to have therapy at both the hospital and the university clinics most mornings while every afternoon was spent in Lab School and on walks or bike rides. After school started, we planned a short getaway over to Indiana for a weekend with my mom and sister at Irish Fest. On a warm and dusty September afternoon, we parked the car in downtown Indianapolis and followed the sounds of the fiddle, the pipes, and the harps. Before Ewan was born, we often went to Scottish and Irish fests as a way to connect Skye to a larger part of her history and family. My dad's family is Scottish and Irish, and if I couldn't have my father, then I wanted to connect with the things that meant something to him. Skye is named for an island off the coast of Scotland, and she needed to know that the generations before her were so much more than just part of her DNA. As a lover of history and the past, I wanted her to see something bigger than just the here and now. She had to know her roots went much further back than to just

Indiana and Illinois. Going to Irish Fest was not easy; I had a communication device slung over my shoulder, a couple of pictures in my pocket, and a lemon shake-up in my hand. Signing to Ewan was not easy, and he was so overstimulated from the music and the crowds that he didn't quite know what was going on. He fixated on a bouncy house for a long time and hit meltdown range when he had to leave for the next child's turn. Other people's rules were still difficult for him to understand and follow. In an attempt to calm him down, we sat down and watched the bands play, hoping Ewan's new love of music would distract him from his confusion. As the pipers went by in full kilt regalia, Ewan used his Talkbox to say, "She?" All the therapy on proper pronoun usage had not taken into consideration the men in kilts issue.

Smiling, I said, "No, Ewan they are not wearing dresses, they are wearing kilts, and those are men. Kilts and plaids are important, Ewan, your daddy married me wearing one." Giggling at what I had told him, I continued, "Someday Ewan, when you're older, you may get married, too, and you'll wear a kilt just like that. It's part of who you are, and it's the reason your name is Ewan. Your name is your connection to your past and to your Grandpa Terrill." Not knowing who this Grandpa Terrill was, he grew tired of the conversation and flitted away to spin in circles while the pipes droned on in the background. I watched him turn around in the streams of sunlight and falling leaves, wondering how much he understood. Spinning faster and faster in time with the beat, he was reaching out to his past without words. He could identify with the music, but would he ever truly relate to the past? Would he ever truly know who his Grandpa Terrill was?

This connection with our roots emphasized how important the past was to Anthony and I. If Ewan was going to understand who his grandfather was, a man who had become a part of history, he had to understand the abstract concept of yesterday. We wanted to hear more than just what was happening as it was happening, we wanted to know about the past. We wanted to know what Ewan felt about the future and everything in between. It was time to hear more than just this concrete connection to the here and now. Slowly, the concept of yesterday, today, and tomorrow was weaved into his Talkbox, therapy sessions, and our afternoon walks. It was not an intuitive task for him. Commenting on the present moment was hard enough, but we were asking Ewan to understand the abstract concepts of past and future. One unusually cool September night, as I went to tuck Ewan in for bed, he placed his hand on the icy, frosted window. His fingers traced around and around following the swirls on the glass. After a thoughtful silence I said to him, "It's pretty isn't it? The ice crystals look like snowflakes to me."

A quiet minute passed by when he said more thoughtfully than I ever thought possible, "Brrr, that's cold Mommy. Remember when we went down the hill. The hill at Grandma's house with all the snow? That was fun Mommy."

With tears in my eyes, I put my hands on both sides of his face, kissed his forehead, and said, "Yes it was, Ewan, yes it was." Not only did this boy just utter 24 words at one time, he had just made a connection to his past, a past from the previous winter. He was describing a moment in time, a moment that he had been unable to communicate to me when it had happened. It had taken him eight months to express himself. A world of history and of days gone by had just entered his life. As silly as it may sound, in that moment I could see my four year old boy grown into the man, discussing his life with someone. I could see the man talking throughout the night, sharing his past and hopes for the future with someone he loved. Ewan had just discovered one of the most fundamental elements of the universe. *Time.* He was now on the path to understanding yesterday, tomorrow, and maybe someday, even his namesake.

For all the growth and maturity we were seeing in our son, there were so many other parts of his life that he needed help with. He was now four years and three months, and he was not potty trained. He was trying, but there were times that we could tell he simply wasn't ready. Socially, on the playground and at Lab School, he continued to struggle with anything beyond chasing classmates and riding bicycles. There were days when everything would fall apart, and no amount of devices and pictures helped him through it. One particularly rough day for Ewan stands out in my memory. Vaughn also attended Lab School in an adjacent toddler classroom. As Ewan began to cry inconsolably over a change in the routine, Vaughn ran out of his classroom and into Ewan's where he slowly patted his back and said, "It's ok Ewan. Take a deep breath."

Vaughn and Ewan sat in the corner slowly breathing in and out until the world righted itself once again, and Ewan repeated, "It's ok," and joined his classmates in circle time. But everything really wasn't ok with Ewan. That same day Ewan could hardly swallow any liquids at all without coughing and gasping for breath. At dinner, his drink came back up and out his nose, milk running down his face and onto the table. We had seen Ewan cough with liquids before, but nothing like this. It was as if he had forgotten how to swallow. Taking a step back, we acted as if he had simply forgotten and wrote Social Stories (TM) about swallowing, focused therapy on swallowing, and even used our pink puffball friend from his favorite Gameboy game to teach Ewan how to swallow again. But this time, all the teachable moments in the world couldn't help him.

It felt that for every step we took, some invisible force pushed us back. Ewan was eating more, but at the same time, he developed strange coughing behaviors that went from sporadic oddities to everyday occurrences. He was running away from the table in tears again and no one knew why. There were days I felt like we were right back at the Creole Incident. As much as we progressed, it was clearly not the type of progress that we had hoped for. It wasn't as if this child went from eating nothing to eating everything. There was interest in food and he loved to learn about it, but that interest didn't always translate into some miraculous change in diet. We had provided Ewan with the means to try new foods and had pushed out from those 10 foods he had before, yet it wasn't enough. We would get so far, only to find ourselves being held back by some invisible tide. We pushed, my God, how we pushed, and yet we only moved inches compared to his typically developing peers. It didn't matter how creative I was in showing Ewan the world of food, somehow the cornucopia was still slipping away. It wasn't enough for him to want to read about food. I wanted more than just interest. I wanted him to eat the food he seemed so excited to learn about. He would attempt, he would reach out, he would try so hard, and yet it wasn't enough. We didn't know what it was that kept us from the Holy Grail of eating; we only knew that we were frustrated and tired. It felt as if all the work, all the time and effort had taken us right back to square one. What was one day an epiphany, was a failure the next. For as much progress as we made and as many ideas that flowed between us all, something just wasn't quite right with Ewan.

He began to get worse rather than better. He developed dysphagia, or severe problems swallowing, and he seemed sick all the time. In the middle of dinner at a local restaurant, Ewan started choking on his food. He was grabbing his chest, and in a panic, he tried shoving his hand down his throat. He vomited all over the table right then and there. Behaviors hit the roof after that. I was being bit left and right by a child who grew angrier and more frustrated every day. Unable to tell me, even with the help of his communication device, what was wrong, I was left simply guessing. Confused, frustrated, and tired, I found myself stacked against a slew of therapists and doctors. No matter how hard I tried to say that what we were seeing was something 'more,' something beyond autism, sensory and language, something much more insidious, no one would listen to me. Doctors told me I was looking for what wasn't there. Our trusted pediatrician flat out told me, "Well, he *is* autistic. He's probably making himself do these things, it's called rumination. He may even like it." Therapists had given me up as an overprotective parent. Other parents began to think we wanted something else to be wrong. People thought we were in denial about what the true problem was.

But I can tell you this, I know what autism is and I know what it isn't. And I knew what we were dealing with was so much more than just what autism could ever explain. As Ewan got angrier and more frustrated with me, I grew angrier and more frustrated with all those who were supposed to be supporting him. It seemed as if everyone fell back on that 'well, he *is* autistic,' catch phrase and if they didn't say those words, they merely scratched their heads as to what the problem really was. One day I found myself in Stacey's office venting in front of her and one of her colleagues. Her colleague listened to me rail on about Ewan trying to choke himself with his fists, choking on his foods, and vomiting at the table, and I knew without a doubt she didn't think this was anything beyond the autism spectrum. Yet in all the times I'd read the DSM-IV, not once did I see dysphagia as a characteristic. Other people in Ewan's clinical life tried to suggest that maybe I was making a mountain out of a molehill, but I knew I had front row seats to a rapid deterioration of health and well-being. Staff at the university clinic where Ewan went for extra speech sessions were neither helpful nor supportive of Ewan's needs and joined the group of naysayers about the reality of his health. In our frustration, we ended up discontinuing their services as we sought out care only from those I felt could improve his life. When we could get him to eat something, Ewan would grab his chest in pain and gag or even vomit right there in front of us. This was so much more than just a texture problem with the food. Ewan would take a drink of water only to cough violently until it came back up through his mouth and nose. The last thing I wanted to lose was Ewan's ability to drink, as the milk seemed his only lifeline to keeping weight on. Ewan couldn't even handle everyday life at this point. He was so stressed and out of sorts that we often spent day after day in the dark. He would scream and cry at the light, and day after day my living room became more and more cave-like. I couldn't put my finger on what this was or why it was happening, I only knew that it was. Something was unraveling, but not one person could point me in the right direction. What I did not know, what I could not know, was that we were getting ready to travel down a path more demanding than the one we had just emerged from.

Acknowledgements

To my son, Ewan—without your life, this book wouldn't exist. Every step you take, every word you speak, every thought you share is an absolute miracle to me. You are truly my source of inspiration and awe. Your life has always been a life of possibility and hope. May you find all your dreams come true in this life.

To my father, Terrill—there are no words to express **all** that you have given me. You always told me the world was without limits and that I could do anything if I set my mind to it. I hope you can see my children and how beautiful they are. I hope you see me and are proud of the woman I've become.

To my husband, Anthony—you have been, and always will be, the love of my life. Thank you for giving me three amazing children and a life of purpose and meaning. Thank you for putting up with endless pairs of pajama pants, cups of coffee, and boxes of snack products over the last year. Thank you for ignoring the piles of laundry and stacks of dishes while I finished this book. Now buckle up, we've got three more books to go!

To my children, Skye and Vaughn—While this book may not always be about you or the amazing accomplishments in your life, every minute of your life has given profound depth and meaning to my own. You are every bit as special as your brother, albeit in different ways. You each have changed me and your father, and I know, without a shadow of a doubt, that the future holds great promise and endless possibility for the both of you.

To my mother, Linda—thank you for being there for me and my family time and time again. Without your support, we simply wouldn't have made it to today. Despite our differences, your example has made me the tough, resourceful mother that I am today. May you always remember the woman in the old white farmhouse and remember that you *are* independent, you *are* resilient, and you *are* strong. I hope you can see that Anthony is my Terrill, he is truly my heart and soul.

To my sister, Heather—I will never be able to repay you for the hours and hours of free therapy advice and unwavering support. Without you, I would not be the mother and advocate that I am today. Without you and Dennis, I don't know where Anthony and I would be. And I really don't know where we'd be without your pool in these long, hot summers.

To my stepfather—Don, I am so thankful to have you in our lives and I am eternally grateful to see my children have someone to call 'grandpa' again.

To my editor, Brianne—it was only through your greater vision that this book evolved into so much more than just a how-to guide. Without your guidance and insistence to slow the narrative down, this book would be superficial and a mere shadow of its final self. You are an absolute genius and shall forever after reign over the endless lack of commas in my prose. You are truly the Queen of the Red Pens. Now get out a pencil and write, you have a story to tell and people waiting to read it.

To Tera Swango—thank you for taking Ewan's drawing and turning it into a work of art. The book cover is absolutely perfect.

To Kaiya Mann—thank you for reading draft after draft after draft and giving me the feedback and encouragement I needed. Without your feedback, my work would have never made it to Brianne's desk. May our motto always be: writers helping writers! Now hurry up and publish yourself, I'd like to read your own book sooner rather than later.

To Dr. Mark Fishbein—thank you for pushing me to write this book. The night we stood in Fraker's kitchen, after a long conference weekend, you encouraged me to share Ewan's story with the world. I would never have written a single sentence without that initial big push. Thank you for caring about Ewan over the years; without your thoughtful care, Ewan would not be the healthy child that he is. May you always remember Ewan's story and always remember that quality of life truly does matter to each and every child and family to walk through your door.

To Cheri Fraker—thank you for having a kitchen so that we could stand in it and talk about me writing a book. Without your kitchen, well, there might not be a book. In all seriousness, without your help my son wouldn't be eating and I wouldn't be the advocate I've become. Your determination to help as many children as possible before you croak is what makes me get up and answer emails at 2 a.m. to scared and frustrated parents. Between the two of us, we will change the way people think about and see children with (dis)abilities. Thank you for the inspiration, but more importantly, thank you for saving Ewan's life. It was your eyes and your brain that gave him a chance at a life free from pain and suffering. May you always think of Ewan and his life as each child enters your clinic—may you always think of the family behind the child and know that it is only through your support and care that they will succeed.

To Stacey Vitale—you have changed my son's life and you have changed mine. Without your guiding hand, we would have been sucked into a black hole of hopelessness. I hope Ewan will always remember the woman who helped give him a chance at a richer, fuller life. I have never met another therapist that has matched your spirit, your drive, and your creativity. You are truly special. Stacey, it has always been your energetic determination to keep pushing forward that has inspired me to do more, be more, and give more of myself to every child I meet.

To Sibyl, Cheryl, & Laura—without the feeding team, I would still be trying to force feed shrimp creole to my son. Our world would be a smaller, darker place without your wisdom, guidance, and of course, humor. Thank you from the bottom of my heart for making the world of food a safe and enjoyable part of our life.

To Dr. Frances Murphy and Ms. Karen Hart—thank you for giving Ewan a chance to be a child. In your care, Ewan was just a child—not a child with autism or a child with disabilities. Thank you for making his childhood more than just a series of therapy and doctor visits. Thank you for showing me the way to give Ewan a full and happy life complete with play and creativity. Thank you for teaching me to elevate play above all else. You both have forever changed the way I think of child development and education. I pray that future generations of toddlers and preschoolers continue to benefit from the timeless wisdom flowing through the halls and cubbies of your program.

To Debbie—very few people can say that two hours of their time has altered the trajectory and quality of another person's life—you are one of the few. Without you, Ewan wouldn't have had a communication device. Without a communication device, Ewan might not have seen the power of language and expression. Without language and expression, we might not have seen the beauty and depth of his mind. Thank you for giving Ewan a chance to speak to the world.

To all the early intervention therapists in Ewan's life—without your dedication and determination, our life might be very different. It was the hours and hours of therapy that gave me hope and an ability to connect with my son. Not only did you change my son's life, you have forever changed mine. For so many days and weeks and months, we felt lost and out of control. You each empowered Anthony and I to be the parents Ewan needed and deserved. Thank you for giving me patience, understanding, and the knowledge I needed to be the best mother possible. Every single day I see a child and family who needs you and your guidance to make it through another day. You were the hope I needed when times were darkest, and I will continue to fight for early intervention the world over because of that. I support early intervention today, tomorrow, and forever after. For those of you reading, please join me in the fight to save these services on Facebook at **I Support Early Intervention**.

To all the student clinicians at the university speech clinic—thank you for all your hard work and attempts to bring the world of syntax, semantics and pragmatics into Ewan's life. It's not always easy work, but it has given Ewan the ability to say more and more each day. May you continue to challenge yourselves as speech pathologists, and may you remember that creativity walks hand in hand with a good therapist. May you remember to put away the clipboard and embrace your inner child—put the *fun* in functional for every child you meet.

To the *good* doctors in Ewan's life—thank you for caring for the *whole* child in front of you, not just the autistic child. May you continue to help children and families day after day after day. May you remember that one word, one minute, one visit can truly change a patient's quality of life.

To all the fans at The Autism Life on Facebook—thank you for your support over the years, and I hope we continue to walk this road together. As long as there continue to be Ewanisms, there will continue to be laughter and understanding and acceptance. Get ready for the next few books and a host of Ewanisms I've collected over the years!

To all the families raising children with autism—you are my support and inspiration. You amaze me every single day. Thank you Abbi, Anne, Bert, Bil, Cassie, Cheryl, Chris, Clint, Ellen, Eric, Jan, Jen, Jenny, Jennifer, Jennifer S, Jesse, Joy, Julia, Kass, Kellie, Kenny, Kristin, Kyla, Larry, Laura, Lyndsey, Matthew, Marjorie, Maxine, Melanie, Nealy, Pam, Patty, Robin, Robyn, Shelly, Tammy, Terri, Tori, Teresa, Tracy M and Tracy G. You are all the most dedicated and courageous group of parents I've ever met!

To all the children and adults with autism that I've known over the years—you have given me more than I will ever be able to give to you. I have learned more from you than you will ever learn from me. I believe in you, and I fully believe in a life of possibility for each and every one of you. May you continue to challenge prejudices and outdated beliefs about what people with autism can *really* do. May you show the world the meaning and value of seeing the world from another perspective.

Definitions

Aphasia: Aphasia is a language disorder that can run the gamut from word retrieval issues to complete lack of language and even affect a person's ability to read and write and may be temporary or permanent, ranging from mild to severe.

Apraxia: Apraxia is a brain disorder that can affect a person's ability to do or say something, even if they already know how to do it and they understand what to do.

Augmentative and Alternative Communication: AAC is an alternative form of communicating for those who cannot always rely on verbal speech. It includes sign language, Picture Exchange Communication Systems (PECS), low-tech devices, and high tech communication systems. You will find that iPod now has several low cost AAC apps as well.

Autism Spectrum Disorder: Autism is a complex neurodevelopmental disorder that presents with specific characteristics such as impairments in language ability, social functioning, and behavioral issues. It is difficult to diagnose a child with autism due to the unique expression found in each child and adult.

Congenital Sucrose Isomaltose Malabsorption Deficiency: CSID is an extremely rare malabsorption disorder affecting a person's ability to digest sugars.

Developmental Pediatrician: A specialist in the field of medicine focused on developmental and behavioral conditions in the pediatric population. A developmental pediatrician is often a referral for children with, or suspected of having, an autism spectrum disorder.

Dysphagia: Difficulty swallowing that can manifest itself in a variety of ways and can run the gamut from mild to severe.

Early Intervention: A program designed to help infants and toddlers with disabilities to reach their highest potential through therapy, education, case management, and referrals.

Encephalopathy: A generic term for brain disorder and dysfunction.

Food Chaining: A program that uses Flavor Mapping, Flavor Masking, Transitional Foods, and Food Education as a way to promote a more varied and healthy diet for children with selective eating patterns.

IEP: Individualized Education Plan for students with disabilities. It is for students age 3-21 and requires an evaluation by school officials.

IFSP: Individualized Family Service Plan for families enrolled in an early intervention program and includes six month reviews, goals, and specific information for each child age 0 until the third birthday. It is the document that guides the family and clinicians towards independence and increased functioning.

Moro Reflex: An infantile reflex that typically developing infants display from birth until approximately 4-5 months of age.

Neurotypical: A way of describing typically developing individuals.

Parallel Play: A phase of play where children play next to each other, but not with each other. It is typically found in children aged 2-3 years.

PECS ™: Picture Exchange Communication System is a form of AAC where a person uses a picture of something and gives it to a communication partner as a way of exchanging information. For more information visit www.pecs.com

Pediatric Neurologist: A specialist that can help diagnose neurological disorders and developmental disorders and is often recommended for children with, or suspected of having, an autism spectrum disorder.

Pragmatics: The social use of language

Reciprocity: The back and forth exchanges that we see between people in thought, conversation, social situations, and in play.

Self-regulation: The ability of an individual to regulate his or her internal environment and can include anything from sensory systems such as vestibular, proprioceptive, tactile, olfactory, gustatory, auditory, and visual systems, as well as, emotional, cognitive, and autonomic body systems and functions.

Sensory Diets: A concept that allows for a child to use various activities as suggested by an Occupational Therapist as a means to achieve a sense of self-regulation, balance, and calm. It is highly individualized and requires evaluation and constant access throughout the day in order to be effective.

Sequencing: The steps we go through in thought, action, and conversation that get us from point A to point B.

Sign Language: A language tool that allows people to convey expression and emotion through the use of hands, gestures, body language, and facial expression.

Social Stories ™: A system devised by Carol Gray to help children and adults understand a skill, situation, or concept. For more information please visit The Gray Center at www.thegraycenter.org

Sotos Syndrome: A rare genetic syndrome characterized by a large head with cognitive, motor, and language impairments.

Wilbarger Brushing Protocol: A program designed by Patricia Wilbarger, M.Ed., OTR, FAOTA to help with sensory defensiveness that uses deep brushing and joint compression as a way to treat sensory dysfunction.

Resources

The Autism Life: For those of you curious to hear about the Ewanism of the Day or to find out more information about autism and connect with other families please see The Autism Life on Facebook.

Brains, Trains & Video Games: For those of you looking to connect with me or find photographs of people, places, and events mentioned in the book please see Brains, Trains & Video Games on Facebook.

I Support Early Intervention: For those of you seeking to support early intervention across the country, join me in a national effort to spotlight such valuable and underfunded programs at I Support Early Intervention on Facebook.

Food Chaining (Copyrighted): Food Chaining is a program developed by the authors of the book: Food Chaining: The Proven 6-Step Plan to Stop Picky Eating, Solve Feeding Problems, and Expand Your Child's Diet written by, Cheri Fraker, Mark Fishbein, Laura Walbert, and Sibyl Cox. More information about this feeding team can be found on Facebook at Food Chaining.

AAC: There are many device manufacturer producing quality high tech augmentative communication systems. For those of you considering a device, please contact a speech pathologist familiar with AAC and comfortable using all forms of technology—from no tech, to low tech, to high tech. A good evaluation with an experienced SLP can do wonders! A good place to start is with your state's assistive technology lending center.

Dynavox: For more information about the Dynavox products that my son used or the latest models on the market, please see the Dynavox website at www.dynavoxtech.com

Thomas the Train: For those of you raising a train fanatic, I urge you to find out more about this great toy at www.thomasandfriends.com

Chris Rock: For those of you needing a comedic break and don't mind adult language, I can't recommend Chris Rock enough (just wait 'til you hear about the big piece of chicken)! Check out his work at www.chrisrock.com

So I Married An Axe Murderer: Watch it. Now.

About The Author

Alicia Hart is a wife, mother and advocate for children and adults with autism spectrum disorder. She has worked for various autism related agencies, early intervention programs, and has consulted with schools, hospitals, and other programs regarding autism spectrum disorders, feeding aversions, and augmentative and alternative communication. Alicia continues to write and has planned a series of books surrounding the autism life. The next book, Foods, Moods & Isms will be out soon. You may find out more on Facebook at The Autism Life or Brains, Trains & Video Games.

Sneak Peak

A sneak peek at the next book in our journey, *Foods, Moods & Isms: Still Living The Autism Life*:

October 2006

  Three a.m. will always be the hour of my worry. In the darkest part of the night the world is still and quiet while thoughts fly about my brain, gliding between neurons at the speed of light. While everyone else sleeps, I stare at the moonlight seeping through the curtains. Worry doesn't sleep. It is the world's worst insomniac, watching and waiting to shepherd your thoughts towards all the things that have been pushed aside throughout the day. Eyes grow heavy and burn with exhaustion, worry knocks inside the skull, jarring sleep into fear. Fear holds the heart in its frenzied talons, as a cold sweat trickles across the brow. A racing heart pounds against a cage of bones. Worry drives the weary body from the bed and into a wordless pace around the slumbering house. Feet padding silently across carpet, a cough suddenly signals a distress call. A heaving retch echoing from down a long hallway as the light turns on, flooding the room and pupils with a radiant artificial sunrise. There, in the middle of a white bathroom, lies a child with his cheek pressed against the cool relief of the tile floor. Dark, fathomless eyes look up, pleading in silent help against the second wave. Hands reach down to hold and comfort the nameless affliction coursing through his veins. Mother and son are left on the unyielding tile floor, as night passes into day.

  For the previous four years, my son, Ewan, had been down a long winding road of development. He had started life as the original worrier, constantly robbed of the relaxation and rest of sleep. The swish of air from an opened door would drift across his skin and drive him from the land of Nod. The click of an ink pen left his limbs shaky and restless. An addicting thirst drove his every need and consumed his every thought. Day passed into night, night after night passed in a constant vigilance. The infant insomniac grew into the mystifying toddler orbiting the tracks and trains strung throughout the house. A word given in a small clinic room branded his forehead, *autism*. His obsession obscuring the beauty of the world until the day technology baptized him into the realm of things.

Suddenly, there were names and labels for even the most mundane of items. His voice had found its place among the frequencies and waves of vibration. With words came language. With language came an identity. With an identity came a connection to the universe. He had found his place among the generation of men that had come before him and those that would come after. With the good comes the bad, and as Ewan finally stood before the world, he was pushed to his knees in a nameless pain. Doctors saw not the symptom, but the brand. Not seeing past autism, no one dared to see the picture through the pixels. We were left adrift in a sea of sickness, drowning in the avalanche.

    Ewan could speak with his mouth and with his communication device, but for all the adjectives in his arsenal, he could not adequately describe the nature of his pain. He could label and categorize every item in the house, yet could not catalog the suffering. Twisting and contorting his body, shoving hands down his throat, seeking relief and finding none. Frustration and suffering spun around his heart in a cruel dance of dysfunction. The obsessions could not draw his thoughts away from the endless ache. Afternoon walks to the pond granted him no relief. The sun on his face brought no warmth. The breeze in his hair no longer a caress. The world had grown gray and cold, leeched of comfort and passion. Pain had eclipsed the landscape, corrupting the taste of joy and euphoria of childhood. Most days were spent in the somber darkness of a shadowy room. We were left in a spiral of deterioration, directionless and off course from the path. With no name for the cause, there was no comfort to his pain. One word dictated the course of his treatment. One label, a mask over his self and his body, concealed the true nature of his discomfort.

    Only one person reached out to see more than just the label. Ewan's speech therapist, Stacey Vitale, had been with Ewan since we had moved back to Illinois in 2004. Stacey tried her best to help us, but she is a speech therapist, not a medical doctor, and even the miraculous Vitale has her limits. She did what she could and she fell back on what she excelled at, writing Social Stories ™ and connecting with Ewan through his communication device, a Dynavox MT4. Over the previous few weeks, Ewan's ability to swallow deteriorated to the point that drinking anything from soda to water left him sputtering and coughing. It was as if he had woken up one day and just had forgotten how to swallow. It started happening with more and more frequency until this also happened with food. He would grab his chest in pain or shove his finger in his mouth trying to gag and dislodge the stuck foods. He was vomiting at home, at clinic, in the middle of the day and in the middle of the night. There was no rhyme or reason to the gagging and retching. I would wake up to find him sound asleep on the bathroom floor, his tiny body curled up by the toilet. He was biting himself, me, and everyone else. Pushing on his stomach and chest, he would say over and over, "I'm sick. I'm sick. I'm sick."

    We ended up at his pediatrician's office several times for many different visits in those days. Thinking at first, it was a virus, he ignored it. When we kept coming back, his doctor said those fateful words, "Well he *is* autistic, he's probably ruminating," leaving me no comfort or plan whatsoever. The label autism had narrowed the field of possibilities to only one: a self-injurious behavior involving a disgusting voluntary vomit and swallow sequence. Had Ewan been any other child, his answer would have been different. His thoughts would have jumped from possibility to possibility, ordering tests to determine the nature of the beast. He reluctantly put him on a small dose of a proton pump inhibitor hoping to reduce the acidity in his stomach. He emphasized the need to get a behavioral evaluation for Ewan and possibly send him to a mental health facility for an overnight stay. His parting words were, 'This kid doesn't need a GI eval, he needs psych. He *is* autistic and after all these tests are said and done, all it will tell you is that he is *still* autistic." After finally agreeing to a barium swallow test, he couldn't resist one parting shot, "Things are going to come up in Ewan's life because he is autistic, but as soon as one thing gets straightened out, another behavior will pop up in its place. You will always be putting out fires with him." He left the office giving me no other guidance, no cause for concern because, well, Ewan *was* autistic.

Made in the USA
Lexington, KY
12 January 2012